D1416883

DATE DUE

Building Solutions in Child Protective Services

Other Books by Insoo Kim Berg

Family-Based Services: A Solution-Focused Approach

The Miracle Method: A Radically New Approach to Problem Drinking
(with Scott D. Miller)

Solutions Step by Step: A Substance Abuse Treatment Manual
(with Norman H. Reuss)

Working with the Problem Drinker: A Solution-Focused Approach
(with Scott D. Miller)

A NORTON PROFESSIONAL BOOK

Building Solutions in Child Protective Services

Insoo Kim Berg and Susan Kelly

W. W. NORTON & COMPANY
New York • London

The text of this book is composed in Palatino
with the display set in Trade Gothic.
Composition by Bytheway Publishing Services.
Manufactured by Haddon Craftsmen

Library of Congress Cataloging-in-Publication Data

Berg, Insoo Kim.
  Building solutions in child protective services / Insoo Kim Berg and
  Susan Kelly.
      p.   cm.
  "A Norton professional book."
  Includes bibliographical references and index.
  ISBN 0-393-70310-X
    1. Child welfare—United States.   2. Child welfare—United States—
  Management.   I.   Kelly, Susan, 1943–   II. Title
  HV741.B47 2000
  362.7'0973—dc21   00-039416

W. W. Norton & Company, Inc., 500 Fifth Avenue, New York, N.Y. 10110
www.wwnorton.com

W. W. Norton & Company Ltd., 10 Coptic Street, London WC1A 1PU

1 2 3 4 5 6 7 8 9 0

To families who have allowed us into their homes,
in admiration of their strengths and solutions

Contents

Acknowledgments   ix
Preface   xi

Part I   Child Protective Services in Context
1.   Introduction to the System and Our Approach   3
2.   A Brief History of Child Protection in the United States   20
3.   Creating a Context for Change   37

Part II   Child Protective Services: The Nuts and Bolts
4.   Beginning with a Phone Call: Responding and
     Going Beyond   55
5.   Useful Tools: What and How to Use   94
6.   Investigation as Intervention and Prevention   141
7.   Case Closure: How Good Is Good Enough?   187
8.   Supervision, Consultation, and Ongoing Training   204
9.   When You Need to Place a Child Out of the Home   226

The Future of CPS: A Vision for Tomorrow   259

References   264

Appendices
     A.   Handouts   271
     B.   Visioning Process for Local Communities   284
     C.   Focus Group Process for Local Communities   288
     D.   Worker/Supervisor Surveys   290
     E.   Tools for Supervisors   295
     F.   U.S. Child Protection Legislation at a Glance   302

Index   305

Acknowledgments

WE THANK COUNTLESS COLLEAGUES, FRIENDS, AND COWORKERS WHO HAVE encouraged us along the way; our editor, Susan Munro; Shannon Brower, Janet Findlater, J.D., and David Berns for their thoughtful comments on an earlier version of the manuscript; and especially:

- families we have met who inspired us by their resiliency and strengths
- the children who deserve to be protected by their parents
- the Michigan "Partnership for Safety" Advisory Group
- the Michigan Families First specialists, trainers, and quality assurance team
- Martha Tjhin, Program Manager of Michigan Families First
- JoAnne Nagy, Director of Michigan Child Protective Services
- all the CPS workers and supervisors who showed us that they want to make a difference in the lives of the children and the families they serve
- our colleagues and friends around the world, who spent countless hours listening and challenging our ideas
- our families whose patience and support make it possible for us to stay focused on this work

Preface

TRUE REFORM OF THE CHILD PROTECTIVE SERVICES (CPS) SYSTEM NEEDS THE support of workers, supervisors, administrators, and the public. It also requires thinking from "outside the box"—not doing more of the same things that do not work. True system reform not only deals with the external, systemic issues that affect a child welfare system's potential to make good decisions, but also hinges on the frontline workers, who are often the first contact clients have with the government.

One of us, Insoo Kim Berg, has long worked as a therapist, consultant, trainer, and teacher to initiate changes within individual family members and various child welfare services. The other, Susan Kelly, a public child welfare administrator, has management, policy, and administrative experience and a vision for a more effective system. Together we have developed a unique program for training frontline CPS workers to investigate cases differently and better. Our solution-building paradigm allows workers to interview, investigate, and intervene in such a way that the client is better off having had the contact with the CPS system. The hallmarks of this training effort are recognizing the client's own vision of a more desirable future, paying attention to what the client is capable of doing and what he or she has done toward this vision, and encouraging and supporting the client as he or she moves toward realizing this vision. The result is an investigation that is respectful, empowering, and enlightening to clients and workers. Our hopes are that workers will feel a sense of accomplishment and clients will emerge stronger and more competent so that changes are long-lasting, resulting in a reduction of re-referrals to CPS and other child welfare systems.

In *Building Solutions*, we suggest ways in which managers, administrators, and supervisors can help create a context that promotes solution-building in the public child welfare system. Ultimately, the goal is to create client-driven services that make common sense. The book is *not* designed to be a manual. Rather, it is a challenge to step out of the traditional CPS "box" and to think differently.

At the same time, this book is a work-in-progress. In large measure, all CPS work is a work-in-progress. We can never be smug about our accomplishments. We are always on the lookout for ways to improve the services to families and children who are least able to fend for themselves.

We hope the ideas we present in this book will begin conversations about how the CPS system can be more helpful and respectful. In an ideal world, there would be no child protective services system. Because we aren't in an ideal world, we need to look for ways that the CPS system will help families get what they need to care for their children.

Families are unique and resourceful. Most parents want to guide their children to be responsible and caring adults. The CPS system should touch families in helping ways and leave them more confident and competent. We hope this volume contributes to that goal.

This book is a challenge to all of us working in child protection to be a positive and sensitive source of change—to leave the system better than we find it today. We know we are not finished with this book and hope that you too will share your vision and strategies for building solutions in the CPS system.

In our five years working together with CPS systems, we have met dedicated and well-meaning CPS workers who care very much about the families on their caseloads. We have met administrators who are willing to risk changing the system to insure better outcomes for families. Most importantly, the many families themselves, resilient and competent, have helped us craft many of the ideas we share here. As we have observed many interactions between CPS workers and families, good things have happened. Those good moments, those respectful interactions, have inspired us to share the best of those moments with you.

Part I

Child Protective Services
in Context

Chapter 1

Introduction to the System and Our Approach

WHY ANOTHER BOOK ON CHILD WELFARE? BECAUSE WE THINK IT CAN MAKE a difference for children, families, and those who work with them in the child protective services (CPS) system.

It is no secret that everyone has opinions about child welfare services—child protection services in particular—and that the universal opinion is that the system is broken and that something needs to be done to fix it. However, most people have no comprehensive ideas on how to "fix" the problem and any discussion on the subject generally deteriorates into complaints about everybody else.

CURRENT STATUS OF CPS

It seems that almost no one thinks CPS is doing a good job of protecting children in the United States. Often the child welfare system is portrayed as understaffed, undertrained, and jeopardizing child safety. Protecting children is a difficult and stressful job. The following data describe, in part, the serious issues facing child protection today.

Nearly 3 million children were reported in 1995 to child protective services (CPS) as possible victims of child abuse or neglect. Of those reports, 52% were for neglect, 25% concerned physical abuse, and the others were for sexual or emotional abuse.

- Since the 1970s, state and local CPS agencies have been charged with investigating reports of child maltreatment and protecting the victims. These agencies are accused of both interfering in family affairs and failing to act to protect threatened children.

- State laws require professionals and allow laypersons to report suspected abuse or neglect to CPS.

  - Half the reports come from professionals such as teachers, police, and doctors; the other half come from family members, neighbors, and anonymous individuals.
  - The number of reports of alleged child maltreatment has tripled in the past 20 years.

- CPS investigations in 1995 identified nearly 1 million child victims of abuse or neglect, but limited agency resources mean that not all these children or families received assistance.

  - About one-third of reports to CPS are substantiated as violations of state law.
  - Children are removed from home in about 1 case in 10.
  - One-fourth of the cases involving substantiated maltreatment receive no services at all.

- Federal, state and local governments spent about $11.2 billion on child protection in 1995. Governments spend an estimated $813 per case on investigations, $2,702 on services to families, and $22,000 per case each year on residential and foster care.

- Caseworker decisions about specific cases are the heart of child protection, but the CPS system has only a limited capacity to tailor its response to individual conditions:

  - Fewer than one-third of CPS direct-service staff hold social work degrees.
  - In 1995, the median salary for caseworkers with master's degrees in social work was under $33,000.
  - Large caseloads in CPS and cuts in community services curtail agency efforts to help troubled families.
  - The effects of treatment programs on families with differing risk profiles are not well understood.

- Resources beyond CPS are needed to prevent and respond to child abuse and neglect.

  - Family poverty makes maltreatment more likely, especially if parents are unemployed, use drugs, or lack parenting skills.
  - Government efforts to reduce poverty could therefore help to prevent maltreatment and relieve pressures on CPS.

- Informal community resources should also be mobilized in the fight against child abuse and neglect.
- CPS reforms are often driven by media attention to individual child tragedies, but such reactive reforms do not yield a balanced and flexible system for protecting children.
- State legislatures have the power to define the public responsibility for children's safety, and they provide the funds that CPS and service providers need to carry through on the public promise of child protection.*

A series of Michigan Focus Groups on CPS, held during 1997, confirmed that the CPS system is misunderstood by the public, who has widely varying expectations about what its role is, or should be, in communities. Responses about its effectiveness ranged from that of "a life preserver," "helpful, an agent of relief" to "threatening, nonresponsive, uncaring, and ineffective."

Although Insoo has worked side by side with the child welfare programs and their workers for many years (Berg, 1994), outside the system she was among those who lamented the broken system but did not have a comprehensive idea about how to "fix" it.

Susan worked within the system and knew some of what needed to be done. For more than ten years she has worked with the public child welfare system, successfully developing and institutionalizing prevention programs such as Families First, a short-term crisis intervention program which is strength- and skill-based. Families First is an alternative to foster care for high-risk families. The caseloads are limited to two families per worker and services are provided at the convenience of the family, not necessarily during the traditional workday. In Michigan, 66,000 children and their families have been served through Families First since 1988 and many children (85%) have been able to stay safely with their families as a result of this model of service.

Michigan's CPS workers have been the primary source of referral to Families First. Although they see the support provided by Families First and the sometimes amazing changes in families, many CPS workers are reluctant to fully accept its philosophy, which is that *the best protection for children usually comes from helping parents become more capable of adequately caring for their children.* CPS workers were initially skeptical that family preservation was compatible with child protection. They needed to be convinced that the "best interests" of the child were

*From *The Future of Children*, Spring, 1998, Volume 8, No. 1. Reprinted with permission of the David and Lucille Packard Foundation. *The Future of Children* journals are available free of charge by faxing information to: Circulation Department (650) 948-6498.

best served by trying to keep the child in the family and promoting family safety. After ten years, some acceptance and trust in family-centered practice by CPS are evident, yet the prevailing approach remains much more a "child rescue" framework. Many managers and administrators within the system support the belief that CPS rescues children. It seems as if some are not looking at the human cost on children of "rescuing" them. When visiting a family in the throes of a crisis, we heard one very wise child say, "Please help my Mom! She deserves it." She wasn't saying, "Get me out of here"; she was saying, "Please help us."

Over the last ten years, in Michigan out-of-home placements for reasons of abuse and neglect have remained stable while they have risen dramatically in other states (Wulczyn, George, & Harden, 1995), but they have not decreased as we had hoped. Why not? CPS staff and local managers in county offices often say that keeping some children home isn't safe and they need to remove them. Yet, almost 80% of the children removed by CPS are returned to their birth parents—most within six months. The question we have is, if children are returned so quickly to parents, why don't we remove the risks instead of the children in the first place? Children deemed in "unsafe" situations often wait up to six weeks for a "safe" placement. Often this wait is without services to the children or the parents. What if supportive services were provided with the aim of removing the risks? We think far fewer children would be removed in the first place, eliminating the revolving door in and out of placement with enormous human cost, emotionally and psychologically, to the children we hope to protect. Instead of waiting up to several weeks for a "safe" placement out of the home, why not keep the children home and provide services? Changing schools and placements frequently, as many of the children in foster care do, can be emotionally damaging (Fahlberg, 1991). The goal of safe family preservation services is to keep children home if safety can be provided—that is, to remove risks instead of children. The hallmarks of programs like Families First are building on family strengths while treating clients as colleagues, capitalizing on the family and social support networks, and respecting the family's goals and aspirations for their children. These principles should also be the hallmarks of the entire child welfare system. Placing children in foster care only when there is no safe in-home alternative and assisting families who do not need to be in the system to secure resources to keep their children safe is the child welfare ideal.

What Susan realized after ten years of trying to institutionalize a family preservation program was that CPS workers, who are the first decision-makers in a child welfare case, are the ones who have the most power to keep children in their families or to remove them. She acknowledged that even the best family preservation program could not be an effective resource unless the CPS worker decided to use it. The CPS system is a valuable resource with many dedicated workers and supervisors, but seems to lack a unified vision and philosophy about working with at-risk families and their children.

We needed to step back and look together at our common goal: how to build solutions in child protection. Our initial work with Michigan's CPS is heartening. Our vision for working with vulnerable children and their families is very strength-based and solution-focused. Solutions will come when there is a consistent "top down" and "bottom up" approach that acknowledges the need to balance protection for children with efforts to stabilize, strengthen, and preserve their families, to put family safety as the first priority. Safe families will keep their children safe. This challenge is daunting, as bureaucracies often find it less threatening to protect the status quo than to shape a new vision. Given that reality, and knowing the difficulties of the current system, we think we have found some practical ways to implement some of the needed changes. If the will is there to do so, we think it can be done.

In this book we want to describe some of the steps that Michigan's large social service system has taken to implement changes from within the system. Such change required the cooperation of many key players within the system, whose commitment, experience, and skills we describe in this book. Their vision, commitment to implement some difficult changes, and knowledge of how the system operates were the resources that we needed to capitalize on if we were to succeed. As many of you know, vision without techniques is not enough, and operating with techniques alone, without a vision of how to fit them all together into a coherent picture, makes no sense.

We want to emphasize that this is still a work-in-progress and we are still in the midst of multitude of changes. Our view is that any such work is always a work-in-progress and that everything is a process, particularly in a large government agency such as a statewide social service agency. Beginning or ending is an arbitrary marker. We realize that some of you will read this book through a lens different from ours, that is, another way of looking at the same data. We welcome your challenges and your feedback so that we can move into the next stage of this evolving process.

A WORD OF CAUTION AND CHALLENGE

We are not writing a new CPS manual. You already have enough of those. Each state has manuals of policy designed to fit within existing state and local laws and regulations. This book is not designed to replace those. It is designed to challenge you to think differently about families and the child protection laws and practices.

This book has suggestions and many examples. It is not a "fill in the blank" approach for every family. It is a loud and persistent plea to everyone who works with families to see each family's unique strengths—one family at a time!

There are many good "best practice" books written for child welfare workers; we have read many of them, as we are sure you have. However, this book is not one of those either, although you will see some best-practice elements from a solution-building perspective on the issues of how to treat our clients as colleagues and on substance use, domestic violence, cultural diversity, supervision, management, and many emerging topics of interest to CPS workers. We did not try to do a comprehensive treatment of these subjects. You will also not see specific discussions of each state's risk assessments or step-by-step decision-making according to each state's protocol or statutes.

What is this book about then? It is our modest proposal and challenge to those in the field of public child welfare to examine, in a solution-building manner, the everyday work at all levels of child welfare and to suggest ways to inspire and strengthen practice to better serve those most in need of high quality service.

The 1998 Adoption and Safe Families Act (ASFA) presented many new challenges to states to reexamine their child welfare practices. With the passage of ASFA, the pressure to do it "right" at the front end has increased. Financial incentives and penalties encourage states to look carefully at how child welfare workers work with families when they first enter the system. The preamble to the new ASFA regulations includes several suggested court actions that might be used to reduce unnecessary out-of-home placements and to ensure the safety of the child. The courts may ask the CPS workers the following questions, which are designed to guide them in how they intervene with families:

- Would the child's health or safety have been compromised had the agency attempted to maintain him or her at home? Was the service plan customized to the individual needs of the family or was it a standard package of services?
- Did the agency provide services to ameliorate factors (physical, emotional, or psychological) present in the child or parent that would inhibit a parent's ability to maintain the child safely at home?
- Do limitations exist with respect to service availability, including transportation issues? If so, what efforts did the agency undertake to overcome these obstacles?

These questions are heartening to us because they reinforce the importance of balancing the risks with the need to provide services that strengthen families before removal might become necessary. By asking such questions, courts may actually promote a solution-focused approach to keeping families safe and together.

Too often, families try to negotiate the legalities of the court or CPS system when what they really need is support from helping hands. That is not to say that some families do not need the CPS investigative process to proceed; indeed, for some children that process is their road to safety and stability. What we are saying is that CPS needs to balance safety with the family's strengths as well as risk factors. Too often, the risks are the sole focus, leading one to look only at the child—not at the parental potential. The other half of the CPS mission, promoting change through assessing family strengths, is then lost. Both assessing for strengths and identifying risks can keep the safety of the child and his or her family in balance.

State CPS statutes use broad language when defining neglect, which allows many possibilities for workers, supervisors, and managers to individualize and humanize services while adhering to legal mandates. We ask you to step out of the legal box and discover how to walk within the CPS laws flexibly. Each CPS intervention will dramatically affect the families the CPS system touches. We think there are many possibilities. We also think administrators and managers must take the lead in making change happen. At a recent training, CPS workers, when asked about their work, said, "We aren't empowered to do anything different" and "We need to have some administrators in the room to hear what is helpful . . . maybe then we would feel empowered." We hope you will listen to the story of our journey and join us in our hope that children can be safe.

THE BEGINNING

In the spring of 1994, I (IKB) was invited to an informal dinner during a large statewide child welfare conference in Michigan. The conversation turned, naturally, to CPS issues, but with a considerably different emphasis this time. During this conversation, unlike others about what's wrong with the child welfare system, policy, workers, and so on, the director of CPS showed me some statistics as she voiced her concerns. I was stunned by what I saw—not by how many more cases of alleged complaints of child abuse and neglect there were, as usual, or how many children are abused, maimed, killed, or neglected by society, but by what I saw between the numbers.

I want to describe for you what jumped out at me. The following statistics were collected by the Michigan Family Independence Agency (FIA) formerly the Department of Social Services, in 1995. These data, as we described earlier, are quite similar to those of other states across the United States and match closely to what we have known since the United States government started collecting data in the mid 1970s (Government Accounting Office, 1997).

- Michigan population: Approximately 9.3 million
- Abuse and neglect complaints received: 121,000 calls (annually)
- Cases actually investigated (at least 1 home visit): 57, 917 (47% of calls)
- Phone calls not investigated (screened out): 64,000 (53% of calls)
- Substantiated cases: 12,194 (21% of those investigated; 79% are not substantiated)
- Re-investigation of previously substantiated cases: 5,300 cases (43% of 12,100 cases)
- Average number of re-investigations to the same family: 5
- Average length of stay in out-of-home placement: 12 months
- Average number of placements: 3–5
- On average, most "removals" of a child occur 4–6 weeks after opening the case.

The following is what impressed me the most about these data and where I saw the troubles and possible solutions. I invite you to follow along as I describe what I saw, the side that most professionals who are well-informed, knowledgeable, and concerned may not see.

1. 53% of 121,000 calls CPS receives are screened out. How do the CPS intake workers make the right decisions this often? Obviously they know something about those cases because essentially this system has worked fairly well over the years. What do they know?
2. Out of those 57,914 cases (47% of all phone calls) when a worker actually visits the family for the purpose of investigation, only 21% (12,194 cases) are actually found to have cause for concern and therefore need some action or services. It means that in 79% of those cases (45,720), a worker made at least one home visit and found no evidence of abuse or neglect. What happens to those cases where a worker makes one home visit and closes the case? How can we make this single visit more useful to families? Can this single visit be used in a way that is useful to the caretakers?
3. As of 1995, the total number of children in some sort of out-of-home care is 14,942. When you consider that each year 10,246

children are placed in out-of-home care, the majority of these children (80%) are returned home. It shows that the average length of stay in out-of-home care is 12 months. If 80% are returned home, shouldn't many of them stay home from the beginning? How does leaving insure their safety?

4. About 43% of those being investigated had been previously investigated and enough evidence found to substantiate abuse and neglect. Does this mean these parents were deemed to be good/safe enough parents to have the children left with them? How does this happen? The average number of re-investigations is five; rather than repeating the first contact five times, is there some way to look at these cases as having five home visits? How can these visits be used more productively?

5. Each year approximately 64,000 Michigan citizens make phone calls to voice their concerns to CPS. Confidentiality laws prohibit giving follow-up information to interested citizen callers. Most callers taking the trouble to make a call to a government office are left with no idea of how the information they provided on behalf of a child is being used or whether they did the right thing by calling. What is done to address their concerns for a child's safety and well-being? Can the caller be informed about the CPS process when the call is placed?

6. The majority of out-of-home placements occurs four to six weeks after the case is opened, that is, most children remain with their parenting person while the investigation continues. One would expect that the consideration of a move as drastic as separating a child from his or her familiar environment would need immediate action. Why does it take four to six weeks to decide whether the child remains with the parenting figure? What happens to this child and caretaker during this investigation period of several weeks? Apparently the home is considered safe enough so that the child is left with the caretakers. What goes right with caretakers during this phase? Is safety really the issue here?

These are some intriguing questions I voiced while we were looking at the statistics on the dinner table. A series of meetings followed to determine whether some sort of exploratory consultation studies could be done to address these issues. Numerous dinner meetings later, we agreed that the first step was for me to go down "in the trenches" with the workers and their clients. After more meetings, we agreed on a pilot study to test out my ideas and to study further where the answers lay. We selected a mid-sized county, where the poverty level was higher than most cities but comparable to Detroit in some ways, where 25% of children live below poverty level. It was close enough to the large, sprawling urban city of Detroit to have problems with drugs and gangs and a high unemployment rate.

On the Road with CPS

In order to comprehend what really happens "in the trenches," it was agreed that I should get a close look at CPS work not only in a large urban county, but in small rural and mid-sized counties as well. This would give me a wide-ranging impression that would cut across size, culture, unemployment, and economic differences between counties. I followed workers around a very large urban county where the problems of drugs, poverty, violence, and child abuse and neglect are rampant, and where CPS has several branch offices. I also visited a rural county where each worker does everything from financial aid and adult protective services to child protection investigation. The economic conditions and service needs in small, isolated, and sparsely populated areas differ greatly from large urban areas, but in some ways the solutions are the same. During this period, I also visited Albuquerque, New Mexico. I also have extensive experience with the very troubled Milwaukee County CPS system, as well as a northern Wisconsin county where the seasonal employment increases the level of poverty and sets the cultural tone and texture of the lives of the residents. It is much like the Upper Peninsula of Michigan.

In all, I followed over 35 child protection workers and close to 100 cases in various stages of the investigation process in 6 different counties of various sizes, settings, and special configurations of needs. In order to get a rounded view of everything that happens in the child protective services, I wanted to learn everything a CPS worker does day in and day out. As a part of this research, I began at the beginning. I saw how a case enters the system, how a case is referred, and how an intake worker on the phone makes a decision about whether to screen out a case, that is, determines there is no need to make an investigation visit or to follow up the phone call with an initial home visit. I listened in on the phone conversation to find out how a caller presents a concern about a child's safety and welfare and how we can maximize this phone call. Frequently, I followed the same phone call as the case was assigned to a worker. When there was a sense of urgency about the phone call, I observed the workers engage the "client" in conversation. I will describe this observational process in more detail in a later chapter.

I also followed workers to their second, third, and fourth visits, as well as to their "ongoing" cases where workers decided to provide some necessary services. In ongoing cases, clients and workers are more familiar with each other and the worker has much useful and some not so useful information about the family or the child. This type of ongoing case and the worker's interaction with the family will be described later.

The most time-consuming aspect of any CPS worker's job is related to those cases that will end up in the courts, as every CPS worker will attest. I spent hours in courtrooms in various counties and observed worker-client interactions related to transfer of custody, termination of parental rights, etc. Later I will offer some concrete suggestions for productively utilizing this "waste of time."

Both Susan and I also have witnessed the removal of children from their homes, one of the most gut-wrenching aspects of CPS work for everyone involved—the children, the parent, and the worker. As the saying goes, "It's a dirty job, but somebody has to do it." We also have some ideas on how to improve this aspect of the service.

I sat in on the staff meetings and observed supervisor-worker interactions. I listened to workers describe their relationship with their supervisors as both a lifeline and a millstone. I also participated in regional, administrative, advisory, and executive meetings of the state welfare administration.

By and large, what I have found are overwhelmed, overworked, and unfortunately some unappreciated workers, supervisors, administrators, and managers all trying to do the best they can with the poor and vulnerable families in our society. The culture of this work is unique and generally unknown to the rest of child welfare because so few writers in the field of CPS have actually spent any length of time in the trenches. As I spent time driving from one home visit to the next, to schools, trailer parks, housing projects, dirty houses, courthouses, judges' chambers, hospital emergency rooms, and so on, at all hours of the day, evening, and night, I talked to the workers, picking their brains, so to speak, learning about them as persons, listening to their aspirations and dreams. I began to understand their daily grind of working with the poor and neglected, and listened to their ideas of what would help them do their jobs better. I came away awed that they are willing to do the society's most difficult work most of the time. I was frustrated by their lack of training and skills, but fascinated with their undiminished desire to "make a difference" in somebody's life. This book is in part about the clash of cultures, values, and world views and how to make a difference in spite of the enormous differences and gaps. It is also about how to fix both clients' and workers' broken hearts, salvage what we can, and strengthen their spirit and sense of self in such a way that they feel like they can not only climb the next mountain in life, but also be inspired by the one they just climbed.

AN INSIDER'S PERSPECTIVE

In contrast to Insoo's outsider's perspective, I (SK) bring an insider's intuition and understanding of how to make some changes to the system from the inside out.

Both Insoo and I voiced concerns about the CPS system, yet intuitively we knew that something could be done about it—something very different in thinking and design from the many models that previously had been tried. Our common goal of wanting to make a difference brought us together, along with many others, on a project in Michigan called "Partnerships for Safety." We believe that there are tremendous strengths not only in the workers and the system, but especially with families who one way or another came to the attention of the CPS system. Unlike the traditional view that places the responsibility for safe children on the shoulders of the workers on the frontline, we conceptualized that this huge responsibility must be shared as a partnership involving the worker, the parents and family, the child welfare agency administrators and managers, and the community. Nothing more, nothing less. Together, we bring almost 60 years of experience working in the most difficult circumstances, some with success, some without, and yet our commitment to make a difference has not changed. With Partnerships for Safety we were able to sort out some of what worked and some of what did not and, at times, even why.

This book is designed to help those involved in the CPS system find ways to return to the original mission: to strengthen parents in such a way they feel empowered by their encounter with CPS, not broken or destroyed by it. Ultimately, CPS workers want caretakers to feel able and willing to protect their children and nurture them so that the children's lives turn out better, even better perhaps than the parents'. We want parents to ensure safety for their children and to take pride in having done so much with so little.

PROBLEM-SOLVING PARADIGM

The traditional problem-solving model that has been the foundation of social work during the past 100 years has been increasingly challenged by a new breed of thinkers and practitioners (Saleeby, 1992). This problem-solving paradigm, sometimes called "positivistic" or the "scientific approach" or "medical model," begins with a detailed assessment of the problem. This paradigm is rooted in a long cultural tradition of Western thought and belief systems, which hold that the world is knowable through scientific means and that nature can be manipulated. Further, this approach holds individuals accountable for their own actions and responsible for their lot. Saleeby (1992) and others object to the use of this paradigm by the social work profession. The challenge comes from the new social constructivists (Franklin & Nurius, 1996), who advocate for a return to the unique professional identity or a social worker as someone who works with the "individual in the environment."

In the problem-solving paradigm, the professional "expert," one who has been trained exclusively in a specific problem, usually performs the assessment and the next task, the design of the solution. Only the client implements the solution. In the view of social constructivists, the relationship of the client and social worker is a joint venture. This means that the worker is not the "diagnostician" alone. Rather, the client participates and collaborates with the worker in the assessment, treatment, and solutions. The assumption is that the client is competent to know what is good for her and her family, and can, with support, uncover solutions.

CPS risk assessment tools, designed to provide a uniform way to determine levels of risk in vulnerable families, provide a good example of the traditional problem-solving model. Workers arrived at a client home to do an investigation with a checklist and set about to find out in detail the "problem" that brought the client to the attention of CPS. The design of these early tools focused on the risk factors or negative behaviors present in the family that could be documented and thus determine the degree of risk. This expert-driven ("I, the worker, will uncover what is wrong with this family") tool presumed that the professional or expert would match solutions to the problem. In this paradigm, the role of the expert was to carefully study what was lacking or missing in the client and prescribe solutions to ameliorate those deficits. With this approach, the client was told what was wrong and what the professional thought should be done to fix it. It also reinforced an imbalance of power, that is, "If you don't do what I think you should, you may lose your children."

We use the issue of risk assessment as an illustration of how tools such as these can keep one in the problem-solving paradigm, preoccupied with deficits and barriers. In such a paradigm it is fairly easy to see how parents can be relegated to a supporting role and become bystanders as the worker becomes solely responsible for the child's safety.

We know that risk assessments have improved, but we believe many of them stay firmly entrenched in the problem-solving paradigm. We realize that those who know and do good CPS risk assessments may not agree with our broad-brush characterization, presented here to illustrate the potential for these instruments to focus on the negative. We give more specific attention to risk assessment in later chapters, where we address in more detail the danger and safety issues.

A NEW PARADIGM

Perhaps the public child welfare agencies can rely on some lessons learned from the recent developments in mental health practice. The field of mental health is undergoing a reexamination of how services are delivered, who delivers them, and what the results are. It has begun to challenge the traditional view of the expert-driven, prescriptive model (DeJong & Berg, 1998). Of course, this push for reexamination came, in part, from the pressures of managed care and numerous cutbacks and budget constraints. The result is a nagging feeling that there is something missing in this expert-driven medical model. From the field of systemic and family therapy, innovative thinkers and practitioners (Steve de Shazer, Michael White, Insoo Kim Berg, Jay Haley, Milton H. Erickson, etc.) have emerged to challenge the traditional views with alternative approaches to human problems. More models based on this new approach are detailed in literature about family therapy, family-based services, wraparound services, client empowerment, and intensive family preservation services. These alternatives to traditional child welfare work are emerging to show that clients do change, do have aspirations and goals, and can find and maintain their own solutions.

The new thrust has come from the culture of empowerment, the desire of professionals to work "with" the client in an egalitarian, democratic manner that respects and values a client's individual views and way of being in this world (Berg & DeJong, 1996; de Shazer & Berg, 1992; Furman & Ahola, 1992; White & Epston, 1990). The culture of empowerment is becoming the accepted slogan in the mental health field, which, of course, has had a spillover effect on the social work field. Michigan's Families First program is one such empowerment model. It has emerged as a safe alternative to foster care because it is based on a solution-focused approach. Families First has shown that, in most cases, when parents are supported to provide care for their children, they can do so, and do it for the long term.

We believe that it is time for those in CPS and the child welfare field to institutionalize the paradigm based on respect and empowerment. We want to propose a different way to conceptualize and practice, a way that puts the client center stage as the main player, where he or she is listened to and trusted to carry out his or her hopes and dreams. We need a model that supports building on existing strengths and skills. We need to begin to support and encourage this indigenous knowledge and wisdom so that parents can expand and build on these resources for their families. This new approach encourages the worker to see the client as a repository of resources, not a pool of pathology and deficits. We invite you to step outside the social work paradigm and discover new ways to think and behave, to return to the basic social work principles that taught us to "begin where the client is" and look beyond the individual characteristics and problems to understand the client's wishes and hopes, within the context of his or her environment, both social and familial.

Solution-focused therapy, as developed by de Shazer, Berg, and their colleagues, offers effective and efficient ways to utilize this new paradigm. We think it offers an exciting alternative to the traditional approaches in child welfare practice and supervision, and empowers those involved to find solutions to the serious social, professional, and personal dilemmas they face. In the solution-building paradigm, the client takes center stage (Berg & Miller, 1992; Berg & Reuss, 1997; DeJong & Berg, 1998; de Shazer, 1991, 1994; Dolan, 1991; Turnell & Edwards, 1999; Walter & Peller, 1992). It begins with the assessment of solutions, that is, a detailed study of the client's ideas of desired outcomes of contact, the client's achievements so far in realizing those hopes and desires, however small, and his or her existing skills, strengths, and resources. Using the client's own words and images and building on his or her experiences of successes, these listings of resources become the central interventions. Collaboration becomes the key concept; the solution will be generated together, with the worker supporting the goals of the client, and tailored to fit each client's unique circumstances.

With the solution-building approach, the worker offers cooperation *with* the client, rather than demanding cooperation *from* the client, thus creating a collaborative loop of interaction. The worker adapts to the client's way of doing things, thus respecting the unique individual, cultural, and ethnic traits that each client brings to the situation. The worker uses her skills and knowledge to generate and construct solutions that will help the client to move toward the desired outcome.

When we work with the client's own ideas and successes, it is easy to see that the concerns for resistance will diminish and the client can easily own up to the successes. Thus, the responsibility for the safety of the child becomes the parent's, and the worker plays a supporting role in this unfolding drama. You might say, "This all sounds good, but how can you do this?" We will describe in detail the nuts and bolts of this new way to conceptualize, implement, and sustain this hopeful and positive frame in a daily practice "in the trenches."

What we propose and have implemented is a combination top-down/bottom-up philosophy. This approach involves the workers, supervisors, managers, and administrators, who together focus on improving outcomes for families and children who come to the attention of CPS. The hallmark of this kind of approach is the inclusion and participation of everyone, especially the families, in planning and decision-making. The focus of our work is child protective services and its everyday cases—not those headline-grabbing cases that tend to portray CPS as a massive failure and give the impression that nothing works. We want to address the myths and realities of what it is like to work in the CPS field and offer suggestions.

This book combines our many years of experience in working with the poor, the children caught in the web of a system that does not value them and fails to give them adequate support so that they can catch up with the rest of the society and maintain their dignity. We share a commitment to offering a helping hand to those who are least able to fend for themselves. At the same time, we believe that the children and parents we have met over the years have the incredible ability to manage their lives in such a way that they not only survive against all odds, but also thrive and prosper when only a little bit of help is given to them at the right time. It is this constant reminder of resiliency that compels us.

NEW HOPE

We stubbornly refuse to become pessimistic about the potential of children and their parents and we refuse to give up, even though there are many days when we wonder if we are making a difference in even one life. But we have learned to count the small things, the baby steps of change that we know are the building blocks of self-sufficiency, integrity, and bigger successes.

We hope you become encouraged, as we have been inspired, to maintain your optimism in this work. Clients, CPS workers, community leaders, policy-makers, teachers, police officers, doctors, nurses, judges, and many others have inspired us to see them through new lenses, and we have been awestruck with admiration for their dignity, strength, and good will. As you will see, at times we ask more questions than we suggest solutions. Please join us in finding new avenues to build lasting solutions.

Chapter 2

A Brief History of Child Protection in the United States

THE UNITED STATES PLACES A HIGH VALUE ON PROTECTING CHILDREN, BOTH from abusive parents or caretakers and from systems that oppress and exploit children (e.g., child labor, pornography). Since colonial times, the United States has held that children have a right to be cared for, if not by their parents then by the community. This right has its basis of the English Poor Law enacted in 1601.

The United States gives significant attention and resources to its CPS system, which has been shaped by several historical movements dedicated to the protection of children, as well as by legislation that establishes the protection of children as a government function. The system attempts to balance the recognition that parents have a right to be supported so that they will adequately care for their children with the obligation to protect or "rescue" children from abusive or neglectful parents.

To understand the current CPS system, it is helpful to understand its evolution from voluntary, religious, and charitable movements in communities and neighborhoods to a legal, regulated government system. This CPS system has as its mission the safety of children and their protection, whether by their parents or by substitute families, and mandates investigations of certain allegations of maltreatment. Over the last several decades, the federal government has worked with states to help shape local statutes on child protection and has provided leadership on the issues of abuse and neglect. The federal government also provides significant funding to ensure that the provisions of child protection are carried out in all state and local jurisdictions.

Following is a very brief historical overview of some of the significant trends, movements, and events that have influenced the child protective services system we have today in the United States. The information in this overview is based on a more comprehensive look at the history of child protection done by other scholars (Costin, 1985; Schene, 1998).

CHILD PROTECTION IN THE EIGHTEENTH AND NINETEENTH CENTURIES

The legal basis for protecting vulnerable children in the United States is found in the English Poor Law of 1601. This law, like many others, "immigrated" to the United States with some of the early English settlers, and is one of the foundational laws of the American legal system. Under the English Poor Law, townspeople were given responsibility for the care of the poor, including children. The doctrine "parens patriae" in the Poor Law, which translates as "ruler as parent," was the justification for governmental intervention into the parent-child relationship. This law forced parents to care for their children appropriately or to give the ruler (the townspeople) the right to arrange substitute care. In the United States, the focus of this law was primarily on children of the poorest families, orphans, or those labeled "unsupervised." Using this law as a justification, children of the "unworthy poor," many of whom were immigrants with different languages or family customs, were "saved" by separating them from their parents who, in many cases, could not speak English and who could not earn enough money to care for their children. They often did not know their rights or understand what was happening to them or why their children were taken from them.

Historians view this child-saving era as one where actions taken to protect children were justified on moral grounds and the law came to be used as a tool of social control. Children who begged on the streets or who were homeless were often separated from their parents and sent to almshouses or homes for the poor. Often these children were housed with mentally ill adults or the adult poor. Some children, many as young as nine or ten, were indentured to wealthy families to pay for their care in these facilities. Eventually, in the late nineteenth century, growing criticism of these practices and deteriorating conditions of the almshouses led to the establishment of separate facilities for the children.

In response to widespread immigration and urbanization in New York City, the Children's Aid Society, founded by Reverend Charles Brace, began a ministry to respond to the influx of children of poor and immigrant families. The mission of the Children's Aid Society was to round up and "save" poor and needy children. These "saved" children were often put on "orphan" trains to the Midwest to live in Christian homes and to labor on farms. These mostly Protestant "child-savers," convinced that immigrant parents, most of them Catholic, were inferior, saw no conflict in taking children from their parents and giving them to other families. Homeless children living on the street, hungry children, children not attending school, and those who couldn't speak English were "rescued." The child-savers hoped that this would result in a better life for the child. It is difficult, in retrospect, to understand how the bonds between children and parents and the cultural and ethnic differences of new immigrants could be so disregarded. Differences were seen as deficits, not as strengths, and new immigrants were judged for their child-rearing practices and inability to assimilate quickly. New York was a major port of immigration and people from all over Europe and elsewhere were flocking to the city, many without work, language skills, or an understanding of the dominant culture or the pervasive religious bigotry. The child-savers rescued over 150,000 children over the course of 75 years, often permanently separating them from their parents.

Some Midwest rural states set up systems to care for their needy or dependent children. For example, between 1866 and 1899, 50 homes were established in Ohio in which farm families cared for wards of the county for $1.00 per week per child. These homes were forerunners of the current family foster care system.

CHILD PROTECTION FROM 1877 TO 1920

The New York Society for the Prevention of Cruelty to Children (SPCC), the first anticruelty society for the protection of children, was formed in 1877. The current CPS system has its roots in such societies. The formation of the New York SPCC was triggered, in part, by the Mary Ellen Wilson case of 1874. A nurse visiting in the home of Mary Ellen was shocked at the brutal physical abuse of this child. The nurse made headlines when she publicly demanded that Mary Ellen receive at least the same protection and help that an abused animal would receive. There was a great deal of public outcry and attention given to this case and many questions were raised about how to respond to the needs of abused children.

In part as a result of this case, New York State passed a law in 1877 to protect children and punish those that would abuse them, especially parents who maltreated their children. Following New York's lead, most states began to pass laws to protect children. By the beginning of the twentieth century such laws were widespread and had laid the groundwork for the nation's juvenile court system, begun in 1898 in Chicago, Illinois. It was hoped that good protection laws and a child dependency court would give special attention to the needs of abused or neglected children in a more sensitive and humane manner.

By the early 1900s, more than 300 SPCCs were operating, mainly in the Northeast and Midwest, often in partnership with the American Humane Society. Initially, SPCCs were punitive toward parents and often dismissed parents as "cruelists." Little attention was given to the need to help families alleviate the risk factors and stresses affecting their parenting. Some SPCCs had the authority to remove children if it was deemed such action was necessary. The philosophies of individual SPCCs ranged from simply rescuing children to helping families provide appropriate care for their children by offering counseling and other services.

The Massachusetts SPCC, departing from the New York and other conservative SPCCs, began to focus on the idea that the responsibility for caring for maltreated children was a parental duty and saw as its mission, in part, to help parents reform. "We fully approve of the practice of the return of children when the parents reform and establish good homes" (Costin, 1985). The Massachusetts SPCC urged remedial and supportive services to help parents appropriately care for their children. It also stressed that SPCCs should not be just prosecuting agents and child rescuers; rather, they should broaden their role to look for and help alleviate root causes of child neglect and maltreatment. The Massachusetts SPCC promoted the strengthening and supporting of families as the primary vehicle for child protection and suggested that more attention be given to keeping children with their families when it was possible and safe to do so (Costin, 1985). These ideas were not embraced widely by all SPCCs, and chapters were clearly divided on the issues of prevention and how to respond to abuse and neglect. In 1907, C. C. Carstens, director of the Massachusetts SPCC, positioned child protective work in the camp of progressive social action when he suggested that SPCCs should organize against "individual neglect" as well as "community neglect." Carstens recognized the complexity of protecting children in light of the problems of poverty, cultural differences, and other risk factors. He urged recognition of these issues as well as families' strengths and resources in the movement to protect children. He promoted the idea that families are affected by their environments and that parents in difficult and poor situations may need extra support to care for their children. He was a leader in promoting family safety as the best way to promote child safety.

In 1909, at a White House Conference on Children, a landmark policy statement on child protection was issued. The policy stated, in part, that "No child should be removed from the home unless it is impossible to construct family conditions or to build and supplement family resources as to make the home safe for the child." Echoing that, Dr. Vincent de Francis, a leader in the American Humane Society, promoted the philosophy of child protection this way: "The best way to rescue a child is to rescue the family for the child" (Schene, 1998). Carstens' ideas and the federal government's leadership gave a needed balance to the overemphasis on "child-rescuing" as the primary response for the protection of children.

In 1912, the federal government began to take a prominent role in child welfare issues with the establishment of the federal Children's Bureau. The Children's Bureau was issued a congressional mandate at its inception to "investigate and report upon all matters pertaining to the welfare of children . . . among all classes of our people" (Costin, 1985, p. 57).

1920–1959: GOVERNMENT INCREASES ITS ROLE IN THE PROTECTION OF CHILDREN

In 1920, the Child Welfare League of America (CWLA) was formed and Carstens was named its first director. The CWLA's philosophy was to preserve the natural family whenever possible, and when that was not possible to encourage quality out-of-home options. Working with the American Humane Society and the SPCCs, the CWLA set up a national (but private) system of temporary out-of-home options for dependent children. Its mission of promoting child welfare causes continues today. The CWLA is a strong advocacy and membership organization throughout the United States.

The emerging child protection movement during this period saw a gradual shift away from the law enforcement, child rescue mentality toward an emphasis on child safety encouraged by providing services to support and strengthen parents' ability to care appropriately for their children. During this time, the Great Depression and World War II put incredible stress on many American families struggling to care for their children.

In the 1930s, many families were unemployed and had no means of providing for their economic needs. Welfare and federal government support for families were established during this period. Also during the 1930s and 1940s, state and local governing bodies, juvenile courts, and other protective associations gradually assumed the work of the humane societies and SPCCs. The provision of child protection as a government function began to take shape. The child-rescue model as the only way of protecting children was eroding.

Realizing that poverty affects a parent's ability to care for children, the leaders of the Children's Bureau asked the President of the United States to include Aid to Dependent Children (ADC) in the landmark Social Security Act of 1935. This was seen as a way to insure minimal cash assistance so that poor mothers without economic means of support might keep custody of their children. The leaders of the Children's Bureau recognized that without economic support dependent children were at risk of neglect and separation from their mothers. In addition to ADC, a less known provision of the Act, Title IV-B, was included, which provided limited funding to the states for preventive and protective services for children. The Social Security Act also provided funds for homeless or dependent children. This foster care funding, made available to all states, was governed by federal regulations and ushered in an era that professionalized child welfare; child welfare was emerging as a "business." Because states used the majority of the monies in these entitlements for foster care, prevention services for families whose children were not removed from their homes were not seen as equally important and were significantly underfunded, as continues to be the case.

1960–1980: MEDICAL MODEL AND MANDATORY REPORTING LAWS

Child abuse began to be treated as a parental malady in the 1960s. In part, the medical profession contributed to the passage of mandatory reporting laws that required certain professionals to report alleged abuse or neglect to the governmental child protection system or suffer legal consequences. While many factors contributed to the CPS statutes now in existence in each state, in some measure the efforts of the medical community focused the attention of the public on the sad reality that some caregivers inflict intentional injuries on their children. With the availability of modern medical tools such as x-ray machines, doctors began to discover some previously undetected injuries to children that appeared to be repetitive and serious. Doctors brought their case to the media and began to diagnose these situations as the "battered child syndrome" (Kempe, Silverman, & Steele, 1962). The battered child syndrome, originally identified and labeled by Dr. Kempe in the 1940s, began to be used frequently as a diagnosis in the 1960s, as the medical profession's concern for these children grew. Doctors alleged that not only did some parents intentionally inflict these injuries but then these same parents sought care for their children at multiple health care facilities to avoid detection. This practice was called hospital-hopping. As the number of child abuse reports rose, efforts were made in the medical profession to document child victims and their perpetrators. Widespread national attention promoted the call for hospitals to register abuse cases so parents who allegedly inflicted such abuse would not remain undetected.

In 1974, as a result of the national focus on child abuse and neglect the federal Child Abuse Prevention and Treatment Act (CAPTA, PL 93-247, 1974) law was passed. It encouraged states to pass mandatory reporting laws and required public social service agencies to keep track of perpetrators by establishing a state registry. CAPTA also established the National Center on Child Abuse and Neglect, which, among other things, developed national standards for responding to reports of child neglect and abuse. State statutes established professionals who deal with children as mandatory reporters and required them to report suspected neglect, physical abuse, sexual abuse, and exploitation. CPS agencies then were required to investigate alleged child maltreatment. All states were required to develop a registry of perpetrators and child victims. CAPTA provided grants (of limited size) to states that met national standards to develop CPS programs. Those grants continue today as incentives to states to maintain and/or enhance child protection efforts.

By the end of the 1970s, child welfare was no longer a voluntary, charitable, or community endeavor; it was a formalized national, state, and local governmental system.

By 1980, 75% of all child welfare monies was spent on foster care rather than on services to support and preserve families and keep children in their own homes (Burt & Pittman, 1985). Since the 1980s, levels of funding for out-of-home care have continued to increase; spending for prevention and/or protective services has increased, but not proportionally.

1980s–1990s: STATE-MANDATED SYSTEMS

The national attention to the issues of child abuse and neglect and the implementation of state mandatory reporting laws led to sharp increases in reports of child maltreatment. Between 1973 and 1993, official reports of abuse and neglect rose 347%, stretching the capacity of child welfare systems to respond. With significant federal funding available for foster care, the number of children removed from their homes also increased dramatically. Many of these children remained in out-of-home care for long periods of time.

Disturbed by the dramatic rise in the numbers of children in foster care, in 1980 Congress passed the Adoption Assistance and Child Welfare Act (PL 96-272), requiring states to make "reasonable efforts" to prevent unnecessary out-of-home placement or lose federal funding. Its intention was to encourage states to make out-of-home care a last resort, not a first option. It also meant to alleviate "foster care drift" and urge safe and expeditious reunification. While this law required states to make reasonable efforts to prevent unnecessary out-of-home placements, it was difficult to enforce and the courts weren't prepared to implement it adequately. Few resources were dedicated to prevention for the cases screened out of the CPS system but still in need of supportive services. Children in foster care often remained in care for long periods of time due to lack of adequate reunification services.

The unprecedented growth of foster care prompted Congress to pass new legislation in 1993 to provide some funding for family support and in-home care for at-risk children and their families. The Family Preservation and Support Act (PL 103-66) amended the Social Security Act to provide limited funds ($1 billion for all states over the course of 5 years) for prevention and crisis intervention services for families in their homes and communities. While welcome, these new dollars were minimal compared to foster care funding. The Family Preservation and Support Act encouraged states to assess their child welfare services, to define child welfare more broadly, and to include other partners in the protection of children. The law encouraged child welfare agencies to collaborate with parents, services providers, faith organizations, and other governmental entities to create better ways to prevent child maltreatment (ACYF-PL-94-01). In 1997, the Family Preservation and Support Act was reauthorized but renamed "Promoting Strong and Stable Families." A new emphasis on the safety of the child was highlighted and congressional sponsors were clear that the preservation of a family was not to compromise the safety of children.

A public policy framework for a strong prevention and family support agenda does not exist in the United States as it does in other countries, such as Norway or the Netherlands. Many western European countries have substantially better subsidies for poor families or single mothers who are raising children. CPS in many other countries do not have the disproportionate numbers of poor children in their systems that the United States does, where the pairing of neglect with poverty is more of an issue. The United States relies on a crisis-reporting and reactively financed children welfare system. The scope is narrow and, while the value of prevention and family support services is recognized as a mechanism to keep many families out of the formal system, prevention services remain underfunded.

CURRENT CPS: OVERWHELMED WITH HIGH EXPECTATIONS

Today, CPS remains a function of state or local government with investigation services conducted by public child welfare agencies. While CPS is primarily responsible for responding to calls from mandatory reporters and others, the notion that one agency can be totally responsible for the protection of children seems to be changing. Schools, businesses, faith communities, senior citizen networks, domestic violence programs, and community residents are encouraged in some communities to take on some of the responsibility for child protection.

CPS staff is usually located within state or county child welfare agencies along with other publicly funded child welfare services, such as prevention, family support, foster and kinship care, and adoption services. CPS workers must investigate complaints, draw conclusions about allegations, determine safety issues for children, and decide whether to involve law enforcement, courts, other service providers, or support services. To deliver necessary services to families, CPS usually involves other community resources. While CPS's role has narrowed significantly since the 1970s, the public usually still expects a full range of services from CPS and, unfortunately, is quick to blame the CPS system when a child dies or a case of abuse is highlighted publicly.

Contact with CPS can carry a stigma because of presumed allegations of parental abuse or neglect. Parents often feel that there is little regard for their opinions or needs when they are involved with CPS. Because CPS has eligibility requirements, CPS usually pays for services *only if* clients meet specific categorical criteria. Many families are screened into the CPS system solely to receive services. Many states are moving to a new system; for example, Michigan recently enacted new legislation that will assist a family to receive necessary or helpful services but will not require parents to be "substantiated" for neglect or abuse just because they need services. The new law requires substantiation only for those serious cases of abuse or neglect that require a swift and firm response because of safety and risk issues.

Fundamental challenges to CPS remain. Some of them are:

- deciding which situations require formal and involuntary involvement of a CPS agency to protect children, and how to investigate families in a more respectful, mutually responsible manner (Schene, 1998)

- working to bring the broader financial and human resources of a community together to strengthen parents and families so they can better protect their own children (Schene, 1998)
- improving family assessment tools to balance the risk factors in a family with their strengths and resources
- making the removal of a child a last resort instead of a first option when a child cannot be protected in his or her home or family
- improving training for workers to help them deal effectively with racial, cultural, and religious differences between families so that the CPS system does not disproportionately discriminate against children of color, children of the poor, and children of other minorities
- finding more appropriate ways to train CPS workers to assess complex family situations and determine risk of harm to the child in the face of multiple risk factors such as poverty, substance use, mental illness, and domestic violence

CPS workers struggle with high pressure and high expectations. Combining risk factors with other issues, such as ethnicity, language barriers, and different cultural, religious, and spiritual practices, adds to their difficult work. The challenge is formidable. As the system of child protection has evolved, it seems clear that an effective contemporary system must not only work toward ensuring the safety of the high-risk children and families who become part of the formal system, but also support parents not involved in the formal CPS system to keep their own children safe from harm in their homes and communities. A wide range of partners is needed to assist in this challenge.

CURRENT ISSUES FACING CPS

Poverty

Each year, CPS receives three million reports of alleged child maltreatment. Twenty-five percent of the allegations involve physical abuse; less than 23%, sexual or emotional abuse; and 52%, neglect (Packard, 1998). Over half of the reports to CPS are not alleging physical or sexual abuse; rather, 52% of families on whom a report is made are families alleged to be neglecting their children. Neglect, as defined by state CPS statutes, is open to varying opinions and has great latitude in terms of definition. In many cases, though, neglect is tied to economic and environmental factors (housing, beds, heat, water, etc.). Sometimes the lack of economic support is exacerbated by the misuse of alcohol or illegal drugs. Parents without adequate economic support, for whatever reason, might be labeled as "failing to protect" or "threatening harm" to their children. If the children are not removed from their parents, which they often are, they may be offered counseling or parent education classes, as if these classes will miraculously change the economic realities of their life. Parents tell us that they cannot send their children to school in the winter because the children do not have shoes or boots. All the counseling in the world will not remedy that and provide boots and coats. Forty-nine percent of children who attend Detroit Public Schools qualify for free or reduced-cost lunches (Michigan Department of Education, 1998). The latest poverty figures show that over 41% of Detroit's children (ages 0–17) live in poverty (Michigan Family Independence Agency, 1999b). Michigan figures reflect similar realities in other larger urban areas and in many rural areas across the U.S. The CPS system nationwide, not just in Michigan, is a system that has significantly high numbers of poor children and families on its caseload.

As our review of the history of child protection in the United States shows, our system of child protection has its roots in part in the child-saving motivations of private individuals and organizations, which often focused on poor families (Wexler, 1996). It seems that the United States has continued that trend of servicing significantly high numbers of poor children in a system meant to deal with the most severe cases of abuse and neglect. Unlike many other countries (e.g., Norway, the Netherlands), which recognize the connection between poverty and a family's ability to provide safe and adequate care for their children, the United States has basically ignored the link between poverty and neglect in its broad child welfare policy framework. Richard Wexler notes that historian Barbara Nelson, writing on the history of the 1974 CAPTA legislation, states, "In an effort to get the law passed the connection between poverty and maltreatment was purposely blurred. In fact, strenuous efforts were made to popularize [child] abuse as a problem knowing no barriers of class, race, or culture. For some politicians, particularly [Senator Walter] Mondale, this was part of a conscious strategy to disassociate efforts against abuse from popular poverty programs" (Wexler, 1996). Prospects for changing this strategy in the near future are unlikely, given welfare reform measures.

The number of children living in poverty is increasing, despite the United States' relatively stable and positive economy (Michigan Family Independence Agency, 1999b). What will this mean to the public child protection systems for the future? While there is never a good reason for child maltreatment, why do so many alleged "neglect" cases become part of an overburdened CPS system? Does "poor" mean "neglectful"?

Or is CPS a system where families without other resources know they may receive help?

No one argues that wealthy and middle-class children are never neglected, but significant documented evidence shows a clear connection between poverty and what is currently defined by most CPS law as abuse and neglect. In 1996, the *Third National Incidence Study of Child Abuse and Neglect* indicated that abuse or neglect is 22 times as likely to occur in families with annual incomes of less than $15,000 than in families earning $30,000 or more.

Richard Wexler, president of The National Coalition for Child Protection Reform, provides the following information from his research (Wexler, 1996):

- Courts in New York City and Illinois routinely take away children and separate families unnecessarily and often for lengthy periods of time because those families lack decent housing.
- In California, children in homeless families were given emergency shelter only on the condition that they be separated from their parents until a successful lawsuit put an end to the practice.
- Jerome Miller, who had been placed in charge of the Washington, DC, child welfare system by a federal court, estimates that between one-third and one-half of the children now in foster care in Washington could be safely returned home if they had decent housing.

Wexler states that, based on studies of U.S. populations, there is overwhelming evidence that the vast majority of child abuse and neglect cases, or at least what the system calls abuse and neglect, are clearly, obviously, directly, demonstrably linked to poverty. He asserts that this shouldn't surprise us, as child neglect and abuse have been linked to stress, and poor families tend to be under more stress than those who are better off economically. But even more importantly, the poor are regularly defined into the system by most state neglect laws. States have wide latitude with which to interpret CPS state statutes regarding neglect and often misjudge poor parents as maltreating parents. What poor parents need is access to concrete necessities and support to cope with the stress of poverty so they can adequately care for their children. However, given the current federal fiscal incentives for caring for neglected or abused children, it appears that federal and state fiscal policy-makers are much more willing to pay foster or substitute families to care for children than they are willing to promote and fund adequate fiscal support to birth families to help parents learn to appropriately care for their own children. The human cost and toll on children are often ignored. A Chapin Hall-University of Chicago study on a small sample of foster care children suggests that, except where abuse is severe, children do not want to leave their families, schools, or siblings. Many of them want to be with their parents (Chapin Hall, 1989).

Too often, economically deprived families stay in the system or show up again and again. Their situation is not likely to improve. These families are labeled "chronically neglectful." This is the population that overwhelms CPS. This is not to say that there may not be harm to the children, but it raises significant questions about how we deal with these families, families whom CPS workers often say are the most difficult to work with.

Substance Abuse

In 1997 the Government Accounting Office (GAO) reported that one of the most difficult problems facing CPS workers is substance abuse. A substance abuse problem exists in 75%–90% of the families reported to CPS (GAO, 1997). Substance abuse has existed in epidemic proportions for many years; the crack cocaine problem escalated in the 1980s and had devastating effects on children and families. Alcohol and illegal drugs are often present in CPS cases. The challenge of balancing the safety and care of children whose parents are seriously abusing substances with efforts to find adequate community treatment, especially for the poor, many without health insurance, strains the imagination and creativity of CPS staff. There are limited drug-treatment slots, and the demand for them far outweighs the availability. Relapse is high. There seems to be no consistent prioritized effort to address this national emergency to make treatment that is appropriate (e.g., gender-specific) and community-based available. Parents, especially mothers, may need to continue to receive treatment and aftercare services while maintaining care for their children, and many parents are unable to do so. We both have walked into homes where every single piece of furniture had been sold to buy crack. Substance abuse treatment centers had not been prepared to deal with this drug, nor others used in high volume like heroin, and did not have facilities for children who needed to accompany their parents when they sought treatment.

Substance use is a risk factor that needs to be balanced with other factors affecting the safety of the child. In a recent report by the National Center on Addiction and Substance Abuse (CASA) (National, 1998), researchers identified several promising strategies and treatment programs and stated, "Comprehensive treatment that is timely and appropriate for parents is the linchpin of strategies to prevent further child abuse and neglect by substance abusing parents." Recommending a tailored and comprehensive approach that recognizes that most of the parents caught in child welfare substance abuse system are women, it further suggests that only a comprehensive treatment strategy holds out the hope that the family may be held together or reconstituted if services are available and accessible. Several specific examples of proven treatment programs are presented in the CASA chapter entitled "Promising Innovations: Bringing Substance Abuse Expertise to the Frontline." Innovative case studies from several jurisdictions are highlighted, and specific suggestions are made about what is needed to truly help children and families affected by drugs and alcohol. As child welfare systems try to address this very serious problem, CASA suggests two guiding principles:

- Learn to integrate services across agency lines.
- Prepare and change organizational culture and practice—one employee at a time.

Although adequate funding is not available to serve the record numbers of families who need such services, the delivery of home-based services in Michigan has shown that workers who are respectful and who have an understanding of the issues and dynamics of substance abuse can keep children safe and with their families during ongoing treatment (Jiordano, in press). This perspective keeps many families together who might otherwise be separated. CPS is inconsistent about addressing this issue, and the chapter on substance abuse provides specific suggestions to address this pervasive dilemma.

All parents who use drugs do not use them in the same proportion. Nor does substance use impact parenting and child safety in uniform ways. While it is true that many addicted parents neglect their children while abusing drugs, many do not. Some substance users have the help of relatives or friends while trying to participate in treatment programs; social support is one of the keys to a lasting recovery. Many substance-abusing parents need better access to services and better services. Many of these parents need drug treatment, but some do not belong in the CPS system because they do provide for the safety of their children while using drugs. However, many of these families show up at the door of CPS again and again. Drug-affected families should be presumed to need and benefit from long-term (through varying in intensity) support. Substance abuse programs do work, as do follow-up support services such as intensive family preservation services, which assist the family to focus on the safety issues while learning to balance care for children with positive social support and treatment.

Domestic Violence

It is estimated that between 3.5 and 10 million children live in homes where there is domestic violence (Edelson, 1999). Many of those families are reported to CPS. While there is not much data on the numbers of families in the CPS system who are experiencing domestic violence, a study conducted by University Associates (March 1995) showed that 37% of families involved with Michigan's Families First program self-reported domestic violence as a significant issue for their family. A 1991 study of the Massachusetts Department of Social Services found that 33% of CPS case records mentioned domestic violence (Whitney & Davis, 1999). The few data we do have point to an ever-increasing overlap between domestic violence and child abuse.

The issue of domestic violence is complicated, and the actions of battered women are often misunderstood (Dobash & Dobash, 1979). We know that women who stay with their perpetrator often stay because of their children. It is also true that many victims of domestic violence leave their home and economic security because of their children. Victims of domestic violence show incredible strengths and creativity in their efforts to protect their children.

Many women who are victims of domestic violence also have substance abuse problems, a history of sexual abuse, or mental health issues such as depression, isolation, or anxiety. All of these are risk factors that need to be balanced by a mother's coping strategies and resources. Despite the seriousness of many of these issues, a parent often has a safety plan in place to insure her child's safety. Workers need to carefully ask about such plans, and listen to the victim convey what will be helpful.

There has been longstanding mistrust and suspicion between domestic violence advocates and child protection staff. As a result, in many cases CPS staff are not offered access to the advice, case consultation, and resources that are available from domestic violence programs. Nor have domestic violence programs taken the time to understand the issues and constraints of the CPS laws. Today, domestic violence programs are receiving significant funding from the federal Violence Against Women Act (VAWA, PL 103-322, 1994) and many programs are collaborating with other systems, including child protection, to enhance the safety of women and their children (Edelson, 1999). CPS programs are also working to train domestic violence advocates about child protection services and laws. Fox example, Michigan has institutionalized regular training on domestic violence for all of its family preservation and CPS staff.

Respect and Diversity

According to the latest United States census data (1999), there are 273 million U.S. residents. Seventy-two percent of the population is white, 14%, African-American, 12%, Hispanic, 4%, Asian or Pacific Islander, and less than 1% are Native American or Eskimo.

The United States is still predominantly white, and top bureaucrats and administrators of larger organizations, such as departments of social services, are white (Michigan Family Independence Agency, 1999a). Yet workforce and education trends compel us to see the magnitude of diversity that characterizes our youth-care and child-welfare populations. In the United States approximately 45% of additions to the workforce in the 1990s were nonwhite, and at least half of them were mostly from Asian and Latin countries.

While African-Americans represent only 14% of the total population in the United States, they represent 27% of the children in the child welfare system. This is due in part to the reality that African-American parents live in poverty at a higher rate than white parents. In 1997, the poverty rate for white families was 8.4%, while the poverty rate for African-American families was 24%. As stated earlier, poverty is a condition that increases the risk of child maltreatment. In New York City, 71% of children in foster care are African-American and 24% are Hispanic (Swarms, 1999). Racial prejudice is deep-seated in our society and children of minorities often suffer needlessly because of their race, ethnicity, or spiritual practices. This prejudice is present in the healthcare system as well. For example, although past-year illegal drug use is roughly the same in African-American and white families (12.1% vs. 11.3%), in one recent study health officials were ten times more likely to report African-American women who were using drugs to the child welfare agency. Respect for diversity in cultural, spiritual, and ethnic differences is critical for an effective child welfare system. Creating a child welfare system that recognizes a family's history, culture, spirituality, and ethnicity in the case assessment and treatment plan is crucial. Child welfare administrators must insure that CPS staffs are culturally sensitive and culturally competent. Lifestyles, values, beliefs, and customs, which are so important to all of us, must be considered in each and every CPS case. CPS workers need to be aware that many clients will be different from them. Effective cultural sensitivity requires:

- avoiding labeling, judging, or operating from racial, ethnic or other stereotypes
- respecting each client family with all its cultural, ethnic, and spiritual diversity
- eliciting information from the client about unique traditions, family beliefs, and child discipline practices, and how these practices affect family behaviors and family functioning

Workers need to be aware not only of individual family differences, but also of the differences present in extended families, neighborhoods, and communities where their clients live. Recognizing that resources in the community may reflect the cultural and economic characteristics of the families using them, CPS staff should make every effort to tap appropriate culturally relevant support for families in their own neighborhoods and with their own specialized cultural service providers. Some of these services may be informal or untraditional, but may reduce the need for more formal service interventions. CPS workers benefit from identifying and capitalizing on local informal supports to assist with special populations, especially translators or interpreters, spiritual leaders, and health care providers who are familiar with the particular customs and traditions of specific cultural groups.

Statistics such as those mentioned above serve to point out that the child protection system needs to creatively and respectfully support its frontline staff in receiving training and support to deal with the diversity of its caseload. It is not surprising that, faced with the complexities of poverty, substance abuse, domestic violence, mental health issues, and sexual abuse often present in multiproblem families, many CPS workers are criticized for their performance and case handling. They may not have specialized training in each of those areas. The challenge is to help CPS staff value and use the rich and varied informal supports that diversify the provision of services to our multicultural and diverse families.

The rich history of CPS reminds us that there have been many people invested in trying to improve the lives of vulnerable children and families. To improve frontline practice and provide more adequate service we must strike a balance between continued incremental improvement (ideas about which we offer in this book) and envisioning and working for a fundamentally restructured system. Restructuring the child welfare system is an ambitious project requiring comprehensive local, state, and federal changes. We hope our ideas will serve as the foundation for the broader reform of the system, beginning, at the very least, with great respect for the clients we serve.

Chapter 3

Creating a Context for Change

THE CHILD WELFARE SYSTEM IN THE UNITED STATES IS OVERWHELMED BY the complexity of family situations, the volume of cases, the high turnover of staff, the lack of appropriate resources, and the pressure of not letting children fall through the cracks. Child protective services as a system requires fast-paced decision-making, critical thinking, and appropriate judgment calls.

In 1997, focus groups were conducted by the Michigan Family Independence Agency as part of the "Partnerships for Safety" strategy. We wanted to know in detail our CPS's strengths, weaknesses, and future challenges and discuss with the public its role in helping CPS protect children. A wide range of community residents participated, including hospital staff, education personnel, board members, employment specialists, grandparents raising grandchildren, neighborhood residents who made referrals to CPS, and CPS workers, supervisors, and managers.

Ten questions were asked during the focus group:

- Who are the key players in protecting children?
- What is the current public image of CPS?
- What's the ideal public image?
- What's a realistic public image?
- What should be the key messages from CPS?
- What external factors impact on CPS?
- What internal strengths does CPS staff have?
- What internal weaknesses exist within the CPS system/staff?
- What accomplishments have been made for the protection of children?
- What challenges are ahead for CPS staff?

Results revealed an inconsistent image about the role and effectiveness of CPS. For example, the current public image of CPS ranged from helpful to nonresponsive and threatening; the ideal CPS would be well staffed with caring problem-solvers, educators, and miracle-workers who would act in the best interests of the children. Workers were seen as brave, open-minded, and optimistic, but also as having unrealistic expectations, being poor communicators within the agency as well as with the schools and public, and passing the buck. Future challenges included breaking the cycle of returning (rereferred) families, developing positive alternatives for children, reducing workloads to reduce stress and staff turnover, and involving community organizations and volunteers in the process.

Faced with such complex issues as domestic violence, mental illness, substance abuse, and significant poverty, and with families being reported to the CPS system in unprecedented numbers, it is no wonder that the CPS system is overwhelmed. CPS workers sometimes narrowly focus on the child in isolation or order the family to comply with the worker's mandate. It is common to hear "Because it's policy" or "It's my job to protect the child" among the reasons given for removing a child or for not looking below the surface of a family's problem to see its strengths or resources. These responses come from many places: a lack of clear interpretation of policy, fear that they will do the wrong thing, or because a worker thinks that ordering a family to comply is all that needs to be done to do the job adequately. However, most workers follow the guidance of their supervisors, which is why supervisors are such an important resource for workers.

SUPERVISORY SUPPORT

CPS supervisors in Michigan, and perhaps elsewhere, do not regularly, as matter of policy, have structured case consultation for their staff. Nor is there a consistent forum where workers can receive advice, consultation, or help with their cases from their peers. Supervisors who give clear, positive guidance and consultation are key in training workers to be family-driven, not rules-driven. When one of us asked a worker why he spent all day with a family, without any sign of progress, he said, "I don't know what else to do." He was doing what he knew, but it wasn't helpful or effective or efficient. It would have made a difference if that worker had been able to receive guidance, support, and suggestions from both experienced supervisors and peers. More important is the reality that he didn't know to ask. When asked about that, he said he just didn't think about asking for help; he felt the case was his responsibility. While many workers do ask for advice, they usually do so in an informal situation, one on one. Generally, a case consultation format that provides an opportunity for helpful feedback is not structured into the daily business of CPS. Many supervisors do not join workers to observe or support them "on the job" with families. That is not to say they do not want to do that—often they don't have time or they just haven't thought of a way to do it effectively.

When a group of CPS supervisors attending a solution-focused training were asked what they thought their workers would want them to do for them, the supervisors said:

- "Give me more direction."
- "Support and affirm my work."
- "Take time to listen to me."
- "Listen to *my* frame of reference."
- "Give compliments and positive feedback."
- "Be available."
- "Put ideas into practice."

Given these responses, creating a structure to assist supervisors to support their workers would make good sense.

No one disagrees that the CPS system is overwhelmed and CPS staff often highly stressed. Discussions with many CPS workers confirm that they feel incapable of meeting the demands of their job as it exists now and as is expected by their managers. Much of this centers on the appropriateness and complexity of families coming to the attention of CPS today. We would argue that over half of the families that get screened in do not belong in the CPS system. If CPS staff had the flexibility at the very first point of contact with a family to assist with access to other, more appropriate services for the families asking for help, the CPS system might be able to function more efficiently. Sometimes workers open cases because it is not clear to them what is needed; rather than risk something going wrong, they open the case just to be safe. The CPS law for Michigan and in other states gives workers latitude, especially in areas of neglect. If they are uncertain they can use "threatened harm": to open a case and give themselves more time to make a decision. We suggest that enhancing CPS workers' family assessment interviewing skills will enable workers to better determine what support a family needs and whether, in fact, that support requires a full CPS intervention. Though some would argue otherwise, there is wide latitude in CPS law to screen in neglect cases; workers can define the problem to insure that the case is opened.

Supervisors also feel great stress. In a CPS supervisors advisory group, when discussing the possibility of solution-focused training, they quickly listed 68 separate tasks they already perform. They felt adding "another task" to their menu would overwhelm them, not help them—they saw this potential help as an "add on." Part of the burden of CPS comes from having so many families in the system that do not belong and should not be part of the system's caseload. Yet they remain there because the CPS system itself doesn't know what to do with them. It is a never-ending circle of frustration. This frustration has led to the reality that as many as 45% of CPS cases have been referred before the current referral. These referrals are often for the same or similar allegations. While there is debate about why families are re-ferred multiple times, it is clear is that either families have not sustained changes in their behavior to keep them out of the system or that some-one thinks they are not caring adequately for their children.

The CPS system in most jurisdictions is somewhat linear and hierar-chical; frontline workers feel a tremendous solo burden for the children on their caseload. When a child dies or is seriously hurt, it is often these workers to whom the finger points. In fact, this burden should be shared by all within the organization. Given the multiple issues that surround each case coming into the CPS system, common sense says that training frontline CPS workers and their supervisors should have the highest priority. The investment in training and technical assistance would have an immeasurable return. Workers who are well-trained and supported by enthusiastic and knowledgeable supervisors would be able to deploy, in a solution-focused manner, a full range of strategies to assure child and family safety and improved family functioning.

Currently, though, many states limit their in-service training to new workers—and sometimes even that is unavailable (Schene, 1998). Many states do not see ongoing training as critical and essential. Some of the least trained and least experienced workers are assigned complex and tough cases that would challenge even the most experienced therapist. When staff are undertrained and underskilled, they often misinterpret family issues and make bad decisions, resulting in bad outcomes. More problematic is the fact that workers sometimes are treated as if they were incompetent by their supervisors and by judges and courts with whom they regularly interact. It should not be surprising that these workers, treated in this manner, in turn blame their clients and focus on how to assure their own "safety" in the system instead of working with clients to help keep their children safe.

The New York Times reported in August 1998 on the death of a child in the Connecticut CPS system. The governor's reaction was to fire a child welfare supervisor and transfer five managers. He declared, "In the world I *wish* I lived in, I'd fire all these people." While the death was heart-rending and apparently preventable, and, while clear mistakes were made, the story shows how quickly the public and its representatives blame CPS workers and supervisors.

Jonathon Kozol, in a *Time* Magazine editorial on the tragic death of Elisa Izquirdo in 1995, in New York City, stated, "We wring our hands about the tabloid's criticisms . . . but do not volunteer our cleverness to change it." Kozol said, "The more we know the harder it is to grant ourselves an exception." He went on to say that in a conversation with a student in the South Bronx about such dilemmas, the student said, "Somebody has power. Pretending they don't so they don't need to use it to help people—that's my idea of evil" (Kozol, 1995).

Workers need to hear that their contributions are vital when they are doing a good job. They need to be mentored, supported, and well-trained. They need to be challenged to improve. Supervisors and managers themselves must model what they expect: respectful, collegial, supportive, solution-focused work.

COMMITMENT TO TRAINING AND PROFESSIONAL DEVELOPMENT

One of the functions of administration is to promote and expect high-level training and staff development. There has been a great deal of discussion about how to improve training for public child welfare staff. Models emerging across the U.S., as well as the one now being used in Michigan, combine (1) "on the job training," which may involve an experienced peer or colleague mentoring a new worker; (2) "shadowing," where new workers observe experienced workers from the beginning to the end of the day to see how they handle day-to-day tasks; and (3) traditional classroom training.

In classroom training for child welfare workers, it is expected that everyone will master "core competencies." Achieving a minimal proficiency standard prepares new employees for the exciting but often complicated task of giving respectful and responsible customer service. Recently, a few newly hired trainees in Michigan who could not demonstrate an adequate knowledge of the core curriculum or whose attitudes demonstrated a less than desirable mindset about public welfare were fired before starting the job. This is an important step toward "raising the bar" toward professionalism.

The use of technology such as videos, computers, and other state-of-the-art audiovisual equipment has greatly improved training efforts. Interactive video conference equipment for remote large and small group trainings, consultation, and discussion will soon be common-place in every public welfare office and training site in Michigan. Unlike video lectures or teleconferences, remote video conferencing offers the capacity for interactive discussions between two or more sites. The equipment allows for conversations and small group discussions to take place as if the participants were in the same room. Experts like Insoo can readily set up an hour or two of consultation with CPS staffs in Michigan without even leaving her Milwaukee office. Video conferencing has the capacity to provide more immediate and personal access to consultants. It will revolutionize the remote consultation.

In addition to introducing strategies like mentoring and shadowing and providing a more competent training curriculum, a reorganized career development training branch in Michigan's FIA will focus on the professional development needs of staff, promoting financial support for career development, such as advanced study and leadership training. This office of professional development will focus on the lifelong development of competent professionals and promotion of highly competent public agency staff.

Beginning Steps, but Long Journey Ahead

In Michigan, "solution-focused interviewing" is now a standard core module in the curriculum for all new specialists both in child welfare and in the Temporary Assistance for Needy Families (TANF) and food stamp programs. Insoo and Peter DeJong assisted in the development of the materials and are regularly asked to teach, train, or consult with public welfare specialists. "Advanced" solution-focused training also is available. To Michigan public welfare staff this is a dramatic change from training focused on paperwork competency, information transferring, and policy and regulation expertise.

Replicating the essence of a model that has worked well in Michigan's Families First program would greatly enhance training efforts in child welfare. Each of the Families First trainers has been either a frontline worker or a supervisor in the program. In other words, each trainer has done, and continues to do, the frontline work. This brings a great deal of credibility to the training sessions. Annually for two months each trainer "returns to the field" and takes cases again. This makes all the difference in the world. Instead of saying, "When you take your cases . . . ," the trainer says, "When I took my last case, the family I met . . . " Real experience and practice bring ever-increasing skill and competency to classroom training.

In addition, the Michigan public agency training office was recently split into three distinct divisions: (1) child welfare, (2) professional development, and (3) the TANF programs. This division of functions emphasizes mastering of core competencies in each of the specialties. More emphasis within the agency on addressing unmet training needs in a consistent professional manner will lead to a higher standard of practice. Thinking in ways that more closely align public welfare to business models that provide coaching, mentoring, on-the-job training, and lifelong development may result in a more competent and skilled workforce.

If at First You Don't Succeed . . .

The CPS Partnerships for Safety initiative in Michigan allowed us to keep working for better ways to train CPS workers. We tried several. Originally, we tried training CPS supervisors without their staff; we then attempted to train CPS workers with their peers. Neither approach brought about the commitment and change in practice that would enable frontline workers to interact consistently with clients in a solution-building manner. Workers told us that they "loved the training" but when they went back to their offices they often didn't feel that there was a "solution-focused climate." In other words, they were not encouraged to use the skills that they learned in training. We came to realize how important a "top down–bottom up" approach was. Instead of training isolated groups of frontline CPS workers and supervisors, we engaged five local county field offices where managers and staff were willing to work with us. We worked with the staff—going on home calls with workers, holding supervisors' strategy and skill-building sessions, working with supervisors to conduct unit meetings to staff cases, and using role plays to demonstrate solution-focused strategies. We, the outside consultants, were and are regularly in the field offices. Supervisors and managers made us a part of their teams. Our presence became a symbol of the commitment to make "solution-building" an important part of "training in action." Recently, the supervisors and manager in one of the counties designed and led a staff development day for all frontline workers—one more step toward building a solution-focused staff.

Neither of us realized how difficult changing the culture of local CPS teams would be. Nor did we realize how entrenched teams could be in practice methods passed on through long-term staff. Nevertheless, CPS staffs were open to us when they saw we were willing to spend time with them and respect the realities of their very difficult jobs. It meant a great deal to them that we would listen to them and acknowledge their strengths and the ways they were using solution-focused strategies. We developed a worker observation checklist that we used on home visits (see Appendix E). While using many training strategies in our work—mentoring, coaching, role playing, listening, consulting, teaching, observing, challenging, laughing with and supporting the teams—we have seen how solution-focused strategies can improve training.

Both of us believe training must be ongoing, consistent, and individualized. We have seen firsthand the results. Training of public child welfare staff must continue to be a priority if first-class services to CPS families are expected.

COMPLIANCE VS. CHANGE

Those working in today's CPS system are beginning to recognize that in order to bring about lasting change they need to join with families in respectful partnerships that result in safe and adequate care for children. This contrasts with the view of some CPS workers that it is easier to impose a solution on clients. They seem to believe that if they tell families what to do, blind compliance will follow. They impose what they believe will bring about necessary change and often point to rules or policy to justify what they are ordering families to do. The high recidivism rates in CPS remind us that ordering change doesn't work. The reality is that, unless the solution is the family's solution, the best that will occur is compliance—until no one is looking. Imposed mandates are very different from mutually agreed upon goals between the workers and families. This allows clients to work on building their own solutions.

A CPS worker who does not listen but only dictates begins a relationship with a new client that is based on mistrust and then may act as if the client is not to be believed. When the client perceives this skepticism, he or she reacts with equal mistrust and skepticism. This attitude confirms for clients that this person is not a "helper" but someone sent to document deficits and take action against them and perhaps take their children. Is it any wonder that this attitude fails to lead to trust, engagement, and partnership? The view of the client as an adversary or someone not to be trusted spills over into the intervention itself and sets a course that is unproductive and littered with half-truths. The crisis that brought the client to CPS often does not diminish, or the worker judges that the children are not safe. Often this mistrust keeps workers from getting useful and complete information to help the family determine an appropriate course to remedy the situation.

Most CPS policy is general enough and broad enough to allow respectful, solution-focused interaction. However, sometimes the interpretation of policy and lack of appropriate training on policy have led to the view that the family needs to be told what to do in a prosecutorial or "soft police" manner. This can result in blaming the client instead of working cooperatively to find safe solutions. Again, we see the importance of training and supporting the frontline workers. Workers who feel competent rely less on ordering change than on helping families bring about lasting change. When workers do not feel competent, they do not treat clients as competent.

Some supervisors also see their role as enforcing rules and policy rather than supporting, teaching, leading, and motivating for change, and sharing with workers how families might build their own lasting solutions. When workers cross the threshold of a family home, they have tremendous power. They have to rely on their interpretation of the policy, law, and agency rules, as well as their own judgment. Supervisors who have found ways to help workers by initiating consultation and support in these very important situations are seeing promising results in case decisions. When workers make judgment calls on their own, with no consultation, they may miss and/or ignore the hope and the strengths. It helps when a supervisor or peer confirms the reality that all individuals, especially parents in chaotic or very troubled families, have aspirations and dreams for themselves and their children.

While positive changes are slowly being seen in the CPS system, including making necessary state statute changes and providing more funding for family support services for families who get screened out of CPS, many within the system continue to view their task as implementing rules and policies to "make their client change." In the following chapters, we suggest some strategies and skills that will move CPS from a system that sees the same families over and over again to one that see parents as "experts" on their own situations and effective agents of change in their own lives. The suggestions we make do not require new resources—just a new mind-set.

SOLUTIONS THAT SUPPORT

Child welfare today, especially CPS, has become political and polarized. That is in part because we are focusing on programs and categories. Sometimes it seems the best interests of the children are lost in the frenzy. We've fallen into the "either/or" syndrome—if you believe in placement, you don't believe in family preservation. Child welfare is in the throes of responding to these major competitive forces. CPS also carries the burden of society's unrealistic expectations.

We are not so naïve as to think that there are simple or easy answers to the needed changes in our overwhelmed child welfare system, but as Schorr noted in her recent book, *Common Purpose*, "Together we can be sustained by the conviction that we have resources—material, intellectual, and spiritual—to assure that every American family can expect its children to grow up with hope in their hearts and a realistic expectation that they will participate in the American dream. Together we can share and together we can achieve, our Common Purpose" (1997, p. 385). We do not know where we will be in five years, but we do know there's a lot to be done and that together we can make a difference for children and families.

Every day, hundreds of thousands of frontline workers have the privilege of working with families to keep children safe. They will respond to many difficult situations requiring wisdom, good judgment, and empathy. We believe those frontline workers do what they do because they want to make a difference—and they *do* make a difference! However, supervisors need to do better at insuring that these workers have the tools and skills they need to do the job we ask them to do and, most importantly, that they have the support of their supervisors, organizations, and community.

Workers cannot respectfully listen confidently to families if they are not well-trained to listen and if they are not receiving respect, support, and breathing room from their own managers. Nor can they find and broker resources if they feel everything depends on them alone, which is why communication with staff and working in partnership with them is so important. That's why supervisors must be there for their staff, not just when things go wrong, but to notice and affirm when things go right.

How we reach our goal is very important. We've crafted a few rules to keep ourselves focused:

1. Keep the child and his or her family first.
2. Be a great listener—grow big ears!
3. Show respect. It's key and it goes a long way.
4. Notice a job well done.
5. Thank people; appreciate them.
6. Celebrate your successes and those of your clients, families, staff. Talk about that job well done.
7. Exceed customer expectations—as well as your own expectations.
8. Be a leader; don't just talk the talk—walk it.
9. Value diversity, the fabric of our lives: race, culture, gender, religion. See diversity as the blessing it is.
10. Be solution-focused; remove obstacles, don't create them.

These rules seem simple and perhaps idealistic, but overwhelmed systems are filled with overwhelmed people—solutions start with one person at a time, one compliment at a time, one positive thought or action at a time.

Finally, and most importantly, our remedy for easing the burden of feeling overwhelmed is to take time for ourselves so that we have the energy to continue to make a difference in our clients' lives. When we are too tired and unfocused, it is easier to see the broken and the negative. The vision is clearer and the strengths evident when we have energy, which comes when we support one another.

CPS supervisors must thank themselves and their staff often—for the dedication and respect they bring to their work and to those they touch and who touch them. Their gifts, especially their hope, will help staff help children and families find their own power. We've come a long way toward making a customer-friendly system. We have new words, new methods. We've made significant gains, but those gains can only be maintained if we become the change we seek.

ADMINISTRATIVE SUPPORT

In the child welfare field, there are calls to do much more with fewer resources. Living with that reality, how do managers succeed in motivating staff, building morale, improving outcomes, and encouraging frontline workers and supervisors to do high-quality work? How do we help them care about the families they see? How do they know they are doing a good job? Public service is an important and worthy profession. Child protective services is demanding and quick-paced work. The need for good judgment, accountability, and assessment documentation is paramount. We hear regularly from child welfare workers and supervisors that caseloads are too large, supervisors have too much to do, and nobody cares much about what they do until a tragedy occurs. Many workers and staff do not believe their managers will stand behind them in bad times as well as good times.

A range of management styles and a variety of ways to support one's staff exist. As a manager in a large bureaucracy, I (SK) have seen the results of solution-focused management. Incredible staff have produced incredible work. A staff person recently said, "I've been with this agency a really long time—and I am so happy to be working here. It is such a hopeful place to be." He has a wonderful supervisor who requires hard work but provides lots of thanks and manages from a solution-focused perspective. All the ideas in this book aimed at improving outcomes between clients and workers can be adapted as tools for managers and supervisors. The philosophy that clients are experts of their own situations and have ideas about how to improve their lives is true as a management paradigm also. The message that we give workers—that we expect them to listen to their clients with respect, to encourage clients to use their own power to effect solutions that are long-lasting, and to work with clients for positive outcomes and change—is the same message I try often to give my staff. Embracing a vision and philosophy that works with both clients and staff sends a powerful message.

Managers have both an opportunity and a responsibility to model and mentor solution-focused strategies. If we try to operationalize without a solution-focused approach, resistance and mistrust will be common among staff. Management by directive will, more often then not, bring grudging compliance but not wholehearted acceptance and change.

Creating a system based on this new paradigm requires that all of us in public human services agencies make significant investments to change the way we work with each other and with families. These changes include personnel practices, workload and paperwork changes, gatekeeping strategies (i.e., determining which families should be in the system), supervision strategies, strength-based, solution-focused, and family-centered policy, high-quality staff training, and evaluation strategies that focus on outcomes. While each child welfare system must articulate its own vision, the following reflects what is possible from the "top down" and the "bottom up." We envision a child protective services system that will:

- respond to and investigate reports of alleged child maltreatment in respectful, client-driven, and solution-focused ways
- hold parents responsible for the safety of their children by providing collaborative, respectful, individualized services that promote and ensure child and family safety and parental autonomy
- divert families whenever possible from CPS involvement when community-based resources would sufficiently diminish risks and promote family safety
- remove children from their families only as a last resort, not as a first option, and only when all services that would safely maintain a child in the home have been exhausted
- value families' strengths that make it possible for them to maintain their dignity while thriving with integrity and self-sufficiency
- work with parents when the removal of a child is necessary to make changes that will enable swift reunification of the family or, in very serious cases, promote the safety and stability of the child by finding a safe and permanent home with kin or an adoptive family

To be successful in realizing this vision, a commitment to redirect the core values of the current service delivery method within the public child welfare agency is required. This involves:

- making changes at the very top levels of administration
- moving from a bureaucracy-driven service mode to a client-driven, coherent model of service—one that is supportive and helpful to families in crisis with children at risk
- finding safe, strength-based, and lasting solutions in partnerships between parents and workers (treating parents as the "experts" of their own situation, capable of finding their own solutions; using the CPS system as a consultant and helper to families)
- creating respectful customer-driven services that make common sense

CREATING THE VISION, SUPPORTING THE CHANGE

In *Leading Change*, John Kotter (1996) says, "[As] an observer in organizations, I can say with some authority that people who are making an effort to embrace the future are happier than those clinging to the past . . . that those people at the top . . . who encourage others to leap into the future, who help them overcome natural fears, . . . provide a profoundly important service for the entire human community. We need more of those people. And we will get them" (p. 186). Child welfare managers can lead others into the future—and really make a difference, especially through their efforts to work in a solution-building, strength-based paradigm.

We do a lot of talking in this book about what needs to change, but what is this change for? What is the fundamental vision that will drive this change? Managers of child welfare programs need to have a vision that CPS can be different than it is now and be willing to provide the context and support for such a transition. All the suggestions in the world about supervision, consultation, training, and frontline practice will not matter if, when faced with a crisis or poor outcomes, managers step away from the vision. If managers and supervisors are unclear about the vision, everyone gets critical or confused when things go wrong. So first and foremost, it is crucial to have, know, and communicate a vision. An effective vision keeps everyone focused. What do we want CPS to look like? What are the expected outcomes? Who should make that happen?

We have been asked, "What is your vision for CPS?" If we had an ideal world our vision might be different. We believe that, given the current system, our vision is in *how* to provide services. The CPS system grew out of a child advocacy movement and the focus remains today too narrowly on child advocacy. What is needed is a focus on family advocacy. When families are strong and healthy, children are not abused. Our vision is one that looks at both child safety and well-being and family safety and well-being. Our ideal vision is one that begins and ends with RESPECT. If CPS interventions are necessary, and they are for some families, then families must be touched as lightly and with as little intrusion as possible. For a CPS worker, the question is always, "How would I want to be treated?" CPS workers who can put themselves in the place of the client will find ways to respect family integrity while helping and assisting the parents to appropriately care for their children. This is the vision that has inspired our work.

Does everyone you manage know the vision and work with you to promote it? If you asked ten CPS workers, "What is the vision for CPS?" would you get ten different answers? If we, as managers, cannot clearly describe the vision for CPS in a few minutes, we probably have staff that can't describe it either. A vision isn't just what's written (although that helps), it is what is alive in the organization. It encompasses CPS's role and guiding principles. If it is fragmented, confused, or ever-changing, there is also apathy, confusion, and resentment. A clearly understood vision keeps us from being distracted by the crisis of the moment and keeps the individuals and organizations focused on promoting long-term change. This vision is the mainstay when there are challenges and threats.

Change happens in stages. Having a strong vision combined with a sense of urgency to implement it, communicating the vision through-out all levels of the organization, and empowering staff to keep it alive help to anchor the vision in the culture of the organization. Good managers use the vision to guide change.

We hear from workers that the "central office" often changes what is expected of child welfare. This is confusing for them and often they think things change because of political pressure. Politics is often the reality. Sometimes, because of media attention, or because of the pressure by politicians or legislators, the public child welfare system needs to react by shifting gears and changing behaviors, practice, or protocol to address concerns about child abuse issues. Workers wonder, "Should we protect kids or keep families together?" The fact that they ask this question suggests that a clear and consistent vision is not communicated throughout the organization. It may be that the vision is articulated but not communicated well, in either words or actions. Workers are smart enough to know whether the words of the vision match the action. Successful change depends on this consistency. Managers can help their workers make such changes by giving them information on what is being changed, and how the change came about. It makes for a less resentful atmosphere if workers don't think that they are being blamed or that changes are being made for no good reason.

SOLUTION-BASED SUPPORT

Administrators have a great deal of power. They can make change happen by their involvement, attention, and interest in their entire organization, by giving solution-based support to their staff. Here are some general suggestions.

1. Administrators and managers who want to promote solution-building strategies must live, breathe, and model those principles in their everyday actions. The old adage "Actions speak louder than words" is true. The staff look for their managers' commitment in their behaviors and in how they manage.
2. Top-level administrators could encourage the use of solution-focused, strength-based models and language in contracts, training, quality assurance strategies, outcome measures, and service delivery.
3. Administrators also might encourage their top managers to pay attention to child welfare. As simple as this sounds, managers and administrators often get involved in child welfare only when a tragedy occurs. Otherwise, they take for granted large caseloads, multiple rereferrals, and poor outcomes. Perhaps they do not believe enough in their staff or their clients to think it can be different. Sadly, some administrators do not act as though they believe families can change and care for their children adequately; so, like the workers, they are satisfied with mediocrity. They expect families to show up again and again; 45% of them do. They continue to defend budgets that provide only insignificant results. If there is no acknowledgment by the very top administrators that this isn't the vision, there is no urgency to improve. Administrators, in and of themselves, create visions. What should it be? What do you stand for? How is the vision communicated?
4. Administrators could promote good clinical procedures in solution-focused ways by modeling solution-focused skills in their management interactions. Additionally, administrators might help staff to utilize case-staffing that is strength-based and solution-focused. Goal-setting that actively involves family members and active listening skills should be consistent throughout programs.

5. Administrators should be interested in and really know what is going on with families. Often the gulf is both wide and deep between top-level administrators and the frontline staff. One worker told me that the only time she ever saw the county director was when one of her workers or supervisors was in trouble. The idea that an administrator would be interested in "best practices" of frontline staff and the positive outcomes for families wasn't even on the radar screen for that worker. The investment of time and the reaching down into the organization to talk with those who meet families on the frontline every day would go a long way to improve frontline practice and outcomes for families. For example, administrators could attend a staff meeting of CPS workers and listen to the cases that they deal with every day. It would be helpful if administrators would go out on investigative home calls with workers to see firsthand the issues confronting families and what the service needs are.

6. As managers regularly communicate with their frontline staff, they become more effective liaisons between the workers and the policymakers. This is an important role, as managers also have the responsibility of interpreting policy, that is, connecting management directives with what the worker knows and can put into practice.

Detailed suggestions and tools for implementing a solution-focused approach to supervision are given in chapter 8.

Many barriers remain to effective and positive solution-focused management, and we have not yet seen a state or local jurisdiction putting all the pieces together. But many people and organizations are hard at work tackling the issues to create a new system that is a more comprehensive approach to child protection. We believe we can add to the solutions by using the strategies included in this book. While we do not have all the answers, we do have many suggestions gleaned from our experience as well as from others who work for child protection.

Part II

Child Protective Services: The Nuts and Bolts

Chapter 4

Beginning with a Phone Call: Responding and Going Beyond

ALL CPS ACTIVITIES BEGIN WITH THE FIRST PHONE CALL EITHER FROM SOME-
one who volunteers to take the time to express concern for a child's
well-being and safety or from a person obligated to report incidences
of neglect and abuses of children. The reliance on these callers for
case-finding necessitates that we regard all phone callers as potential
partners and resources for CPS instead of mere "reporters." Rethinking
this partnership with callers would improve the community's perceptions of CPS, as well as improve CPS's services. In this chapter, we
offer some ideas on how to take advantage of this resource while
sorting through the myriad of information to ensure or improve the
safety of a child.

SORTING OUT THE USEFUL INFORMATION

Each year in Michigan alone 120,000 people make an effort to get in
touch with a CPS office (Michigan Family Independence Agency, 1995).
(There are 3 million reports nationwide.) Callers expect that somebody
can do something to take care of their worry, frustration, and anxiety.
How can CPS reassure these callers that their call reports are taken
seriously, so that they do not feel disappointed and without much
hope that something will be done about their concerns?

Because of the volume of phone calls that comes through the county
child welfare offices each working day, telephone intake workers take
up a prominent space in most county CPS offices. The number of calls

over the past 20 years has tripled, and it is important to sort out which merit a serious look. It takes a considerable amount of sophisticated skill and intuitive sense to sort out and make quick decisions based on a limited amount of information. Each phone call is taken seriously because of the many potential high-risk factors. Any phone call might reveal a life-and-death issue. Intake workers are sensitive and vigilant about screening out crank calls (e.g., disgruntled neighbors, angry family members, divorcing parents) and are very skilled at discerning facts from imagination and sticking with the legal definitions of abuse and neglect. As we mentioned before, it is impressive that this process has been as successful as it has been in sorting out the serious from the frivolous. Having listened in on these phone calls, we have come to respect the professionalism of these intake workers, who are the first contact for laypersons and for professionals who are mandated to report abuse and neglect cases. They are truly unsung heroes.

Yet the public perceives CPS as intrusive and as not doing enough. What can be done to remedy this perception? It seems that a great deal of bridge-building with the community is needed. We have come to the conclusion that, like most governmental and large bureaucracies, CPS can and should do a better job of building a relationship with the community and viewing it as a resource.

CPS REPORTERS AS RESOURCES

Back to the statistics. Of these 120,000 calls, 64,000 are set aside and no action is taken because they turn out to be rumors of neglect or abuse or the incidents occurred too many years ago to be able to document the allegations. By and large, these callers are viewed as "reporters" and are politely thanked and then essentially asked to step aside while we do "our thing." For many of these reporters the outcome of the good deed is very obscure and unknown. It is human nature to be curious about the outcome of one's action. We all want to know the ending of the story. When it appears that nothing is being done, it is easy to imagine why some of these 64,000 callers would complain to their friends, neighbors, or even in public forums that the CPS "does nothing," especially when sensational and high-profile cases are reported daily on TV and in local papers. There are people who make repeat calls with the same complaint within a short period of time because they don't trust CPS to do anything without a shove. Some of them have to make repeated calls to get the family connected to the intake worker.

We are very aware of privacy and confidentiality issues related to these phone calls, but we wonder what might happen if these 120,000 callers were persuaded to be our ambassadors? What if each and every one of them said something positive about CPS to a single friend, relative, or coworker? Imagine what might happen if CPS decided to enlist these callers as potential allies when, fairly early in the phone call, it became clear that the allegation was a rumor that the reporter heard or an incident that occurred two years ago. Viewing them as allies and as eyes and ears of CPS, rather than as busybodies or trouble-makers, would build better relationships with the community.

How to Build Alliances with Those Who Report to CPS

What if we changed our thinking and began to see these reporters as resources? What would happen if we used the "utilization principle" and recruited them to be the eyes and ears for CPS? The utilization principle says that, rather than try to change common undesirable behaviors by extinguishing them, instead turn them into something useful and positive (Haley, 1973). Thus, instead of viewing these report-ers simply as "meddlers," the system could invite them to be meddlers of a different sort by asking them to pay attention to the neighbors, only this time with a different purpose. Imagine the creative intake worker saying this on the phone when it becomes clear that this case is likely to be shelved until something more tangible is offered:

> Thank you very much for calling and letting us know about the children next door. Obviously you are the kind of person who cares and wants to make sure that the children are well taken care of. It would be very helpful for us also to know when and how the mother seems to be feeding the children well—how she seems to take care of her children. Would it be all right with you if I asked more questions about what you know about when the mother seems to be doing a good job?

Turnell and Edwards (1999, pp. 84–99) provide much more detail about how to start looking for safety as well as risk to children during the telephone intake phase and demonstrate with a transcript of a lengthy phone conversation. They recommend using scaling questions to obtain the reporter's assessment and the changes over time. We support this approach as an ideal. However, having seen and listened in on the hectic pace of the intake unit in several counties, we are pessimistic about its feasibility without significant structural changes and funding to hire and train more intake workers.

INTERVENING AS WE GATHER INFORMATION

When I (IKB) first began to listen in on the phone calls, sitting in a corner with a extension phone, computer, and notepad, I began to imagine the caller on the other end of the line. Intake workers estimate that the majority of calls are from other professionals in the community. Most are from schools, day care centers, healthcare facilities, tutoring programs, other social services, mental health services, and, of course, the police. These calls are rather clear-cut and straightforward and are generally simple to handle. The worker gets the information, including physical or other evidence, about the child who might be harmed or in danger and assesses the urgency or the potential risk. Sometimes this means taking steps immediately.

When the nature of a phone call is deemed sufficiently serious to warrant an investigation (47% of all phone calls that reach the CPS office), the case is immediately assigned by a supervisor to the next available intake worker, who must start the process of investigation within 24 hours. This rule puts an enormous burden on the worker, since some days she may have two or three new cases assigned to her—this in addition to her ongoing cases that still need further information to determine what kind of decisions need to be made within 30 days (some systems allow 60 days, some others as much as 90).

The decision to follow a phone call with a home visit involves three assessments:

1. Is the reported neglect or abuse one of crisis, such as a child comes to school with physical marks of abuse, a child who reports that he or she was physically abused, or a neighbor's witnessing of a physical abuse?
2. Does the anonymous caller seem credible?
3. Has the caller personally witnessed actual events or signs of abuse or neglect, such as a young child left home unattended?

The telephone worker listens for possible or plausible evidence, such as the child has not come to school for several days and the parents have not given good explanations. When an eyewitness account seems to indicate a high-risk potential for a minor child, then a decision is made to investigate further by making a home visit. This is where the "rubber meets the road" so to speak, because the tone and nature of the worker's relationship with the alleged abuser are determined during the first home visit. Depending on how and what kind of contentious issues emerge and depending on how this beginning is handled, the case could turn into either a "difficult" one or a "cooperative" and productive one.

Before exploring how to avoid creating a "resistant" client and how to place yourself on the family's side, we will take a slight detour and discuss the intake worker's attitude toward gathering all the necessary information.

MYTHS ABOUT COMPLETE INFORMATION

We are aware that the emphasis in CPS is on following correct procedures in order to protect oneself from potential accusations of mishandling a case. The bureaucratic paperwork system insists that procedures are the path to truth: as long as all the procedures are followed correctly, the worker is not responsible for the outcome. Therefore, there is a great deal of emphasis on "complete" information rather than "useful" information.

The general assumption that we need to gather complete information about clients and about their problems is rooted in the problem-solving paradigm (DeJong & Berg, 1998), which implies that once we have the complete and comprehensive information, then we will make a "good" (meaning "perfect") decision. We want to describe the implications of such thinking and how it is detrimental to CPS.

1. This assumption leads to indecision. That is, workers feel that there must be something else around the next corner that will make everything clear. All they need to do is wait long enough, then they will get all the information.
2. This leads to workers' feeling overwhelmed. They have a vague feeling that there is always more to do and thus cannot find closure or make a decision.
3. Having a vast amount of information often leads to workers' having wavering ideas about goals or desired outcome. Yet, they are expected to know everything that pertains to a case and thus they attempt to get even more information, which, unfortunately, leads to more confusion.
4. It is difficult for the workers to sort out information that is useful from that which is not. Often they do not know when they have enough information to take steps.
5. Workers do not always know how to use the information on hand. They usually feel like they might have missed something, but since they do not know what might be missing, they feel uneasy.
6. The consequences to the worker of making a "wrong" or insuffi-

cient decision are severe and harsh, which can paralyze the worker's decision-making abilities.

We contend that it is the quality of information that counts, not the quantity. More is not always better. In fact, what counts is how best to use the information on hand. We want to remind you that only 10% of all investigated cases require such an extreme measure as "removal" from the home and about 80% of those investigated are closed after 30 days of further investigation. For now let's address that 80%. Such a high percentage means that a large segment of CPS work involves making sure that the necessary elements of safety are present in each case. Following the solution-building paradigm, it is important to keep the following in mind throughout the contact, because the answers will guide the worker in deciding what to do:

1. What outcome do both the caretaker and CPS want? Be specific and behavioral.
2. What are the detailed signs of safety for this case? (Every case is different!)
3. What concrete, behavioral, measurable indicators of safety are there already?
4. Where would you rate the existing level of safety in this particular case today?

1	10
Least safe	Very safe

Describe in detail what you see that indicates this family is at this level today.

5. When was the most recent time the family was at this same level of safety? Have family members describe how they accomplished that previous level of safety. Ask them to be specific and detailed about this information.
6. How confident are the family members that they can get back to the previous level?
7. How confident are those around this family (grandparent, friend, neighbor, etc.)?
8. What is the safest, easiest, and simplest way to increase this level by one point?
9. How confident is the caretaker that she or he can achieve this goal of raising the level of safety by one point? What about other significant and supportive people?

10. How confident are *you* that the caretaker can achieve this goal of safety?
11. Who is most invested in accomplishing this goal? The caretaker? Family? You? If it is you, what can you do to turn it around so that you are not the most invested?
12. How will the caretaker and you decide that the safety goal has been achieved? What are the signs of success?
13. How much time do you need to help the caretaker raise the level of safety by one point? What would be realistic to achieve within that time? Describe in detail.
14. What number on this scale in question 4 would indicate that you could close the case?

We suggest this is the minimum level of information needed to assist the family in achieving its goal. Therefore, any other information may not be relevant to you at this stage of investigation. We will address more serious cases that might require removal of a child later.

WHAT IS USEFUL INFORMATION?

Remember that what determines whether information is useful is directly related to the question "toward what goal?" In other words, useful information has the following qualities:

1. It is present- and future-focused.
2. It involves what the client is doing now that is in the direction of the goal.
3. It is directly related to the outcome you and your client have identified as desirable.
4. It demonstrates that the family has the capacity to meet the goal.
5. It includes the caretaker's detailed description of a positive, alternative picture of his or her family's future.
6. It clarifies in concrete, behavioral terms the caretaker's list of necessary steps to insure safety.
7. It elucidates the caretaker's detailed plans for implementing the necessary steps.

The solution-building paradigm offers some useful concepts that can be adapted by CPS. The idea that the client's present and future are created and negotiated rather than predetermined by what happened to the client in the past is particularly useful. This makes it possible to hold clients responsible for change, rather than viewing them as victims of past abuses or neglect—or worse, as responsible for the problem. Another assumption of the solution-building paradigm is that all problems have exceptions; for example, even the most depressed clients have periods, however brief, when they are at least a little less depressed. The basic requirement for reaching a goal is that the client has had a small success in the past that will help him or her overcome the current problem.

ASSESSING FOR SAFETY AND FOR RISK: CHILD-CENTERED, FAMILY-FOCUSED INVESTIGATION

For over 25 years states have been mandating that their public child welfare systems implement "child protective services" for children experiencing, or at risk of experiencing, severe maltreatment. Philosophically, CPS is based on the premise that it is the fundamental responsibility of parents to adequately and safely care for their children and that CPS should only intervene when parents fail to do so (De Panfilis & Salus, 1992; Schene, 1998). From our work in CPS, we both believe the following:

- Most parents do care or want to care for their children.
- Most people can change their behavior when provided with support and adequate resources.
- CPS should provide respectful, individualized interventions.
- Clients should be directly involved in their case plan and decisions about their families.
- CPS services should be the least intrusive possible.
- The safety of the child and family must be at the heart of each CPS intervention.

To determine whether CPS should continue its involvement beyond the initial investigation requires that the CPS system conduct a careful and accurate assessment for risk and safety. Children's safety must be the highest priority in the risk and safety assessment. Local jurisdictions have struggled to carry out their statutory responsibility to identify risk and make decisions about families based on this information. Risk assessment tools have been developed in various states and localities across the United States to improve consistency and accuracy in making judgments about risk and safety factors. While these tools are important, they cannot substitute for the human judgment of workers who are well trained to assess a family's assets, as well as the risks for a child in that family. Making decisions about the future course of action for a particular family is an important responsibility, which must be approached with respect and accurate information. An assessment tool alone does not suffice; worker judgment, often based on common sense, is crucial.

The typical CPS assessment begins with attempting to find out and verify in sufficient detail if the alleged problem, neglect, or abuse really exists. The worker must also determine if the child can be safe with his or her family or caretakers. Unfortunately, some risk and safety assessment tools may leave workers thinking that it is their sole responsibility to find all the family deficits, as they make important decisions about the safety of the children and the parents' capacity to care for them. In part this is true.

A paradox inherent in using risk assessment tools is that they encourage workers to probe for what is *wrong* to accurately meet their statutory responsibility to make solid and clear decisions about *safety*. Workers need to balance all of the information about a family's strengths and deficits and to keep in mind this question: *"How does this information affect this child's safety?"* Sometimes it may be difficult in an initial investigative visit to both establish a modicum of rapport with a client and gather detailed information on the nature, severity, and patterns of alleged abuse. Solution-building interview strategies, described in chapter 5, help workers gather more comprehensive information at this initial stage.

Essentially, CPS workers investigating suspected child abuse or neglect must determine whether information reported meets statutory guidelines for child abuse or neglect. Further, workers must determine how immediately, if at all, the agency must respond to the report. The key issue is the safety of the child and whether there are sufficient protective factors in place.

Sometimes it seems that workers try to garner too much information on the initial visit or that they gather information irrelevant to the safety of the children. When I (IKB) asked a worker why he asked for so much information, he told me he was afraid he might miss something, so he asked about everything, thus leaving the client feeling that the worker was overly intrusive into areas of her life that didn't seem relevant. Yet, crucial information is needed at the risk assessment and/ or initial investigation phase. Workers need to determine the following to make a clear decision about how to proceed:

- if maltreatment occurred;
- if the child is safe at home; if not, what will insure the child's safety and maintain the family unit if at all possible;
- if there is risk of future maltreatment; and

- if appropriate family services exist that will reduce the risk of future maltreatment.

These are the critical issues. Sometimes, not knowing how to get this information, workers gather much more than is necessary to determine safety factors, thus overwhelming themselves in the process. The initial interview can be in itself an intervention. Fully involving parents as partners in the safety and risk assessment is crucial, as this interview sets the stage for all future work with the children and family. Unless a worker is able to establish rapport with the family immediately, an incomplete assessment will result.

The following questions may provide the workers with a way to ask about some of the critical safety issues:

- *To the mother (or caretaker):* "If I were to ask your children (on a scale of 1 to 10, 10 being the most safe) how safe they feel they are right now, what would they say?" Follow up then with "What would they say it would take to get from 6 to 7 . . . ?"
- *To the children:* "If I were to ask your mother (grandmother or father) how safe she thinks the family is (on a scale of 1 to 10), what do you think she would tell me?"
- *To the mother (or caretaker):* "If I were to ask your mother (best friend, sister) how safe you are, what would she say?"
- *To the mother (or caretaker):* "I imagine you've thought a great deal about how to keep you and your children safe. How have you done this in the past?"
- *To family members:* "What do you think would be helpful in keeping you safe (or helping you be more safe)? What needs to change to make that happen?"

Each of these questions opens the door in a nonthreatening way for the client to share with the worker how she gauges the risk and safety factors. This kind of interaction immediately involves the parents in the assessment and give them the power to begin to build solutions, in the manner that makes most sense to them. The questions, of course, may lead to other questions and information volunteered by the client. These can be integrated with risk assessment tools that may be required by state or local jurisdictions.

Both of us have accompanied workers in initial investigative visits to assess for safety and both of us are more convinced than ever that much more work is necessary during this initial visit to conduct a good, balanced safety assessment that does not mimic a deficit-documenting tool. While we know there are solution-building ways to gather information about safety and risk factors, we do not ourselves know of any strengths-based, solution-focused risk assessment tools being widely used in the U.S. As we adapt and finetune existing assessment tools, as we are doing currently in Michigan, we expect to see new methods for conducting investigations that are in themselves solution-building.

The pressure on workers not to make mistakes, especially in very serious cases, is sobering. Often even the most skilled and experienced workers do not know the correct path for a particular family, especially for the children. While the safety of the child cannot be compromised, this does not mean that removal is the first option. When parents are uncooperative or unwilling to give necessary information, it creates a dilemma. The suggestions we make in the rest of this book help workers establish rapport, engage families in the gathering of information, and assist in determining the safety and protective factors that are present. Risk and safety assessment tools are only valuable if workers are trained to use them effectively and accurately and with respect and sensitivity. Full partnership with families both in the assessment and in finding lasting solutions is critical.

Risk assessment is commonly viewed as a factual account of a person's situation. To us, however, it is no more than a snapshot of a time in a person's life, not a life script, as two CPS workers we met described.* In addition, assessment is often one-sided. That is, assessments are conducted as if the client lived in a vacuum. However, there is always an interactional component that the assessment cannot account for. It is invariably assumed that the worker's attitude and behavior have no influence on the outcome of the evaluation. The linear assessment sees the activity as static and can easily ignore the context in which the assessment occurs, including that of the worker's preconceived opinion about the family and a lack of skills and ownership of problems and solutions.

When we read many risk assessment narratives, we worry that the parents in these interviews did not have a chance to voice their side of the story. Some narratives even indicate that the worker believes that a parent behaved in the manner that was not friendly or courteous. But why should a parent be friendly? Consider, for example, the contrast between the two different ways to phrase a question and how they might generate different responses from the parent:

---

*Don MacLean, Shiawassee County Child Protective Services Unit, MI; Terry Smith, Wayne County Child Protective Services Unit, MI.

- Did you hit your child on the head?
- You must get frustrated with him at times. How do you deal with that?

The questions we ask shape the answers we get and nature of the worker-parent relationship. We will discuss this in more detail in chapter 5.

We strongly suggest that the assessment be fluid, organic, and reflect the changing circumstances of the family. In addition, it should reflect the family relationship changes, and the parent's relationship with the children. Looked at this way, the assessment document needs to be viewed as a living, breathing reflection of what the family is like at this particular time. This belief comes from our observation that people's lives are constantly changing. This is especially so among the poor, whose lives often depend on what others will or will not do.

MAKING HOME VISITS: SETTING THE STAGE FOR SUCCESS

Clients' reactions to CPS visits vary. Some clients react to home visits as an intrusion into their privacy and personal space. They see the workers as busybodies who barge in and tell them what to do. At times these sentiments seem perfectly justified and understandable. Such sentiments are colored by what clients have heard from others or their own personal experiences. It is perfectly reasonable for them to be wary of CPS workers, almost like reactions most people have when stopped by a highway patrol. Accepting and normalizing this cautious, hesitant, or even hostile response to a worker's visit can enhance the client-worker relationship right from the beginning.

Strangely enough, we also have observed clients who seem impervious to such intrusions, who in fact welcome the worker. This often seems to be the case when the client has had numerous previous encounters with CPS or other social service providers over the years or when the client grew up in the foster care, corrections, or other social service systems. Many clients come to rely on social service providers as a source of emergency services. Of course, there are stories about how clients abuse social services, using them as their transportation service, emergency grocery store, and so on, but these represent a very small number of people.

Since the home visit is the basic tool of CPS and the channel through which a case enters the system, it may be worth taking a new look at it. Many things can go wrong at this point that may be beyond one's control. For example, we came across a single parent who worked the night shift and had to sleep during the day, leaving the children unsupervised. We knew a working mother who left her children at a shopping mall while she worked nearby because she could not afford day care and did not have anyone to help her out. These may be high-risk situations if they happened repeatedly and are cause for concern if the parent has no stable and realistic solutions to these external circumstances.

Ways to Take Advantage of a Home Visit

Home visits offer a unique way to learn quickly about a client's lifestyle, and this allows us to take advantage of being in the center of activities as they occur, an opportunity that is missed when workers stay in their offices and the client comes to the office. Being in the client's natural environment helps to assess what is available and what is lacking, but also to take advantage of what is there and not there. For example, pictures of the children or the family members, award ribbons the children earned, signs of creative activities such as an afghan on the couch, children's drawings hung on the refrigerator door with magnets, house plants, attractive placemats on the table, and so on can be used as a way to break the ice and acknowledge the client's competencies and successes. Allowing the client to be the expert on plants, a breed of dogs, goldfish, crocheting, knitting, or decorating—and of course her children—is a natural way to begin building a positive relationship.

When friends or neighbors drop in during a home visit, workers can try, with the client's permission, to include these friends as resources. Workers might ask the friends and neighbors to be their eyes and ears by asking questions such as, "You have known Maryann for a long time and you seem to be good friends. What is Maryann like when she does a good job with her children?" When questions are phrased in this way, there is no danger of embarrassing the client in front of her friends or family members; such an approach actually tends to reinforce, validate, and support their existing relationships. When the client is supported in this way, we are more likely to get useful information voluntarily.

Instead of focusing on what is wrong with this home, always begin by commenting on the positive. It does not diminish or negate the danger or high-risk factors; it merely juxtaposes both aspects of the client's life. You can always address the negative aspects later. Many workers are concerned that if they do not immediately address the mistakes clients have made or the problems they have, somehow they are being remiss in carrying out their responsibility. Quite the contrary: Most clients know that their house is dirty or their lifestyle is not perfect and they could do a better job. They are exposed to how other people live through media such as TV, magazines, or visits with neighbors, friends, and family members.

Physical Environment and Safety

We never cease to be amazed that with thousands of uninvited home visits conducted each year throughout the country, there are relatively few cases of violence against CPS workers. We have made many home visits in areas considered dangerous and were continually amazed by how little fear we had, considering the potential for violence.

One of the most striking aspects of making home visits is the assault on our senses when entering the poor neighborhoods where most of our clients live. Like most of you, I (IKB) had heard many stories about the smell in the "dirty" houses we were required to visit and tended to minimize its impact. I had also seen many rescue workers holding handkerchiefs over their faces at scenes of natural disasters shown on television. I never fully understood what it must be like to be those rescue workers until I made visits to some clients' homes. When you enter certain urban neighborhoods, the area looks generally unsafe, not because of a threatening presence of drug dealers or a gang of teenagers, but because of the visible signs of decay, neglect, and poverty. It is not uncommon to find garbage on the front lawn; a huge, rusting car with flat tires that clearly has not been moved in years sitting in an unpaved driveway in a pool of water; missing steps on the porch and stairways; or dog feces and broken glass on the ground where barefoot children are playing. We once saw a rain-stained, dirty, worn-out mattress on the roof of a house as we turned onto a street. Visual assaults are not limited to outside the houses. We have seen green, fuzzy mold on a child's dish, piles of greasy dishes and pots and pans in the same sink with dirty family laundry. The sensory overload can be quite disturbing. We have found ourselves wanting to go back to the office, where we felt protected. The immediate involuntary reaction is wanting to gag or throw up, if not a strong desire to flee, to get out of the area as soon as possible.

We have wondered why most training of novice CPS workers or books and articles rarely mention this reality. Beginning workers are not given any helpful hints or pointers on how to manage such things. We suspect that most trainers, teachers, researchers, or writers of textbooks have been removed from the daily grind of being in the trenches for so long that they have forgotten about their own reactions. Besides, it is unpleasant and impolite to talk about such topics. It is also difficult to talk about this without appearing to be prejudiced against the poor.

Our hunch is that this sensory discomfort contributes to our feeling vulnerable, threatened, and unsafe and enhances our desire to leave as soon as possible. Many veteran workers say that "one becomes used to it"; over time you learn to ignore it. They also build up personal coping strategies, such as thinking, "It could be me." It takes a great deal of discipline to use one's reaction to such environmental factors and appreciate that the client's social environment might impair her capacity to insure the child's safety. One worker, who had been on the job for about a month, said that she certainly felt the impact and found that talking to more experienced workers helped because she came to realize that she was not alone in having such unexpected and unpleasant reactions. When I (IKB) began doing home visits I talked to myself to calm myself down so that I looked calm on the outside. Sometimes, pretending to be calm worked to calm myself inside. Many workers report taking long showers as soon as they get home. I found myself doing the same thing: I used to take long, hot showers at the end of the day to wash away the feeling of grime. While I felt guilty for feeling the grime on my skin, I also felt gripped by the need to forget all the dirt, clutter, and disorganization I saw during the day. I am grateful for this experience. Even though I knew that I would not be doing this for the rest of my working life, I could easily understand why novice workers ask for transfers to some other work within a short time after joining CPS. Of course, there are many reasons for problems with staff retention, but we should never forget the impact of such sensory overload on workers.

An important component of training, then, is to bridge the vast gulf of differences between workers and clients in culture, lifestyle, class, and many other areas. These issues need to be addressed repeatedly and openly and honestly throughout training and staff discussions, since they are all part of becoming acclimated to the job of making a difference in CPS. CPS veterans should be the ones to teach and mentor novice workers because they have so much to offer. (One of those seasoned and highly sensitive workers taught me to wear dog flea collars on my ankles to prevent flea bites!)

Personal Safety Tips

We have some suggestions for you, as CPS workers doing home visits. When you find yourself in this type of home situation, ask the client, "You must have a very good reason for not being able to keep the house as tidy as you would like. Can you tell me your good reasons?" Surprisingly, most clients do not feel offended by this question, since they recognize at some level that their house could be cleaner, tidier, and less cluttered. They may even have been told by someone in their life who cared enough to point it out. One very experienced colleague, Neil Sheeley (personal communication, 1998), told about a client who kept an enormous number of broken-down, rusted cars in his yard and stacks of car parts everywhere, including on top of the roof and around his house. Of course they were dangerous, an eyesore for the neighbors, and mostly ugly junk. When asked about the good reason for keeping this much junk, the client laughed and said it was his "bank account," indicating clearly that the worker should not intrude on his enormous asset.

Many training activities and manuals emphasize your safety as a primary concern and include tips on how to ensure it. Of course, you need to be prudently cautious so as not to jeopardize your personal safety. For example, the decision regarding whether to use the agency's car or your own private car to make home visits varies greatly, even among experienced CPS workers in the same county unit. We know workers who feel safer in their personal cars because they do not want the client's neighbors to know that she is being "checked on" by a social worker. We also met workers who feel safer using an official car because they feel less vulnerable when faced with an angry client who might attack the car, trace the license number to their personal address, or even threaten their children. Clearly, it is a matter of personal preference and how you choose to look at your relationship with your clients, what kind of personal experiences you have had, and so on. In addition, tools such as cell phones, car phones, and pagers give a greater sense of security.

When you hear from fellow staff that a certain family has a reputation of being violent, do not ignore this information. Ask a sheriff, police officer, or colleague to accompany you. Many programs routinely send workers in pairs to certain parts of large urban areas that are known to be high-crime districts. Take advantage of such options. Do not be a "cowboy."

If your office has a dress code, we suggest that you follow its guidelines. Since one cannot predict the situation you will run into, most workers prefer slacks, comfortable and sensible shoes, and clothes that allow freedom of movement. Keep in mind that some clients' homes have missing steps in the porch or stairways.

Many people are afraid of large dogs that seem to be trained to attack strangers; indeed, these dogs are menacing and make threatening gestures when you knock on the door. They jump up on the screen or storm door, acting as though you are an intruder, and seem poised to attack. Don't worry about showing your fear to your client—most people want to be helpful and often rise to the occasion in remarkable ways.

Talking with Angry and Hostile Clients

It is very likely that your agency manual, training sessions, workshops, discussions with colleagues and supervisor(s), and staff meetings have covered this topic numerous times. We offer these useful suggestions to keep in mind when faced with angry and hostile clients:

- Be polite at all times. Don MacLean, a veteran of CPS in Shiawassee County of Michigan relates having had no difficulty with clients in his seven years of CPS work (personal communication, 1999). He relates that he is always polite. He calls clients by their last name, making sure that he uses, Mr., Mrs., or Ms., and addresses them as "sir" or "ma'am." He always asks for pemission to enter. When he is told to get off the front porch, he immediately gets off the porch and continues his business from the walkway, off the porch. When the client refuses to talk, he asks, "When would it be convenient for you to give me your permission to step inside your house?" When the client is upset, he calmly asks, "When can you give me your permission to return and talk to you about your children's safety?" If the client is still upset, he leaves his business card and walks away. Don reports that he always gets a phone call, along with an apology.
- Once allowed inside, always behave as though you are a guest in the client's home. Your respect for his or her turf means that you may need to ask which chair the client wants you to sit in, which room is quiet enough so that you can carry a private conversation, etc. Don told us that he always asks for "permission" to look at children, to talk to the children, to make sure that children are safe.
- Find out what has worked for your colleagues or supervisor in the past. If this client is known to the agency, ask others about what has worked before.
- If the client is drug- or alcohol-affected or irrational, you can always return later. Quietly say to the client that you will return later and will talk when he or she is able to talk. Do not feel compelled to stay in a violent or threatening situation.
- Allow the client space. Meeting in a large space, if available, allows freedom of movement if the person gets agitated. Feeling confined in a small space often makes things worse.
- If the client lashes out at the department, CPS, or previous workers,

do not defend them. Agree with the client's point of view—this is not the same as supporting her view. "I can see how come you feel that way" or "I can see your point of view" or "I guess anybody would feel the same way if they saw it that way." Normalizing the client's anger is not condoning it. In fact, it will help her to calm down faster, rather than inciting him or her to further anger.

- Take your time. Listen to the reason behind the anger with genuine curiosity. Take the complaint seriously without defending yourself or the program. Do not offer advice or suggestions. This approach helps minimize the intensity of the anger. Ask the client what would be a little bit helpful—so that he or she will feel a little bit better.

- Use distraction. Angry people are emotionally upset and so are not thinking clearly. Therefore, they can become easily distracted. Any activity that shifts the focus of their attention to something or someone else, such as moving to a different room or changing seats, can be helpful.

- Always offer choices to clients, even when they are angry, threatening, and hostile. As long as they can carry on a conversation, it is helpful to offer clients a choice. Clients indeed have a choice, but when they feel they are pushed against the wall, they believe they have no choice and tend to become angrier. Thus, instead of saying, "I am just doing what the law says," "I'm just doing my job," or, "That's what the law says," we suggest that you formulate the same idea into a question of choice. "I can see that you really want to protect your privacy and to keep the family together. I will leave right now if you want me to. But, as you know, I am required to file a report and I really want to know your side of the story, since all stories have two or three different sides. I wonder, what is your side of the story?"

- Ask the client what helped him or her to calm down in the past. Since most of your clients have had numerous previous contacts with schools, public and mental health departments, the criminal justice system, etc., ask who was most helpful. What did this person do that was helpful? Listen carefully.

- See the hidden side of the anger. When you notice the person becoming calmer, ask in gentle, soft voice, "Where did you learn to be so independent, to protect your family, to be loyal to your children, etc." "Have you always been such an independent person, or is this something new for you?" Be sure to follow up on your questions. If the client says, "This is how I've always been," then you can respond, "Where did you learn to be so independent?" This implies that the person is independent and that you are only interested in where he learned to be that way. If the client answers,

"This is new and it scares me to find myself so angry at times because I've been a doormat all my life, but I decided I ain't gonna it take no more," you can follow this up with, "I am very impressed that you decided that being a doormat is not good for you or for your children."

- Maintain humor, hope, and gratitude. Do not take yourself too seriously. The tremendous human spirit peeks out in a child's smile or a struggling mother's efforts to do her best. Be inspired and feel privileged when they share their most intimate pain, raw humanness, and fortitude. This is what keeps us going too.

Case Example

CPS received a call about two young children who were left "home alone" for hours. The caller was concerned about the safety of the children. A worker immediately went out to the house and found two young children. Since he could not get the children to open the door for him, he called the police. Two policemen showed up at the front porch and also found the screen locked from inside. Melissa, the 4-year-old, answered that her sister, Heather, was 2, but she didn't know what their last name was, where their mother went, or when she would be back. When the police asked Melissa to open the door, she shook her head and said she was not to open the door for anybody.

"But I am a policeman, honey."

"Unh, unh, my mom says not to open the door for anybody."

"But honey, I am wearing a uniform so you can see that I am a policeman."

More head shaking. Finally exasperated, the police waited for a while and then decided to break into the house through the back door and find identifying information about the children and their mother. The children were "apprehended" and taken to a temporary foster placement and a note was left for the mother, informing her about what happened to the children and telling her to go to the CPS office the next morning at 9:00 A.M.

The next morning the young mother arrived angrier than a wet hen, demanding to know where her children were and threatening to "sue your ass off if anything happens to my kids." The worker angrily started asking questions:

"Where were you yesterday? If your children are that important to you, how come you left them on their own for hours?"

"Well, I did not leave them alone. I had a baby-sitter. What do you take me for? I would never leave my kids alone! I am a good mother!"

"So, what is the baby-sitter's name?"

"His name is Billy something. I don't know his last name."

"You don't even know his last name? Where does he live? What is his phone number?"

"I don't know where he lives and I don't know his phone number. He just moves around."

Both the mother's and the worker's faces were flushed with anger and frustration and their voices were becoming harsher with each exchange of words. Finally the worker said, "You are too angry to talk right now. We can't continue like this. Why don't you go home and I will come out to your house to complete the investigation."

Suppose the worker had begun the conversation with a comment about her daughter Melissa and how well the mother must have trained her children not to open doors to strangers, even policemen. What if the worker casually added, "I wonder how you impressed this important lesson on your children and they listen to you—even when you were not there. Not many children that age would have learned such important lessons. You obviously did something very right with your children. I wonder how you did that?"

What do you imagine the mother's reaction would have been? What do you suppose would have happened to her anger at the worker for "barging in" to her house and yanking her children away from her? Giving recognition to a success does not mean condoning her mistakes or her neglect of her children for so many hours. Yet, we are sure that the meeting would have started in a much more cooperative manner and plans would have been made for how to make sure that this kind of episode would not occur again, and so on. The worker would have saved a lot of time by beginning the meeting this way, instead of making a home visit, which would have taken at least two hours. And the mother might have been more willing to accept the responsibility for her mistake of trusting a baby-sitter whose name she didn't know or being gullible and naive enough to trust children to someone like "Billy something." Even mothers who make poor decisions want to be treated with respect and courtesy, and they are likely to be motivated to become better parents on their own initiative—which is what CPS wants also.

Case Example

The reporter on the phone to the intake unit identified herself as the children's paternal grandmother and told the intake worker that her three grandchildren had been "abandoned" at her door that morning by their mother. She did not know the children very well, and besides, she was in no situation to take care of the "abandoned" children, since she had to go to work. Obviously, the children were not in school that day. She asked CPS to come and take custody of the children immediately. Because the possibility of "abandoning" children was quite serious, the worker checked with the foster care unit to find out if there might be space open for the three children, should it be necessary to take custody of them.

But the worker was also open to listening to the mother's side of the story. The grandmother told the worker where the mother was staying, and she went to interview her. It was clear that the mother was expecting a visit from CPS. She immediately launched into a barrage of complaints against the father of the children, who had not paid child support payment for three months. She was agitated beyond reason. It seemed she could not sit still; instead she paced the room, spouting anger at the father of the children and his side of the family, including the paternal grandmother who had reported the "abandonment." With each sentence, her anger mounted, her voice rose, and her words tumbled out like a waterfall. Yet, it was clear that she was in control of herself, since the anger seemed to be targeted at the father of the children, a long-distance truck driver who had not returned her numerous calls to him, his radio, and his employer. She explained that she had been homeless for three months. She has been staying with friends, two nights here, three nights there, all the while making sure that the children were taken care of and went to school.

The worker calmly listened to the mother for about 15 minutes and then asked in a soft, calm voice, what she thought was best for the children—to stay with their grandmother, to be placed in a foster home, or to stay with her. At first the mother did not hear the worker and continued with how the children's father's family, including his mother and sisters, were all against her from the beginning and how the grandmother had never sent the children anything for Christmas or their birthdays. The worker quietly asked again in an even tone, "Ms. Evans, I can see how important your children are to you, and I can also see how tired and worn out you are from trying to take care of them during the past three months. So, what do you believe is best for your children—to live with their father and their grandmother, to live in a foster home, or to live with you, if we can find a place for you and your children so that they can continue to go to school?" On the third try, Ms. Evans finally slowed down a bit and said, "Of course the best thing for the children is to stay with me." The worker was finally able to establish that the mother's goal was to keep her children with her as the first choice; she thought perhaps the second option was to go to live with father ("so that he will find out how difficult it is to raise three children by himself like I've done all these years"); the last option was for the children to go to a foster home, but only if all of them could stay together.

The worker set to work finding services and resources for the family to stay together. We see here that, even in the midst of tremendous anger and what seemed like an out-of-control situation, a worker can influence the course of the conversation so that a parent can participate in decision-making for her children.

Managing Interruptions, Noises, and a Sense of Chaos

The most common concern voiced by social service workers who make home visits is how to handle the chaos, noise, disruptions, and general level of disorganization when in the client's home. We would like to remind you that this is not a social visit; it is a purposeful visit and you have a task to perform. Therefore, it is imperative to insure that the client's home becomes conducive to conducting business. For example, you should feel perfectly comfortable asking the client to turn the TV volume down. Make your request confidently, not demandingly or sheepishly. Explain that you want to give full attention to the reason for your visit and then your visit can end as quickly as possible. *How* you ask is very important. Instead of saying the TV volume is too high or too distracting, clarify in such a way that the client can see how she stands to benefit. You could also ask, "How do you make sure your children give you some peace and quiet when you need it?" This phrasing implies that the client must be doing it and you are curious about how she does it. Presenting your requests in a calm, quiet, firm voice makes them difficult for clients to resist.

Case Example

I (IKB) have a colleague who is also my neighbor. He and his wife have six children under age 18, plus a dog and a cat. The constant activity of little and big bodies makes their small household seem chaotic and noisy. Usually within an hour of being in his house, I am so overwhelmed that I am ready to escape to the peace and quiet of my own house. One day I realized how different his threshold of tolerance for noise and commotion is from mine. Frequently when I visit, he gives his wife a break and watches the children. In the middle of a discussion about a writing project, Karl might suddenly yell out, "Tony, step down from that chair!" or "Sara, you need to leave your brother alone" or "Tom, stop throwing food at your brother!" Without missing a beat, he then turns his attention to me and continues in a calm voice, "I think we should move this word over here" or "It will sound better if we put this over here instead of at the end of this paragraph." I am amazed that he can keep track of several things at the same time when I can only handle about one hour of it (with great effort). It suddenly occurred to me that his six children did not arrive all on the same day, but came one at a time. That is, Karl became acclimated gradually. Likewise, what might seem chaotic and disorganized to us might make perfect sense to our clients.

Meeting with Families that Fight All the Time

Family members who fight and constantly criticize and belittle each other are not necessarily as angry or hostile toward each other as they appear to be. However, you want to make sure that there is no violence or threat to the physical safety of family members or yourself. Once you have established that, remind yourself that this is a purposeful visit, not a social one. You need to do whatever it takes to manage the meetings in such a way that they are useful and helpful for the client. It is not good for anyone to be subjected to this fighting repeatedly. Most of the time, your use of language, gestures, postures, and voice inflection should be enough to convey to the client that you mean business and that you need to spend some time gathering information that will be useful to the client. Observing one or two of these fights will give you lots of information, such as who says what, what follows, and, most importantly, how the fight ends. However, if you continue to find yourself out-shouted, outnumbered, and overwhelmed, try talking to the family standing up. If that doesn't work, you can break up the family into small groups, such as all the children in one group, parents in another, or even a single person. This will make it difficult to continue fighting and arguing in front of you. If the family fighting is too loud, the temptation is to try out-shouting or talking over them. This is usually doomed to failure. Instead, we suggest whispering to one person in such a way that it is obvious you are whispering. The others might become curious about what you are whispering about and quiet down so they can hear you.

THE LANGUAGE OF CHANGE

Of all the helpful activities we do everyday, the most important is talking with clients. Talking involves using words to express, shape, clarify, and ultimately figure out what to do to find solutions. It also involves *listening*, which is more important than talking at times. Yet surprisingly, the social work profession in general, and the child welfare field in particular, has paid little attention to the link between language and change. All the activities we do daily—assessing, contracting, referring, consulting, supervising, writing reports, building relationships with clients, negotiating problems and identifying possible steps to viable solutions—involve the use of words. Even offering hard services, such as clothing, bus tickets, emergency shelter, food for the children, and money to pay overdue electric bills, involves talking.

A word is an expression of an idea; without words, we would not be able to discuss the ideas that enter our brains. Words make it possible for us to think about things that we have not thought about before. Yet, words also limit us and shape us. For example, suppose a grandparent decided that her grandchild's misbehavior is caused by the fact that the child is "sad" about a friend who moved away from the neighborhood. The grandparent's response to the child would be conciliatory. She would try to soothe, comfort, and reassure the child. But if the same grandparent decided that the same child's misbehavior was due to a "bad" trait she got from her no-good mother who got hooked on drugs and disappeared from the family, leaving her to take care of the poor child, her response to the child would be different. She would scold, compare the child to his "no-good" mother, punish him, and admonish him for misbehaving, and then threaten the child with further punishment. If the same grandparent decided that the same child was "mad," then the response might be to "walk on a egg shells" around the child. She would probably take him to a mental health center for therapy. How we define the problem tells us where to look for a solution; what we call a thing is very important. It is particularly important when "the thing" is a child's future.

In CPS, we have been so preoccupied with the investigation aspect of our work that we separate it into four functions: investigation/ assessment, intervention, ongoing (or other similar functions), and referral for services. Written this way, these functions appear as if they are separate, distinctly different activities. Therefore, in the name of efficiency some large governmental units in large urban areas have separate investigation, ongoing, and intervention departments, which could include a multitude of services. Consequently, they have a large number of workers whose only function is to investigate and then turn the case over to someone else. In addition, because the investigation aspect of CPS has been so heavily emphasized, we have come to believe that its primary function is to investigate. The words that are closely connected with investigation are *right* and *wrong, guilty* or *innocent*, etc. Of course, the guilty one is punished and the not-guilty one receives services. In the midst of all these intense preoccupations—sorting out the guilty from the not-guilty, substantiating abuse or neglect—we sometimes lose sight of the other important purposes of our service: to insure safety of the child. In the majority of cases this can be best achieved by connecting and building a positive working relationship with the parent. Because our primary tool for change is language, through which we enhance clients' motivation to look at their own behavior and decide to change, paying attention to and becoming artful at using the language of change are important skills in child welfare.

Interviewing as a Cooperative Endeavor

A good interview requires the cooperation of both parties. It is not simply a way for CPS workers to get information out of clients. It is a dance that must be learned by both parties. That is, as in a conversation, while we are gathering information we are also giving information. Imagine you are asked the following questions:

1. Have you ever had a job before?
2. How many jobs have you had before?
3. What kind of jobs have you had before?

Although these questions sound rather innocuous, you can surmise from your different reactions that the interviewer (1) has doubts that you ever worked before, (2) assumes that you have had jobs before, and (3) assumes that you have had a variety of jobs before and is interested in knowing about them. Your response depends on which understanding you have of the interviewer's perception of you and in turn shapes his or her next questions. From this simple example it is easy to see how and why you immediately hit it off with some clients but not with others. Instead of blaming the client for uncooperative responses, we must take at least 50% ownership for the interview's progression. Perhaps as professionals we should be responsible for more than half. Of course, there are always clients who seem determined to be uncooperative, but they are actually very rare. If your caseload is largely made up of hostile, angry clients, maybe it is time for you to examine your interviewing technique and the language you use and determine what you can do differently.

Interviewing as Intervening

Every time we knock on a door and make a surprise visit, we are intervening, that is, we are creating a crisis for someone. From the client's perspective, your showing up at the front door is a powerful force to contend with. Given CPS's negative reputation among the general population, it is not surprising that you often see panicked or disdainful expressions on your clients' faces. One scared and angry mother explained later (after she calmed down) that a worker and his student "jumped out of the car" and immediately she became scared and decided that the worker was coming to "grab my son." The worker was surprised to hear this because he had just gotten out of the official car in the usual way and had no intention of removing any child without good cause. Can you imagine the first thought that might enter the client's mind when you ask her how many children she has? Something similar to, "Oh, my gosh, how many of my kids are you going to take from me today?" An innocent question that you meant as small talk can be interpreted as something sinister and threatening within the context of your standing on her front porch and knocking on the door. Every question you ask can have a significance that you did not mean to imply; your questions cannot be separated from the circumstances that brought you to the client's home. It is no wonder, then, that when a client has repeatedly been subjected to this kind of crisis, she would turn passive and attempt to wait out the storm to minimize the disturbance to her life. It is painfully clear how thoughtful we need to be and how much compassion and skill we must have to soften the impact.

Whether or not we like, asked for it, or want it, everything we do during a home visit has an impact and creates a special meaning for the client, depending on his or her personal experience or opinion about CPS, and it behooves us to use this encounter as a vehicle for initiating positive change. The ultimate beneficiaries of this change, whether by design or as a by-product, are the children.

Service and Change, Not Compliance

When we talk about "service," many people assume that we mean hard services, such as providing beds, blankets, shelter, or food. However, these services comprise only a small portion of CPS work. The real service in child welfare is the work that influences our client's behavior so that a family's life is little bit better off because we were there. A child welfare service should bring some measure of change, however small. If we only look at the monumental problems, it is easy to lose sight of some of the small successes that clients accomplish each day—the building blocks of change. Change is a complex process; it involves stacking one block on top of another, moving one step at a time, one client at a time.

You might ask a very profound question: "How do we change people when they don't want to change?" We really don't change anyone. Nobody can change someone else. What we can do is to influence clients in such a way that they believe that it is their desire and in their best interest to change. This is all done with talking. Conversation with clients is readily available whenever we have contact with them. Of course, talking alone does not change behavior, and there are actions clients must take to change behaviors regarding child care, personal hygiene, cleaning the house, being selective about relationships, and so on. All these behavioral changes begin with an idea. Language shapes the idea one has about what and how one wants to change—without words the client may not even be able imagine the state of change. Beginning with your first contact, you can influence the client's idea about what she might want to *do* to shape her life differently. This happens even during your investigation and assessment for safety. Language is a powerful tool—the only one we have in most CPS contacts. It is our responsibility to be skillful in using it.

Genuine Curiosity and a "Not-Knowing" Posture

We agree with Anderson and Goolishian (1992) that helping profession-als should take a not-knowing posture with clients, and with Hoffman (1990), who elaborated on their idea by adding a "negative capability" to highlight this position. We like these concepts because they empha-size that clients "know better." DeJong and Berg (1998) give a more detailed explanation of this "not-knowing" posture. Clients are the experts on their situations, on how they want their lives to be different. They are the only ones who know when they have arrived at the beginning stage of solutions. This posture of not knowing does not mean that the worker need not have any knowledge about normal child development, parenting skills, what constitutes abuse and neglect, and numerous other areas of expertise. It means that when it comes to a particular client's past, present situation, and dreams for a better future, only the client knows those things. It also means:

- We decide HOW to use our expertise on child and family develop-ment, laws related to abuse and neglect, resources in the commu-nity, etc.
- We suspend our years of experience and all the knowledge we have about the nurturing environment that children need to develop into healthy and productive members of our society, beginning instead with the client's context and world view.
- We maintain a posture of curiosity and look at our clients' life as if we were novices and willing to learn from them.

There are many aspects of clients' problems that we cannot possibly know—and that we may not need to know. Building a cooperative relationship with clients requires that we be strong, competent, and humble enough to admit that we do not have all the answers.

Solutions that Fit

All solutions we offer must make sense to clients and fit with their way of figuring out the world around them. Instead of using a single solution for every problem of neglectful behavior, we must tailor a solution with the client in such a way that he or she sees the benefit. Much of what we view as client resistance or noncompliance is due simply to a lack of fit between *our* solutions to their problems/lifestyles. How many times have you as a worker become frustrated trying to find parenting classes that fit the client's schedule? Imagine how the client who is forced to participate in numerous services might feel. Can you blame a client for not following through on everything?

Case Example

When a worker discovered that a mother of four young children was feeding them donuts and cake for breakfast, he was aghast and immediately thought of lecturing her about good nutrition. Instead the worker had enough sense to ask the mother about her good reasons for feeding the children cake for breakfast. The mother said that the children liked it and it was much easier on her than corn flakes or oatmeal, which required washing a stack of dishes every morning. So, instead of lecturing, the worker asked the mother about how she manages to feed her children when she is so busy and worn out all the time. She said that when the children are fed, they get along better with each other, are less irritable and easier to handle, and listen to her better. This meant that she is able to be more positive with them and therefore does not have to yell and scream at them so often.

So the worker began to think that the mother already knew that feeding her children breakfast is important because it made her day easier. The worker also learned that having an easier time managing her children was important to this mother. Clearly, she knew how to be gentle and loving toward her children. Now, all she needed to do was to switch the donuts and cakes with cold cereal. The worker explained that cereal would increase the children's attention span and they would be even calmer and more alert. This made sense to the mother, who was then willing to wash a few more dishes so that her day would go better and run smoother.

If the worker had not asked about the reasons for the donuts, he probably would have given the mother a lecture about good nutrition, which undoubtedly would have fallen on deaf ears, and the mother would have insisted that donuts and cake were the best things to give her children.

Case Example

A colleague of ours, John Leverington of Cedar Rapids, Iowa, describes the creativity of his staff in finding solutions that fit the client. A single-parent mother raising her 11-year-old son was on the verge of having her child placed out of home. All assessments seemed to indicate that the mother, who had limited intellectual capacity, was no match for her bright and talented son, who, with his impressive verbal facility, argued about and challenged every rule she set for him. Mother's frustration about her inability to enforce her rules around the house would occasionally reach a point of mutual verbal abuse and physical blows. While making a home visit, the worker noticed the mother and son sitting on the couch side by side and watching a baseball game on television and they obviously were having fun and getting along famously. Both were avid baseball fans, and the mother seemed to be very familiar with the rules of the baseball game.

The worker came back to the office and described her observation to her supervisor, John Leverington. John got an idea for a solution that might fit this mother and son. He bought the family's favorite baseball team's cap and a referee's whistle. During the next home visit, the worker presented the cap and the whistle to the mother and explained to her, using baseball jargon, that anytime she wanted her son to follow rules, she was to put on the cap, blow the whistle as a real referee does, and tell her son in no uncertain terms what the rules were and what the penalty would be. Not only did this work for this mother and son, but they also started having fun with each other, vastly improving their relationship.

Workers, supervisors, and administrators often ask how talking about such small positive things, as in the above examples, can possibly be turned into a solution when a family has problems so monumental and overwhelming that they seem to defy solution. Of course they are overwhelming. This is the type of case where lots of resources have been applied with apparently little or no positive effect. A comment we frequently hear when we have been asked to consult is that some of the interventions—even with some of the toughest cases—have worked, but "only for a while." The mistake is to ignore those short periods of success. When ignored, these "small" successes become buried under the mountain of problems, unrecognized because they seem small and accidental. We suggest that, instead of thinking of these small successes as accidental, all the professionals involved in the client's "problems" pay close attention to the small pieces of success! Suppose all the workers talked about the client's coping strategies, pointed out exceptions to her problems, acknowledged how much she wants to be a good mother, and recognized what she was doing as her way of being a good mother, and so on. You can see how this approach would make a difference: Once the mother had done something successfully and the worker had recognized her efforts, she would become more and more confident that she could be successful again.

The Concept of Resistance

For a long time, the social service field, modeling itself after the medical field and other fields that specialize in working with "difficult populations," blamed poor treatment outcomes on the clients. The familiar refrain that the client is "unmotivated," "lacks insight," "is in denial," "minimizes problems," or "has not hit bottom yet" is used as the reason for the poor outcomes of expensive treatment programs. There are numerous books, workshops, and conferences devoted to "how to motivate" clients. Complaints about clients' lack of motivation are commonly heard in conferences, case staffing, supervisory sessions, and consultation. Most practitioners' frustrations come from their feeling unable to "get clients to do something" that practitioners or workers know is good for them. This includes such things as failure to take medications as prescribed, keep a promise to go to AA meetings, take parenting classes, take a child for immunizations or a medical checkup, follow up on a treatment of head lice, get the child's eyeglasses fitted in a timely manner, and so on. The list is endless. This phenomenon is usually described as the client's failure to follow through on the professional's prescriptions, suggestions, or court orders and directives. When this happens, the primary responsibility is placed in the client's lap and we begin to call him or her "resistant" or "noncompliant." Furthermore, the client's failure is attributed to flaws or deficits in the client's character—not to an ill-fitting professional intervention. At best, we assume that somehow we mis-assessed the client's needs or deficits and then begin another, more thorough, assessment.

Many practitioners have grown increasingly uncomfortable with this view, saying that it is time to stop blaming the clients for our lack of skills and to reexamine our responsibility. Treatment is increasingly viewed as a collaborative effort. Clients should have an input into (1) what they want to see happen in their lives that the worker agrees would enhance the safety of the child, (2) what they know how to do to achieve what they want, (3) what they might do to move toward that goal, (4) what might be the first small next step toward achieving what they want—that is, what the client and worker need to do—and (5) assessing and evaluating what kind of progress both are making.

When professionals talk about resistant or unmotivated clients, they are implying that these traits are the characteristics of the client. That is, the reasons Mr. Lewis, for example, is so "resistant" is that he is an uncooperative sort of person, he was either born with or acquired a personality that is obstreperous and argumentative, and he is not willing to admit his mistakes. But if you ask Mr. Lewis whether he is a resistant person, he might ask, with a surprised look on his face, "What do you mean? Who, me? Resistant? What are you talking about?" He will then offer evidence that he is not resistant. A look at his entire life reveals that he is a highly respected and valued worker, a good father, a good husband, and a good friend to many fine people. How can this be? In most aspects of his life, he might be a reasonably genial, friendly, God-fearing churchgoer who is helpful to his neighbors. Yet, he disciplined his teenage daughter too harshly for getting mixed up with the wrong kind of friends.

On the night Mr. Lewis reportedly punished his 15-year-old daughter, Cheryl, for violating her curfew and not coming home until midnight, she ran to her boyfriend's house and called CPS to complain about her father's physical punishment. Cheryl claimed that her father put her across the kitchen table and lashed at her legs with a belt, leaving bruises. It is easy to conclude that what the father did was abusive. Suppose the CPS worker stressed this point and began to investigate whether or not he actually "beat" his daughter. Of course, the father would not be much interested in discussing whether his punishment of his daughter was lawful or not—he would not be "motivated" to discuss this issue—but he *would* want to talk about how his daughter disobeyed his rules. He would explain that he set up the curfew because he feared his daughter's running away to her boyfriend's house. Recognizing and giving credence to his worst fears about his daughter, that Cheryl is throwing away her potential and perhaps will even become pregnant, the worker might instead start with, "You must love your daughter very much." This approach would be much more likely to elicit his cooperation in looking for other ways to express his worries about his daughter. In addition, Mr. Lewis might on his own conclude that he "got carried away" with his worries and lost his temper. He might agree that he needs help with his temper. It would be a mistake to immediately decide that Mr. Lewis was "resistant." Eliciting his cooperation would not mean ignoring his mistake of leaving bruises on his daughter. Discussion of the event would be easier to handle when the father felt validated, affirmed, and respected for his "motivation" to do what he thought would work. The worker could follow this up with questions like, "Tell me about when she is doing well," or "What is it like when you get along with each other?" Juxtaposition of what goes well and what doesn't would give us a more accurate assessment of the risk and safety.

We believe that motivation is created through personal interaction with workers, using words. Suppose we were to ask Kathy whether she is motivated. Her answer would be, "Motivated to do what?" Having been sober for eight months, Kathy would say that she is very motivated to stay sober. On the other hand, if you were to ask her whether she is motivated to bring the AA attendance slips to the worker, as he demanded she do, her answer would be, "Absolutely not." The thought that she might be "unmotivated" would never enter her mind and she would vehemently disagree with that description of herself.

Using such negative terms as "unmotivated" is not conducive to building positive relationship with clients. The most common reaction to these words is dread. You want to avoid or postpone contacts with the client because you anticipate that the action will be "draining" and that you will feel "like you are pulling teeth" and that you have to "brace for a battle." Your decision that the client is "unmotivated" determines your behavior. Kathy, in turn, would respond in the manner that confirms your belief about her. A few rounds of exchanges, and the die is cast. The description of Kathy becomes a reality.

Suppose, instead, that Kathy's worker saw her as a person with a "strong opinion" and her tendency to speak up as a positive quality. She might then describe her as "very opinionated," "feisty," "assertive," "independent," or "confident." The interaction between the client and Kathy would be quite different. Kathy would respond in a more positive manner, perhaps even joke about it later when the relationship became more comfortable. Furthermore, both people would find it easier to build a cooperative relationship. We must reach out to clients first, before we can expect them to respond to us cooperatively.

Professional Responsibility

Many thoughtful writers in the field have asked CPS clients for their perceptions of the services they have received (Brown, 1986; MacKinnon, 1992; Mason, 1989; Winefield & Barlow, 1995; Zellman & Antler, 1990). The most common complaint MacKinnon (1992) found—which I (IKB) also heard in my personal interviews with CPS clients—is that the clients are not clear about what is expected of them. As they see it, they work hard to meet the goals set up by CPS only to then have the workers change the goals and raise the expectations with no clear explanation. For example, a client is told to clean up the house; when the housecleaning task is finished, she is told to attend substance abuse treatment; then she is told that domestic violence is the issue, and so on. Client frustration toward the system is seldom taken seriously in our profession. Why is that? In every other business, consumer surveys are conducted and customer service is a top concern. Our field, the social services, which is based on a set of social work ethical principles, the most paramount of which is respect for the client's self-determination and world view, rarely conducts customer satisfaction surveys. Repeated complaints from clients never reach management and administration of the social service system because our clients are, by and large, poor and inarticulate. Their voices do not count.

CPS workers described Kathy, who had been trying for eight months to get her two children back from the foster care, as a client with "an attitude that won't quit." They said she was noncompliant, stubborn, and unwilling to follow the foster care agency's demands. This was in spite of the fact that she made regular supervised visitations with her two boys, had quit drinking for eight months, and was learning a trade as an upholsterer, which she believed she had a talent for. She was frustrated and angry at her worker, whom she saw as making more and more demands on her to go here and there, obliging her to do more and more, even demanding that she bring written proof that she had been attending AA meetings regularly, as stipulated in the parent contract. At one point in our interview, Kathy said in a disgusted voice, "They've [her social workers] got their BAs hanging on the wall. They've got their jobs. They've got their cars, their homes. I'm just a paycheck to half of them."

WHAT TO DO?

1. *Approach the interview with an open mind.* There will always be many opportunities to press an issue. Any conclusion reached in haste is difficult to take back. Always give the client the benefit of the doubt and assume that the client is cooperative and wants to get along with you, until proven otherwise. Keep an open mind while listening to the client's side of the story.

2. *Find out what is important to your client.* Remember that the client is not looking for rapport or a "positive" relationship with you. Clients are generally very pragmatic and realistic. They want to know what you can do to help them get what they want. Address the issues that are important to the client first, not what you think should be most important. Explain anything you want the client to do as a means to get what is important to him or her. For example, do not press the issue of staying sober as the priority if that is not important to the client, but do explain that staying sober will speed up getting "your children back." In other words, staying sober becomes a way of getting

what is important to her: She wants her children back home. Another example: Instead of saying that a client must learn to discipline without hitting her child, explain that learning to discipline without hitting him will help her because social workers will stop coming out to check up on her, if the client indicates that is important to her.

3. *Use the client's exact words.* We should have the humility to respect what makes sense to the client. This includes his or her manner of speech. For example, unless your client asks you to teach her how to talk to her children in a better way, do not insult her intelligence by setting out to teach her how to communicate with her children, such as teaching her about "I-messages." Instead, ask her how well her way is working with her child. Only when she says, "It does not work," and you have permission to teach her a different way to talk, can you begin.

At times, clients use peculiar words or misuse words. Take note of the words clients use and try to incorporate them into your talk with them. At the early stage of meeting the client the first time, you are not analyzing what the client said or pointing out the inconsistency of her story; you are simply trying to connect, to establish a workable relationship, and to build rapport. Using the client's exact words will help you do that more quickly and efficiently. Our job is not to teach clients new way of talking to their children but to find out their desired outcome in an efficient and respectful manner.

4. *Listen to her explanation about her own situation.* Ask the client to explain the events as she sees them, without correcting her or arguing with her, however outrageous her story seems. When—much later—you follow her logic and push it to an extreme, it will come to sound pretty incredible to her also. If the client were forced to defend her position, she would naturally become more and more reasonable.

For example, a young woman was severely abused by her male partner. Many people in her life, who cared about her very much, advised her to leave him. Although she agreed at times with their strongly worded advice, she always returned to the theme of how she was afraid of being alone for the rest of her life and just could not make the break. Soon, her friends and family got frustrated with what they perceived to be her "stubbornness" and her weak character that always gave in to his manipulation and they gradually withdrew from her. When the CPS worker talked with her, he agreed that indeed she might live a very lonely life if she left him. The worker pushed her logic to an extreme and kept asking her to describe how her staying with this abusive partner was better than being "alone for the rest of your life." In addition, the worker asked the young mother to describe to him how her staying with this partner would be beneficial to her young children. This was the concern that drove the point home. Eventually, the young woman decided for herself and her children that the intense sense of humiliation, shame, guilt, and loneliness she felt whenever her partner beat her was in fact worse than her imagined fear of being alone. Many mothers will say that the "straw that broke the camel's back" was her intense desire to protect their children from harm.

5. *It is better to ask questions than issue commands and threats.* Asking questions provides you with several options, such as which thread or comment to pick up, and when, and how, and which one to set aside until another more appropriate time arises. Listening to the client's answers provides further information on what and who is important to a client. When you demand something from a client, you expect that the client will do what you want. The more you issue threats, the more you are compelled to follow up on all the things you demanded. This not only jeopardizes your chance to build cooperation, but also increases your tasks, since you must follow up on those things you demanded. Common sense tells us that all people like to think that they are following their own mind. Aiming for compliance does not work to build a groundwork for lasting changes.

For example, a worker visited Sandra, a mother of two children, ages 9 months and $2\frac{1}{2}$ years old. The initial complaint centered on her dirty house, which was in fact dangerous for the young children. Most unnerving for the worker were the clothes hangers made of thin, flimsy wires, kitchen gadgets with sharp edges, and numerous other objects that were thrown around the floor where the children crawled and ran around with their bare feet. There was also a mountain of garbage and debris and dirty disposable diapers on the floor. The worker was strongly tempted to tell Sandra to clean up the dangerous objects and take them out of the house because the children could very easily fall on them, put them in their mouths, or walk on them, thus hurting themselves. However, the worker took a deep breath and calmed herself down and asked Sandra *how* she would make sure that the children were safe. Initially Sandra looked confused and was silent. This gave the worker a chance to calm herself down further while she waited for an answer. Finally Sandra said, "I suppose I will just have to pick up these things and put them out of the house. Actually, I know that my kids can hurt themselves." Quickly the worker smiled at Sandra and said, "I absolutely agree. So how will you make sure that they are taken out of the house?" Sandra said, "My mom says the same thing. I will have to get a grocery bag and just throw them in it and take it out to the garbage can." When the worker visited Sandra a week later, her little apartment looked different—not quite immaculate, but certainly less cluttered and free of sharp objects. The assumption behind the worker's asking Sandra about her plan for keeping her children safe was that Sandra cared about her young children and would want to protect them and ensure their safety.

6. *Expect and anticipate differences of opinions and standards.* It is perfectly normal for you and your client to have different agendas, different perceptions, and different explanations of how things are, as well as different opinions about what the problem is and what to do about it. It is always more productive to work with the client's view than your own. Of course, you and the client will see things differently because you are in very different roles and have very different jobs to do. Most clients understand this and can work with a reasonable mind-set, when approached respectfully. A clear focus on safety of the children by eliminating or diminishing risk will help.

7. *Do not expect insight.* Can people change without admitting problems? This question comes from the mind-set that one must admit or confess there is a problem before one can change. To go one step further, this thinking postulates that one must understand the reason for the mistake before one can change. This is a very seductive idea that may suit academics, philosophers, or analysts, or serve as grist for the mill of long-term psychotherapy. However, those of us in child welfare do not have the luxury of time to wait for someone to gain insight into their behavior and then learn how to become more responsible. We want this mother to do something about her childcare responsibility today! If you see a young child sticking his finger into an electrical socket, you do not have time to reason with him, to get him to understand that it will be harmful for him to keep doing it; you simply pull him away from the wall so that he will learn that it is a forbidden behavior.

The expectation of insight is related to the idea that we want to hold our clients accountable for their abusive or neglectful behaviors, expecting that once they admit their shortcomings or mistakes they will start to change. Hence an enormous amount of energy and time is spent on extracting confessions from clients, especially when there is a violation of the law or when substance abuse is an important risk factor. It is commonly believed that admission of guilt necessarily leads to change. We believe that changing leads to change. Of course, we do hold clients responsible for abuse. However, focusing on getting them to admit or confess their abusive behavior is not productive. Holding them accountable for change is. We know from experience that admitting to crimes or problems or sins is no guarantee that one will not commit these offenses again—we know of many alcohol abusers who readily say "I'm an alcoholic," but continue to drink year after year.

8. *Holding clients accountable for solutions.* While holding clients responsible for problems is not a very productive activity, holding clients accountable for change is. Over the years we have observed that talking about problems or past mistakes is different from talking about future plans for solutions; similarly, there are different ways of behaving toward clients when we are engaged in problem behaviors and solution behaviors. Notice the contrasting emphasis on past mistakes and holding clients accountable for solutions in the following dialogue.

Worker: Why did you leave your children alone?
Client: I didn't leave my children alone. I had a baby-sitter who was supposed to take care of them until I came back from paying bills.
Worker: So, who is this baby-sitter? What's his name?
Client: I don't know his full name; his first name is Billy.
Worker: So, when did you leave him with your kids?
Client: About 10:30 this morning. He promised me that he was going to wait for me to come back. He seemed like such a responsible kid.
Worker: So, where did you find this baby-sitter?
Client: I met him at a party last week and he said he was looking for some work to make some money.
Worker: So, how can you leave your young children with someone you just met?
Client: I had to go take care of my electric bill because they were going to shut off my electricity. I don't have anyone to watch the kids and I had to take a bus and couldn't drag my kids on a bus by myself.

Well, you get the idea! I am sure you have heard this kind of conversation before. This kind of conversation is all about mistakes, past events that nobody has any control over anymore. You can see that the longer the conversation goes on, the more defensive this mother will become. Contrast the following conversation with the same mother and same worker who this time speaks in a soft, calm voice to the mother.

Worker: I suppose you must have thought about what you need to do differently next time to make sure that your children are safe.
Client: I was worried sick all night thinking about how upset my poor kids must have been when I didn't come back home on time.

Worker: So, you must have thought about how to make sure that this kind of thing will never happen again?

Client: I have thought about it all night. I know better than to leave my kids left with a baby-sitter that I hardly know. I thought it was going to be a short time. It's my fault, trusting this boy that I hardly know and leaving my kids with him. Of course, I didn't expect that I was going to stand in line for a such a long time at the counter but they said someone didn't show up for work and someone else was filling in for her and it took forever. Of course they found problem with my bills and had to dig up all the old records and this lady at the window didn't know her job. I have to have electricity in this heat because I'm worried about my refrigerator shutting down and all the food will spoil. So, I had to stand there and wait for them to do straighten things out. It took forever and of course I was worried about my kids.

Worker: So, tell me again what are you going to do differently next time so that your children are not left alone on their own?

Client: Billy seemed like such a nice kid. I can't believe that he would just walk off, leaving my children alone.

Worker: So, Sandra, tell me again what are you going to do differently next time to make sure your children are safe?

Client: I know what I have to do. My kids must have been scared out of their minds, being left alone like that and not knowing where I was or when I was coming back. I feel terrible about what they must have been through. Poor kids!

Worker: So tell me again, what will you do exactly to make sure that your children are supervised at all time? What are some of your ideas? (What will do you do differently next time?)

Client: I've been thinking about it all night. I don't have a car and it's really humiliating to ask friends every week. I have to go grocery shopping, too. I guess the best thing is to take the kids with me next time I go shopping. I used to do that even when they were younger but you can't carry too much groceries with you because sometimes Heather wants to be carried. So, it means I have go more often so I just go to the little store in this neighborhood but everything there is more expensive, you know. Maybe I can borrow a stroller from my upstairs and we can make it an outing. It will take me all day, but maybe we can make it a fun day instead of thinking of it as a chore. That way, the kids can get out of the house, too. I will just make it a shopping day and we will just take our time and maybe rest under the tree and maybe I can buy some popsicles for them.

Worker: I realize that your children are young and they may not have the right words to say it. But suppose I ask Melissa and Heather how they want you to make sure that you do not leave them alone for such a long time, what do you suppose they might tell you?

Client: My kids are pretty smart, they might tell you that they didn't like the baby-sitter because they want to be with me all the time. Not that I have money to hire a baby-sitter but they want me to take care of them all the time. I don't have a family in this town and so I am stuck with the kids all the time.

Worker: So, how would they say they would like to be taken care of?

Client: They are really good kids, you know, considering what I've been through with their father and all that stuff. They want to know where I am all the time and they get scared when left alone.

Even though the client began the meeting with an outburst of anger and threats to sue, the worker repeatedly focused on what the client will do in the future, rather than debating about what she did wrong, thereby developing a productive and collaborative relationship. This might take a few minutes longer when dealing with an angry and hostile client, but in the end the client is much more likely to take responsibility for changing her behaviors, so that she can feel positive about her parenting.

Changing behavior changes people. That is, they must DO something to change things; just thinking or talking about change is not enough. Talking in details about what, how, where, when, with whom, they are going to *do something different* is the beginning step. Our experience is that once people have an idea of what to DO, then they are usually quite confident about what steps to take on their own and they are already on their way to change.

Chapter 5

Useful Tools: What and How to Use

CONTRARY TO THE SENSATIONAL STORIES PORTRAYED IN THE MASS MEDIA, most CPS work does not involve cases of brutal physical abuse, sexual abuse, or children who are killed by their caretakers. Almost all communities in the Western world adhere to certain standards of child-rearing behavior and will not tolerate violation of them. All of us are quite familiar with what needs to be done with those uncommon cases of brutality. Therefore, we have decided to focus on the cases that test your stamina and challenge your belief that you can make a difference in a child's everyday life. These are the majority of your cases. Some are boring and the tedium of them wear you down. The most difficult and persistent cases, and thus most frustrating, are those that make you feel uneasy, when you do not know exactly what to do.

Some situations seem so slippery that they could fall in either direction: for example, should you substantiate abuse or neglect even though you have doubts about its standing up in court? These are constant worries that are on the minds of many CPS workers. How can you be sure that these children with this depressed mother will be safe and taken care of properly? What can you do about the cases where the standard of care falls in the margin? How can you protect yourself so that you are free of liability issues at the end? Who will protect you?

These are important and reasonable questions. In this chapter we offer suggestions on what to say and how to say it. We will show you how to enhance safety, as well as a client's confidence and self-esteem, in a way that influences a child's sense of security and well-being. Our approach to working with clients will take no more time than you usually spend with a client and it will leave you with a much more balanced view of your client's competence and shortcomings, enabling you to obtain a better quality of information that will help you make a "good" decision.

USEFUL QUESTIONS FOR INVESTIGATION

As we mentioned in chapter 4, asking questions is more useful than telling clients what to do. Getting clients to engage in creating their own solution also helps them become motivated to follow their own ideas, thus enhancing the chances of success. In addition, by asking questions we learn what this parent thinks and what he or she believes is useful and helpful to him or her as well as to the child. Following are examples of questions that will move the interview forward.

Open-ended questions allow the client the widest range of responses. The client's answers reveal his or her frame of reference, what he thinks about his world, his life, his children, and his own assessment of his life and his children. These questions encourage the client to disclose and volunteer much more information than you get any other way, which saves you time and allows you to be more efficient and effective.

- Can you tell me a little about your children?
- What are you most proud of about your children?
- Can you tell me what you are most proud of about yourself?
- Can you say a little bit more about that?
- I didn't quite understand that. Would you say a little more about what you were thinking when that happened?
- Tell me a little about what your children are good at.

Who, what, where, when, and how questions provide structure to the topic and set up parameters for the information you need. You will see that there are no "why" questions, as they tend automatically to make people defensive.

- What happened when you decided not to drink?
- When you decide to count to 10, what will you do differently?
- Where did you get the idea that it will be more helpful to walk out of the house?
- How did you decide that it was better to walk away and "not to lose your temper"?
- How do you get yourself out of difficult situations? What seems to help most?
- How will you make sure that your children are safe in the future?
- Where in the house do you feel most relaxed and calm?

Whenever talking about the future changes, always use "when" instead of "if." "When" implies trust that the person is going to behave better (e.g., control the temper, stay calmer)—it is just a matter of time. "If" implies that they may or may not get better. "If you are in control of your temper, what will you do?" conveys a doubt that the client can control her temper, as opposed to "When are you in control of your temper, what do you do that you are not doing when you are not in control?"

Always use "how come" instead of "why." In everyday, ordinary conversation, we use the question "Why?" to show our curiosity, trying to learn new facts or how things come together. In normal situations, "Why?" creates no complications or difficulties. However, a surprise home visit by a CPS worker is not an ordinary situation—it feels like a crisis to the parent. Therefore, instead of using the very ordinary and common "why," use "How come?" "Why" implies there is a mistake and blame is involved. Of course, nobody wants to be blamed for a mistake, especially when "caught" doing something she should not have done. CPS's presence usually implies that somebody has done something wrong, might have done something wrong, or is about to be found out. A "why" question will only make the client more defensive. It is like being stopped by a highway patrol; there is a vague sense of guilt or fear of being found out—without knowing exactly what is involved. Thus, without its being your intention, the conversation can easily deteriorate into an adversarial, competitive one.

Any question that can be answered with "yes" or "no" is less useful. There is no room for the client to voice his own thoughts and ideas in a yes or no answer, and you will not be able to discern his emotional involvement.

- Did you talk to the attorney today? Will you make sure you do that today?
- Did Susie get to see the doctor yesterday? (Did you take Susie to the doctor?)
- Are you planning to call the landlord about the toilet not working?
- Will you make sure the toilet is working in your house?

Tag questions are least useful. In fact, questions of this type (asking a question and providing an answer in the same sentence) are often ignored.

- You hit your daughter again, didn't you?
- You want to be honest, don't you?

- You got drunk again last night, didn't you?
- You didn't go to work again, did you?

Now, we offer specific types of questions—useful tools—for engaging the client, establishing what the client wants, identifying problems and successes, and enhancing (or instituting) safety measures. Not only will these questions generate solutions that clients create, but in the process of asking these questions you will also discover how creative and resourceful clients can be. It is likely that your anxiety about safety will lessen and you will notice that the client is more motivated and invested in his or her own ideas for solutions.

COPING QUESTIONS

Whenever you walk into an overwhelming situation, or when the client seems distraught, frightened, or panicked, begin with this question. You will immediately commiserate with the client, and thus understand the challenges she faces while communicating to the client that you recognize that her life is difficult. Described as "admiring commiseration" (Janet Beavin Baveles, personal communication, 1998), these questions acknowledge the difficult situation the client is in while at the same time recognizing the client's strengths and resources. Imagine yourself at the receiving end of these questions and how you might respond if you were the client.

- I imagine these children are a real handful. I'm sure they keep you on your toes all day. How do you keep going day after day? What seems to help? How did you come up with the idea of just taking time off and laughing with them? That's very clever!
- I'm sure there are days when you feel like running away from it all. What stops you?
- How did you decide that you want to be a good mother? Where did you learn to be such a good mother? (If the client's self-perception is that she is a good mother.)
- How come you are doing as well as you are doing with all that stuff going on in your life? Most people would have given up a long time ago, but you keep hanging in there. Amazing. Have you always been this strong?
- How come it's not worse, given all the things you are going through?
- Wow, how do you do it? It must have been very tough just to get through the week.

- How did you manage to stay sober for a whole week? Considering how long you've been drinking, and how tough this week has been for you, it must have been very hard to do. How did you find out what helps when you get the craving?
- What would your best friend say about how you are coping with so much?
- What about your children—what would they say they see you doing, even a little bit, that helps them feel a little at ease?

These and other similar questions elicit a client's reason for "hanging in there" and/or identify her purpose in life. Again, most clients have never been asked these kinds of questions or articulated their own answers to such questions. They usually need some time to think about the answers. Do not be surprised if they become thoughtful or quiet in response to these questions. Allow them time to mull them over and formulate the answers in their own words. You will soon find that clients quickly establish a positive relationship with you; they will volunteer more information and sometimes elaborate on how much they have suffered. We ask these questions because of our genuine awe and respect for *how* they keep going in their own way. When clients sense our respect for their fortitude, they are much more likely to view themselves in different ways and respond to us differently. By the way, do not be surprised when a client breaks into tears. This may be the first time someone has acknowledged the magnitude of the burden she has been carrying for so long.

If a client persists in telling you how awful her life is, instead of trying to reassure her that her life is not really that terrible, agree with her and then immediately ask again, "So, when your life is so terrible, how do you keep going?" You may want to go one step further and ask, "When things are so terrible, how do you manage to get up in the morning, like this morning? Many people would have just stayed in bed all day. So, how come you didn't?" This usually brings up responses like, "Well, I thought about it, too. But, you know, I have to get up." From this point, you can easily build up this client as a strong, committed mother who forces herself to get up against her wishes because she takes her responsibility as a mother very seriously, or as a "fighter" who does not give up easily and who is not going to let life destroy her.

"How Do You Do It?" "How Come It's Not Worse?"

These simple questions are variations on the coping question. They are effective not only in extreme situations, where a client has somehow, against all odds, survived horrific experiences, but also in chronic situations, such as having had to endure sustained suffering of sexual abuse, and emergency situations, such as when someone has been physically assaulted or is acutely distressed and talking about suicide or harming others.

When you listen to a client's long history of suffering, extreme deprivation, or horrible, unfathomable cruelty, it is easy to feel at a loss for words. There are no words to adequately express your sense of horror and indignity and shame that human beings are capable of such cruelty. Indeed, there are times when we feel ashamed to be a human being when we learn that we all are potentially capable of inflicting such pain on others. Since you have not experienced the exact same degree of suffering, it is dishonest to say, "I understand" or "I can imagine" or some such words, because you don't understand and you can't imagine. Yet you do know that these things have happened and will probably continue to happen. You can immediately put yourself in the other person's shoes and try to imagine and then say, "Wow, I am amazed. So, how do you suppose you got through all that? You are still here. How do you suppose that you did that?" Simply, you can use intonation and inflection to highlight various aspects of client's success. Hear the differences in "Gosh, *HOW* do you do it?" "How *DO* you do it?" and "How do you do *IT*?" Isn't it amazing?

These and similar questions validate that the client "got through" it somehow and let her know clearly that you are interested in how she got through such an ordeal. An important part of asking this question is knowing how to wait, to give clients space to think about their successes—since it is very likely that they believe that they did not "do it right." Listen carefully and you will hear some amazing, creative, wonderful stories of survival, perseverance, and the human will to do not only better, but also more.

Case Example

Many years ago I (IKB) met a Native American woman whose life was riddled with wounds, both physical and psychological. Her alcoholic parents, aunts, and uncles all died of cirrhosis of the liver. She was regularly beaten by her parents whenever they got drunk, which was almost weekly, and her three ex-husbands also abused her sexually and physically. At times, she barely escaped with her life. Yet, she turned out to be the warmest, gentlest, most generous woman I have ever met. One day I asked her how she managed to be different from her parents and siblings, her aunts and uncles. She said that her grandfather was a very gentle and loving influence on her. When she was very young he told her a secret that kept her alive. I was very curious about what secret could be that useful and helpful to her. She related that her grandfather told her that she was a descendant of a very brave chief, which made her a princess, and that his blood still runs in her in all its glory, nobility, bravery, and soaring spirit. The grandfather also told her that, no matter what happens to her, she must not forget this fact and she must always carry herself with the dignity of a princess. She never bothered to find out whether the story was true, but she decided that, no matter what, she would believe this about herself. She always remembered to carry herself as a princess, which, she says, at times saved her life. It is not just what happens to people that shapes their future but what meaning they attribute to their experiences that influences how they view themselves.

When clients do not have such amazing stories to tell, you can still be helpful to them when you ask, "How come you are doing as well as you are doing?" or "Most people who have gone through what you have gone through would have turned into a basket case by now; how come you haven't? What's different about you?" This kind of question validates and affirms clients' suffering and at the same time asks them to describe their own resources and strengths. Be prepared to see them sit up straight, hold their heads up, and their eyes brighten. This kind of experience can have a lasting impression.

RELATIONSHIP QUESTIONS

Are you willing to do an experiment just for the fun of it? What uncensored, honest words pop into your head when you think about your clients? The most common answers we have heard are: sneaky, lazy, hostile, depressed, overwhelmed, deceptive, abusive, unmotivated, mentally ill, minimizes problems, loves her kids, lacks parenting skills, has an attitude that won't quit, has a chip on the shoulder, tries to hide things, hasn't got a clue, is in denial.

Imagine your immediate impulse about how to respond to the above description. For example, "She is lazy." What would you want to do with this lazy client? You might walk away in disgust or, if walking away were not possible, you might be tempted to yell, scold, shove, or whatever you needed to do to get her to be a hard worker.

Suppose we were to ask your clients to describe you in a very honest way. What uncensored words might pop into their heads to describe their encounters with you? What kind of words might they use? We have heard the following from clients about their workers: nice, nosy, hard-nosed, meddler, Miss know-it-all, snoops around, has a chip on the shoulder, judge, jury, and executioner, just pops in and out, likes to threaten people, won't listen, won't give me the time of the day, just grabbed my kids and ran, never tells me anything.

Now, what do you suppose your clients would say about how they want to be treated instead? Take a few minutes for this one!

You just completed an exercise using relationship questions. Was it difficult? What did you learn from this?

Relationship questions are those that ask for the client's perception of what others think of him or her. It sounds complicated but this is something that all of us do on a daily basis. We constantly wonder how others see us: Do I look smart, foolish, friendly, sexy, angry, attractive? We compare ourselves with those around us and wonder if we measure up. Do we live up to others' expectations? Are we average or not? This is a fact of life. Relationship questions accept this as normal by bringing attention to what clients are doing already in their usual, everyday life. They heighten their awareness and allow them to assess themselves against their own yardstick. Clients are able to see how their behavior affects important others around them as well as how they are affected by them. We find these questions especially helpful with clients whose behavior harms those who love them more than the offenders themselves: substance abusing caretakers, both verbally and physically abusive parents, people who claim to have no control over their behaviors such as violence, drinking, promising things they cannot deliver, and so on.

Some examples of relationship questions are:

- What do you suppose your children would say they like best about your being sober?
- If your daughter could explain, what would she say about how seeing you sober helps her?
- How could he or she tell without your saying so? What would he or she do then?
- What would your best friend say about how she could tell that you are more confident about yourself?
- What would your daughter say about how seeing you smile helps her?
- What would your children say about how they could tell that you love them?
- What would your best friend say about how you keep going day after day when your life is so tough?
- If I were to ask your best friend how she could tell that you are more confident about yourself, what would she tell me?
- How does your mother think parenting classes will be helpful for you?

Notice that these questions never focus on what the client is doing wrong. We are not interested in getting the client to do the right thing yet. Right now, we are interested in the client's deciding to want to do the right thing because he or she thinks it is good or helpful—not because we insist on it. Any changes motivated by compliance alone tend to be short-lived.

When to Ask Relationship Questions

Many of our clients are overwhelmed by life, and the burden of carrying on daily routines is almost unbearable at times. When they plead inability to make changes, instead of becoming overwhelmed by the enormity of their problems, ask questions about exceptions: "What would your daughter say that it took for you to get out of bed this morning?" Even though we are asking about the smallest success this mother may have had this particular day, the success can be built on. This kind of question helps the client to see herself from her daughter's point of view. We have met so many mothers who were written off as "hopeless drug addicts," "battered wives who would never leave their battering men," or as chronically depressed and helpless to change. Yet, somehow they managed to clean up their drug habits, to throw the abusive men entirely out of their lives, etc. When we ask them how they managed to do it, many answered, "It was the children who saved me from dope this time," or, "When I saw what his beating me was doing to my kids, I knew I had to do something about it." These are really touching stories of courage and love. If we hang in there long enough, somehow clients will pull themselves together and will make it.

Case Example
Following a complaint that three children were living in a house with broken windows and no door, with no electricity, no running water, and no food in the house, the worker immediately made a visit. Surprisingly, the mother was inside the door waiting for the worker, but there were no children to be seen anywhere.

When the worker explained that she was concerned because of a report that there were broken windows and no doors, mother reassured the worker by showing the fixed windows that had been broken a few days earlier and front and back doors with locks on the inside. The mother explained that she was in the middle of moving to a different house in a different neighborhood not too far away. That sounded reasonable from the appearance of the house, since there was no furniture of any sort and the kitchen was empty of utensils or equipment.

When the worker asked to see the children to make sure that they were safe, the mother was very evasive and changed her story that the children were with a friend while she was moving. The mother was very cordial but stood her ground that the worker could see the children but not today, that she would have to come to the new address to-morrow.

Realizing that forcing the issue of inspecting the children would only alienate the mother, the worker wisely decided to assess the children's perspectives on their safety and risks. The following questions were helpful in gaining the children's perspectives until they could be interviewed the next day:

- What do you suppose the children would say that they like about the new place? New school?
- What would the children say they like best about moving this time? Like least?
- What would they say they like about the sleeping arrangements in the new place? Anything else?
- You mentioned that you had a break-in recently. If the children could talk, using grown-up words, what would they say about how safe they feel about this new place? Anything else?

EXCEPTION-SEEKING QUESTIONS

All problems have exceptions. Contrary to what words like "abusive mother," "drug-addicted mother," "mentally ill mother," "uncaring father," and numerous other such labels imply, even the most chronic alcoholic, drug addict, or abusive parent does not do drugs or abuse the child 24 hours a day, everyday. Any time, place, or situation that the person could have done drugs, drank, slapped, cursed, or left a child unsupervised, but somehow managed not to, is a treasure chest of resources to build on. Instead of brushing off such small, seemingly insignificant successes, pay attention to the details of how the caretaker managed to avoid lashing out at the child. These can become the building blocks of bigger successes in the future. When you first ask about these small exceptions, the caretaker himself might easily brush them off as insignificant. But do not be put off: With persistence, curiosity, and a posture of not-knowing, ask about how he managed to walk away, count to 10, or take a deep breath. One mother explained that she locked herself in a bathroom in order to stop herself from hitting her child again.

The following questions will help you generate exceptions:

- Tell me about the times, in recent days, when you could have hit Tommy (screamed at him, called him names, etc.) but somehow managed to handle it differently?
- Can you explain to me how you did that? How did you know that just "keeping your mouth shut" would work with Tommy? What do you know about him that told you that it would work?
- In what other situations have you been able to manage your temper in such a way that you did not have to regret it later? How would your supervisor say you did that?
- You are saying that you make sure that the children are in bed before you decide to drink. Tell me about the most recent time when you could have drunk but somehow managed not to.
- You just told me that you decided to lock yourself in the bathroom so that you would not hit your child when he gave you an "evil eye." What did you know about yourself that told you to do that?

As you ask about details of exceptions, expect to be surprised at the client's reactions. You are likely to see him or her become more thoughtful, slow down a bit, and even begin to brag, elaborating on what she or he did to successfully maneuver a difficult situation into a successful outcome. Other clients minimize their successes. They are not accustomed to seeing themselves as successful and may discredit their "small" successes. Be persistent and curious and fairly soon you will see that she or he will give you a visible sign that something is clicking.

If the client has no clue, and can't answer your exception-seeking questions, ask, "What do you suppose (your child, best friend, partner, etc.—anyone who is supportive of the client) would say about how you got yourself to walk out instead of hitting Lamont?" If the client still cannot come up with a positive answer, ask, "What do you suppose Lamont would say that he liked about what you did?" or "Which part of what you did would Lamont say was most helpful to him?" Some clients are very literal and concrete. You may need to explain, "I realize that Lamont is very small and he may not be able to express himself, but suppose he could. What would he say?"

When you get a positive answer to your questions about exceptions to problematic behavior, follow up with questions about how confident the client is that he or she can repeat it. Be sure to use the client's exact words about herself. "What gives you that kind of confidence that you can do this again?" If he or she reports no confidence, ask, "What would your best friend say needs to happen so that you can do this again?"

How and When to Ask Exception Questions

All interviewing is a matter of timing, and the use of exception-seeking questions is no different. We cannot dictate what to ask first, second, and so on—it is not possible to script a conversation. You will need to use a great deal of common sense to judge when these questions would best fit into a routine investigation and the most appropriate way to insert them into the natural flow of the conversation. Again, contrary to the common perception that clients are secretive and always trying to hide and conceal information, you will be surprised at how attentive and responsive clients can be when you address their successes, however small. Their expectations are that most CPS workers are out to find faults or mistakes, so that they can carry out the real or imagined threat of taking their children. We urge you to set aside your disbelief and experiment on your next home visit. Different responses from your clients are the only evidence that will convince you.

Case Example

Theresa left a mark on her 7-year-old son's arm when she grabbed him to get his attention. She explained that Erik kept hitting his younger sister and was too stubborn to stop when Theresa repeatedly told him to. What really got her was not only that Erik refused to stop hitting and talked back to her but also that he used an ugly swear word that she had never heard him utter before. Alarmed and concerned, Theresa wanted to get Erik's attention so that he would know she was very serious about his use of swear words. She admitted that she grabbed Erik's forearm too forcefully, causing a bruise.

The following is a dialogue between the worker and Theresa, who at this point is still angry at Erik. The worker's options are to refer this mother to counseling so that she can gain an understanding of what she did wrong and find strategies for making sure that this will not happen again or to spend a few more minutes talking to her about her past successes and seeing if she is willing to look into solutions. Unless Theresa asks for a referral, she is not likely to follow up on the worker's recommendation that she get counseling, especially if she describes herself as overwhelmed with raising her children and keeping her part-time job. In addition, unless the worker spends time discussing what it means to seek counseling, a referral might exacerbate her sense of inadequacy or make her wonder if she is losing her mind (still a common misunderstanding).

Worker: I can imagine that a feisty child like Erik can get on any mother's nerves, and it is obvious that you really feel bad about this episode of your grabbing him so hard that you left a mark. So tell me, Theresa, there must have been times in the past when you felt like grabbing Erik. What did you do right all these years that you managed to do a good job of raising Erik to be so spirited and full of energy?

Theresa: I feel terrible about this. I should never have grabbed him like I did. I guess I didn't realize my own strength. Since he was a baby, he has always been so full of energy and into things all the time. Sometimes I get so exhausted just trying to stay one step ahead of him. And of course as he gets bigger, he gets into more things and I am afraid that he might really hurt his sister one of these days. I don't know how to protect her because she is so small and she just adores her brother.

Worker: So, tell me again, what worked for you during the past seven years that somehow you managed to do a decent job of raising such a spirited boy?

Theresa: I don't think I'm doing a good job. He is so full of energy and gets into things, but he is a good boy, really. He can be such a devil, but his heart is in the right place. He really loves his sister very much and he is such a smart kid.

Worker: I can imagine. So tell me what works for you so you don't lose your temper more often?

Theresa: I feel terrible about what happened. You know what helps is that I keep thinking about what a nice kid he really is. He will give his lunch to other kids who are hungry and he will share everything he has with other kids, his toys, his pet frogs, anything. I guess I try to see his good side and think about his good qualities and it really helps to slow me down. And he is such a smart little boy.

Although this conversation took no more than five or six minutes, imagine the impression the worker must have left with Theresa. In addition to feeling guilty about having grabbed Erik too hard, she is likely to think about what she did in the past when she did not grab him—that is, she will remember how smart and kind her son is and how proud she is of him. The worker went one step further than performing the task of investigation: He also reminded Theresa that she has done a good job of raising Erik to be a spirited, generous, kind-hearted, and smart little boy. This conversation will have a long-term impact on their relationship, perhaps long after the worker has forgotten the case. Here is a summary of what the worker accomplished during this routine visit:

- normalized Theresa's frustration
- validated Theresa's success in raising a "spirited" child
- helped Theresa to look back and recognize good qualities about Erik
- helped Theresa to remember successful strategies that she can repeat again and again
- drew Theresa's attention to how Erik might perceive their relationship

Without lecturing or demeaning the mother, the worker was able to successfully close the case, feeling more confident about her ability to continue on a positive path than he did when he first walked into the case.

Contrast this ending with one where the worker informs Theresa that she is going to recommend that she seek counseling. Theresa might very well wonder to herself, "What did this worker see that I didn't see? What's wrong with me? Of course, it's Erik, isn't it? Only if Erik behaved better, not so sassy, a little calmer, or listened to me better, I wouldn't have had to grab him like that. I am sure it's that nosy teacher that called these people. What will she think about me now? I will never go near that school again." How might these thoughts influence Theresa's relationship with Erik in the future? Her relationship with the school teacher or others in Erik's life in the future? Remember, if you bring up the issue of counseling without the client's asking for it, you must do it in a sensitive manner, since you are implying that the client needs serious help based on one episode of bad behavior. We will touch on how to make a referral to enhance the chances of successful outcome later in this book.

SCALING QUESTIONS

Scaling questions are a very useful assessment tool that both you and your clients can use to gauge confidence, hopefulness, safety issues, willingness to take certain steps, and many other topics that are often difficult to describe with words. Often your confidence regarding a child's safety will increase when you know that parents have specific plans for what to do and when and how to do it. For example, it is difficult to believe a caretaker who says, "I will never hit him again" or "I will never drink again" unless he or she also tells us the specifics of a detailed plan. Instead of accusing the client of trying to evade, conceal, or minimize the problem, we ask the client to account for his or her perceptions, willingness, behavior, motivations, and so on. We contend that holding clients responsible this way is much more powerful and respectful than threatening or cajoling them in an effort to get them to do something that is good for their children. Working within their world view and their way of making sense of their life is not only respectful, but also pragmatic. Listen to the following dialogue that uses scaling questions. Following a considerable amount of time spent in assessing the safety issues with the father, the worker and the client had the following dialogue:

Worker: Now I want to ask you a different kind of question. On a scale of 1 to 10, where 10 stands for how confident any parent can be in making sure that his child is safe and 1 stands for you are not sure at all, that is, you feel very shaky about your child's safety, where would you put yourself between 1 and 10 right now?

Tom: I am really trying to be a good father, you know, just like my old man was for me. He didn't always do it right, but he tried his best. Look at me, I turned out okay, I guess (smiles). I don't know how confident I am. I guessed on the higher part.

Worker: So, what number would you put your confidence at, between 1 and 10?

Tom: I would say around 5 or 6 and moving closer to a definite 6 because I realize that I could have really hurt him. Of course, I don't want to hurt him, but he is such a difficult child.

Worker: 5 or 6? That's pretty high. What tells you that you are at 5 or 6?

Tom: This time I learned my lesson and now I know what could go wrong if I am not careful and it really scared me. I guess sometimes I don't know my own strength and forget that he is still a small child. I also realized how much I love my kid.

Note: From our 20 years of experience using scaling questions with clients from all walks of life who have been forced to seek help for a wide variety of reasons, we have learned that clients invariably answer at a level higher than that predicted by workers and other professionals.

Turnell and Edwards (1997, 1999) suggest that this kind of scaling is the most consistently useful tool for assessing safety issues. Since safety is never an absolute and is never guaranteed, as any reasonable person will readily agree, scaling questions indicate to the client that it is a continuum. No sensible CPS worker will guarantee total safety or accuse some parent of complete lack of safety.

Our experience is that most adults and children are quite able to respond to the scaling questions. However, for those few who are unable to understand the concept, some creative practitioners have drawn pictures of ladders, steps, or even Oz's yellow brick road and asked the parent, "Suppose the land of Oz stands for 10, and the beginning of the first step on this brick road stands for 1; how close are you to reaching the land of Oz?" You can follow her answer with "What do you need to do to get to the next step closer to it?" As described elsewhere (Berg, 1994), you can also draw simple faces that range from frowns to smiles. You can also use the client's home: "If one side of the room stands for 10, which means that you are very confident that you will be able to protect your child from your boyfriend, and the other side of the room is 1, that is, you have no confidence at all that you can protect your child, where would you say you are today?" Have the client stand on an imaginary line along the middle of the room and step toward one side or the other. You can also have the client describe how it feels to be one step closer toward 10 and then ask, "When was the last time you felt that way?" Using relationship questions, you can also have the parent scale what the child might say about how safe he or she feels and what the child would say it would take to move one point higher.

Young children respond nicely to scaling questions, since such measurement or approximation is something children learn early on. When using scaling questions with young children, you can draw a vertical line on a page and indicate that the top of the line stands for 10 and the bottom of the line stands for 0. Ask the child to mark a point on the line to indicate how serious the problem is, how safe he feels, how comfortable he wants to be (at what number), how he would rank the best time in his life, etc. Not only are the scales flexible but they also allow you to use your creativity when working with clients from diverse cultural and ethnic backgrounds.

Use of Scales When the Client Is Mandated by the Court

We learned this creative approach to using scaling questions from Karen Jick (personal communication, 1997) of University of Wisconsin-Milwaukee and Milwaukee County Department of Human Services. She directs a family reunification program that tries to reunite mothers, mostly drug-affected, with their children who have been placed in foster homes. These mothers have been ordered by the courts to perform specific requirements, such as entering drug treatment programs, getting adequate housing, visiting children in foster homes regularly, protecting children from abusive male companions, attending parenting classes, and many other things, in order to be reunited with their children. These are nonnegotiable goals. Jick and her class of students in the master's of social work program review each item on the court order with the mothers and ask them to scale how confident they are that they can realistically finish the specific requirements. This leads to talking about how they will go about obtaining necessary help they need, and from whom, and by when, and how. The workers also ask them to scale their motivation on a 1-to-10 scale for each item of the court order and to describe what will either move it up or down the scale and what might be the consequences of such a move. Scaling questions are used to identify the process of getting closer to their desired outcome.

Many practitioners find this the most versatile, useful, flexible, and easy tool to use, particularly when working with mandated clients. Only your creativity is the limit, and once you begin to think "outside of the box," you may find yourself becoming more and more creative and innovative. Have fun with this.

Case Example

Twenty-seven-year-old June was recently released after a four-month incarceration for causing severe burns on her 9-year-old daughter, Melody. To get her daughter back, the court ordered her to take parenting classes, enter an alcohol treatment program, get a job, and find housing: a tall order for someone self-described as "a softie" when it comes to being consistent with her daughter. The worker decided to use the scaling question with June about her confidence, motivation, hopefulness, and also her daughter's perception of her own safety and parenting ability.

Worker: I'm impressed, June, that you made a point of calling me soon after the hearing when you obviously have a lot to do. So, let's get started. Let me ask you, on a scale of 1 to 10, where 10 stands for as determined as anybody can be in your circumstances to get your daughter back, how close would you say you are to 10 right now, today? (Holding up a piece of paper, pointing to the top of the page as 10, bottom as 0.)

June: Oh, I want my daughter back real bad. She wants to come to live with me, too, and I keep telling her she will have to wait a little while longer, and that she will come to live with me real soon. She is my flesh and blood and I don't want her to grow up with strangers.

Worker: I can see that. So, how badly do you want to work to get Melody back to live with you?

June: Oh, I'm at 10. I've been waiting for this while I was in there.

Worker: That's very good. Suppose I were to talk to Melody and ask her how badly she wants to come back to live with you, where would she put herself on the same 1 to 10 scale?

June: She will say 10, too, up there at the top.

Worker: Okay, now this time I'm going to ask you a slightly different question. This time, 10 stands for as confident as anyone can be that you will get Melody to come back to live with you, where would you put yourself on the same 1 to 10?

June: (Pause) That's a tough one. I will have to say around 2 or 3 right now. I will have to make sure that I visit her regularly, and I don't have a car yet. I will have to get to treatment, get a job ... that's going to be tough because I want to be honest with people that I've been in jail. But they taught me to stay sober, I've been sober for at least eight months now. I will have to say 2 or 3.

Worker: So, what would it take for your hope to go up to 3 or 4?

June: I will have to get a job first. I have some idea of talking to my old boss because I was a good worker at the restaurant and all my customers liked me. When I get a job lined up, then I will be at 4.

Worker: Okay, that's great. It makes sense, that you want to get a job lined up first. So, what will help you stay at 4?

June: Once I get a job, keep working, stay sober and go to AA, see my daughter, and just stick it out.

Worker: So, this time, I am going to ask you another number question. On the same scale of 1 to 10, how determined would you say you are that you will get up to 4 and stay there?

June: Oh, I'm at 8 or 9. I'm determined to it, but it's not all up to me. Somebody will have to give me a job before I can get a job. So, that's why I say I'm at 8 or 9.

Worker: I appreciate your being very realistic about this.

June: It don't mean I'm not going to try my best. Like I said, my old boss really liked me because I was willing to come in even when I didn't have a baby-sitter.

Worker: How will you do that, June?

June: Oh, don't worry. I'm not going to leave my child alone. I've learned my lesson. I can still go to work everyday; I have some relatives who are willing to help me out that way.

Here the worker is helping June to map out a realistic path to achieving her goal. In the process, the worker is also learning a great deal about

June. Notice how the worker did not push the client but allowed her to build her confidence slowly, one step at a time. You can imagine the worker doing the same thing when talking about sticking with AA, getting an apartment, and so on.

THE MIRACLE QUESTION

The miracle question was inspired by a client who saw no hope for herself or her family. One day in the early 1980s, I (IKB) was talking to a mother of four who was exhausted and felt hopeless about herself and her family. Her husband was serving time for having sexually abused her two daughters, who were showing all sorts of unhealthy symptoms. Her two boys were "wild and uncontrollable" she said, and she had thought about killing herself many times because she just could not see the point in living. All her family and the husband's family were against her for supporting the prosecution of her husband and eventually blamed her for what he did. The children's schools were calling nearly every week to report one problem after another.

Not knowing what to do next, beginning to feel overwhelmed and hopeless just like the mother, I asked, "What do you suppose needs to happen as a result of this meeting today that will let you know that this talking is helpful to you—even a little bit?" The mother heaved a big sigh and said, "I don't know what will help. Everything seems so hopeless." Discouraged by this reply, I sat quietly, trying to figure out what to do next. Then the mother blurted out, "I don't know what will help . . . unless you have a miracle." I knew that I did not have a miracle to offer the mother, but I quickly followed up with her idea and said, "I'm afraid that I don't have a miracle . . . but suppose I did, suppose a miracle really happened—how do you suppose your life would be different?"

The mother thought about this a long time, and then she slowly lifted her eyes, looked up at the ceiling, and started to spell out how each of her four children would change and how she would feel like living again. Hearing a very different tone in the woman's voice, I followed up by asking about the details of this miracle picture that she had started to paint. She began to talk about her dreams for her family, how she wanted a close, loving family. She wanted a family whose members would help each other, support each other, and feel like they were blessed with God's grace. When I followed up with questions about her past—when she felt like she had seen small pieces of the miracle—she described without hesitation in a firm voice all the small pieces of the miracle that she and her children shared, how they used to go to church together every Sunday morning, and how happy she once felt. As she told about times when things had been better she became more hopeful about herself and her children. She visibly changed before my eyes: Her shoulders relaxed, her eyes looked brighter, she sat up straight, and her facial muscles relaxed. She even showed a faint smile, which eventually broadened as she talked more.

Since then, this miracle question has been used with thousands and thousands of clients all over the world. After years of experiment and refinement, this question has become a standard tool to help clients generate descriptions of their dreams, visions, and aspirations for their lives. These visions become part of the intervention goals; clients are very invested in accomplishing their own dreams and visions. Through this question, they dare to dream a better life for themselves, to remember hopes and aspirations they once had but somehow gave up a long time ago. Don't be surprised when a client breaks into tears triggered by the memory of a long-forgotten dream.

The miracle question seems to produce the best results when phrased in the following manner:

> Now, I am going to ask you a rather strange question (pause here). After we finish talking, obviously I am going to go back to my office and you will do your routine—whatever you need to do the rest of the day, such as feeding the children, looking over their homework, watching TV, or whatever. And of course it will be time to go to bed. And when all of your family members are sleeping and the house is very quiet (pause), in the middle of the night, a miracle happens (pause), and the miracle is that the problems that you might have with your children, or that other people think you have (use client's exact words here to describe problems), all the problems you face are solved (pause)—so people like me will no longer meddle in your life. Poof! Gone! But because all this happens when you and your family are sleeping, nobody knows that the problems are all solved (pause). So, when you are slowly coming out of your sleep, what differences will you notice that will make you wonder if there was a miracle overnight and the problem is all solved?

Even when you are this careful in presenting the ideas to your client, the first response many clients give is, "Gee, I don't know," which you need to greet with silence, perhaps for a moment or two. This answer is perfectly normal, since clients have never imagined a different future before. Soon the client will begin to formulate an answer. Answers to the miracle question range widely, depending on the state of mind. For example, one drug-addicted mother described her miracle as "I will get up in the morning and help my little girl get ready for school, maybe comb her hair so she will look nice. When I do drugs the night before, I am just wasted and I can't even get up in the morning and so my children have to get ready on their own. It hurts to talk about it."

Most practitioners' fear—that the client's idea of solution will be out of reach and unrealistic, for example, "winning the lottery," "having lots of money," or "meeting a man who will take care of me and my children"—is unwarranted. Clients' notions of what constitutes a miracle will surprise you. For example, a chronically depressed mother related that her miracle would be that she would be able to get up, get dressed, and put on makeup, because that would be a sign to her that she was ready to face the day. We are always astounded when we hear these small, doable, concrete answers and we wonder, Where did they get the idea about small things being the beginning steps of a solution and a problem-free life? These small steps need to be respected and honored, since clients know their situation better than any professional can.

Your next step is to painstakingly weave the client's vision into a solution that he or she can implement immediately. Listen to the following conversation between the worker and a mother.

Worker: So, suppose you get up ahead of the children, get them up, get them ready for school. What would your children do differently that they didn't do this morning, for example?

Mother: I suppose they will be happy to see me up and bustling around because it means I am feeling good.

Worker: So, when they see you bustling around and getting them ready for school, what would they do different that they didn't do this morning, for example?

Mother: Oh, they will want to get up, get their books ready, get washed up and then come downstairs for breakfast instead of parking themselves in front of the TV.

Worker: So what would the children say that they like about you on this special morning?

Mother: Oh, I know what they will say. They will say they like it when I am up and sending them off to school in a good mood. They seem to have a better day in school when they go off happy instead of getting out of the house all crying and my yelling and screaming at them.

Worker: So, what will be different between you and the children?

With a little prompting, the mother can provide the details about how to get started on a better beginning to the day because she has done it at least once before, and since she has done it she can repeat it. It is very encouraging to the mother to be reminded of a success that she has probably long forgotten. As she talks about her past success, however small, she not only begins to feel a ray of confidence, but also generates more ideas about how to be helpful to her children and to become more competent.

Even if the caretaker blames other people in her life as the problem, such as her stubborn child who has taken after his father's side of the family, it is more profitable to bypass the temptation to correct her misperception about child-rearing and just follow her logic and pursue the solution. At times, clients see the problem as caused by someone else or themselves as victim of what someone else is doing to them. Listen to the following dialogue:

Worker: So, what will you notice different tomorrow morning that will let you know that a miracle has happened and your problem is solved?

Mother: I will have a different child, head to toe. He will wake up feeling good instead of being so grumpy and messing up everybody's day.

Worker: So, how will he be different when his problem is all solved because of this miracle?

Mother: As I said, he will be a different child—like he used to be when he was a baby. He will wake up smiling, in a good mood, ready to face the day and do his best. He will behave himself in school; I won't get a phone call from school all day. If he can do this once in a while, I would say that's a miracle.

Worker: So, let's just suppose he does. What do you suppose he would say about how you will be different tomorrow morning?

Mother: I suppose I will be so surprised and maybe even talk to him nice, like we used to. Yeah, that's what will happen, I will feel like talking to him in a calm voice instead of screaming at him like I do now.

Worker: So, suppose you do talk to him in a soft, calm voice, what would he say about how that is helpful to him?

Mother: I know what he will say. He will say he likes to be my baby. We were very close until I got so involved with Tom and I guess I lost a grip on my life and got swept away with Tom and neglected my kid. I know what I have to do: I have to put my son first. You know, he really needs me because he doesn't see his father and I am sure he worries that I am going to be like his dad.

So, you may rightly ask, "Why should I put so much energy and time into interviewing the client if the majority of our client contacts consist of a single meeting and I am likely to close the case?" The reason is to maximize the benefit of the client's contact with you. Once the mother in the above dialogue has thought through this far, she has very good insight into what she needs to do so that her boy will feel loved and she will feel like she is a good mother. When this mother gets this far with you, she has a clear idea of what her next step is. Imagine how much change you can initiate in a single visit and how much a mother and the boy will benefit from talking to you.

Children's Miracles

Many workers find that the miracle question can be successfully adapted to work with children. You can adapt the miracle to fit the child's age, such as substituting a magic wand, fairy godmother, three wishes, and so on. One little girl was very close-mouthed about reporting her mother's serious drinking problem. The worker nevertheless had a hunch that there was lot going on in the child's life. When the worker introduced the magic wand, the girl's first response was that her mother would not drink so much and so wouldn't yell and scream at her. Another child told about how her cousin would not touch her in bad places when she was sleeping at her grandmother's.

HOW IS THAT HELPFUL? HOW HELPFUL IS THAT? HOW WELL DOES IT WORK?

Whenever we see or hear of clients doing harmful things to themselves and to others, such as drinking excessively, doing drugs, cutting themselves, not eating, leaving the children alone in order to go out and "party," smacking a child on the head or face while talking to him or her, etc., our immediate impulse is to lecture and point out how harmful that behavior is. Most will describe it as a compulsion or say that it is out of their control. Others will tell you that they have tried to quit drinking or have even stopped for a short while or tried many things that didn't work. Your reprimanding, scolding, or lecturing is only doing "more of the same of something that doesn't work" (Watzlawick, Weakland, & Fisch, 1974). The MRI group suggests that sometimes the "attempted solution is the problem." That is, scolding and lecturing actually make things worse, since they only increase the client's frustration level—and yours as well. Of course, nobody wants to be lectured at, and so the worker-client relationship becomes strained. It is time to do something different.

One of the gentler, more thoughtful, and respectful ways to turn things around is to calmly ask, "How is your drinking helpful to you?"

This sentence implies, "You must be trying to help yourself; can you tell me how your drinking helps you?" Imagine the client's surprise; this is a question she or he has never heard before. The client might stop and take a breath before trying to answer because this requires a different kind of response, a more thoughtful one, instead of her usual, "Yeah, yeah, I heard that before, so what's new? You are like all the rest. Why should I listen to you?" Even if the client does not show an immediate response, the question certainly will sit in some corner of his or her brain, thus giving the client a chance to think about it. We are aiming to get clients to think about their own aspirations and how they want their life to be different and better.

"How well is it working?" directs the client's attention to how her repeated, ineffective attempted solution is harmful for both her and her child. You might get answers like, "I just want him to listen to me when I talk to him." This opens up the possibility for you and your client to negotiate what might be more useful and helpful instead of smacking a child in the head or calling him names. This is illustrated in the following conversation that took place with a mother about her "incorrigible child with a devilish look on his face." (The mother's usual punishment was to hit the child on the head and call him "stupid.")

Worker: You must get pretty frustrated with Jay. He is a handful, isn't he?

Mother: You ain't kidding. I can't get him to mind me. I yell, scream, holler but does he listen? No! This is the only thing that gets him to stop and listen to me for a while.

Worker: So, how helpful is it to hit him?

Mother: It works only for a while, then it don't work no more.

Worker: (Curiously) So, how long does it work with him?

Mother: Only about five minutes and then he is right back at it again, so it don't work too good.

Worker: I can see that. So, this is a lot of work for you. What else have you thought about doing to get him to listen?

Worker: I don't know what else to do! I tried everything you can imagine. He is such a wild child.

Having come this far—to acknowledge that her hitting is not working—this mother is now a little bit more open to entertaining some other method to make the child listen to her. Now that the mother is interested in finding a way to get the child to listen to her, the worker immediately repeats the mother's words while negotiating some other approach to get him to listen. The worker follows up on this issue:

Worker: So, when Jay listens to you, what exactly will he be doing that will let you know that he is listening to you?

Mother: That he respects me. A child that young should respect his mother and I try to teach that to all my children but Jay is the tough one.

Worker: Can you explain to me again, what did you do with other children that they learned to be respectful of you and listen to you? How do your other children show that they respect you? What is it that Jay needs to learn, do you suppose?

The idea of being respectful also must be broken down into behavioral signs that the mother can recognize when Jay does what she wants him to do. Often, children do not understand what constitutes listening or respectful behavior. This lack of understanding is interpreted as willful defiance by the mother, especially if the child is quite different from her.

The opposite of an undesirable behavior is not always clear. For example, "Don't bang the door!" does not tell the child what to do instead. A child would understand his mother's directions better if she were to say, "Jay, when you go outside, close the door gently like you did yesterday," or "Jay, you played with your sister so nicely yesterday; let me see you do it again."

You Must Have a Good Reason for . . .

This is another version of "How helpful is it?" This gives you an additional way to connect with your client. Whenever clients are engaged in destructive behaviors, our immediate temptation is to get them to stop. Again, common sense tells you that others close to the client, those who care about him or her, must have repeatedly done the same thing without much success. Instead of repeating the same old tired lecture, you can take a fresh approach by saying, "You must have a very good reason for not eating," or "You must have a very good reason for drinking as much as you do."

Notice the difference in tone and phrasing in the following two questions and imagine how your client might respond to each of them.

- Why do you drink?
- You must have a very good reason for drinking in recent months. Can you tell about that?

The second question catches the client by surprise because he or she has never been asked questions about her drinking this way. The client probably heard many variations of the first question and by now his or her defenses and predictable answers are well rehearsed. The first question comes across as demeaning and insulting, while the second asks for "good reasons" for drinking and says, "I am interested in listening to your good reasons." It alters the meaning of drinking. It is seen as a means to a goal, that is, drinking is only one of many ways to achieve something—we don't know what yet. When you hold the second attitude, it is easy to figure out how to phrase your basic posture and assumptions about clients' behaviors.

The most common immediate reaction to "you must have a good reason for . . . " is to become defensive, since the client has already heard so many scolding comments. Then he or she will tell you his "good reasons" for drinking excessively. You need to listen patiently, try to see things from his perspective, and calmly hear what he has to say. Follow this to its logical conclusion and—with genuine curiosity— ask him to explain things further. When he begins to realize that you are not attempting to shame him, scold him, or make him feel guilty, he will begin to relax and to tell you that indeed his drinking is excessive and he should do something about it. You can then follow up on his idea of what he is going to do about it, and how he is going to do it.

HOW DO YOU KNOW HE OR SHE CAN DO THIS?

CPS workers are often frustrated by parents or caretakers who have unrealistic expectations about what a young child can do. For example, I (IKB) met a mother who expected her 7-year-old daughter to do the family dishes without being told every time, another who demanded that her 5-year-old know what kind of mood she was in, and another who thought her 8-year-should know when his father was "not feeling good" and then play quietly by himself. Some parents, out of their desire to give their children so much more than what they had growing up, expect them to achieve more than what is realistically possible.

We do not want to repeat the same pattern of becoming frustrated and critical. When we become frustrated with the parent for not know- ing that it is unreasonable to expect a 7-year-old child to be responsible for washing dishes for a family of five without being told, then we are very likely to betray our frustration in a manner similar to what the mother uses (unsuccessfully) with her child. Since repeating the same pattern between the mother and the child is not very helpful, we want to engage the mother in a different way of thinking about her child. In the following dialogue the worker talks to a mother who slapped her 9-year-old son in the face because he was being disrespectful to her.

Worker: So, it sounds like you want Jeremy to learn to respect you.
Mother: Of course. I want all my boys to respect their mother and he
is the only one that acts cocky. He thinks he knows it all and
nobody can tell him nothing.
Worker: I can see that you are trying to instill important values in
him. Since you know Jeremy well and since you are trying to be
a good mother, let me ask you something. What do you know
about Jeremy that tells you that he can learn to be respectful to
you?
Mother: How do I know he can be respectful?
Worker: Yeah. You know him well enough to think that he can learn
to be respectful of you. How do you know he can do this?
Mother: Oh, he knows. I've seen him do it when he wants something.
He ain't no dummy; he's smart. When he wants something, he
talks real nice to me; he knows how to talk nice. I taught him
that.

In the above conversation the worker validates the mother's attempts to teach Jeremy the value of being respectful to her and learns that Jeremy indeed has the skills and know-how to show respect to his mother when he wants something. This means the mother taught him the necessary skills that a child his age must ask for what he wants, including being polite and friendly when he wants something from adults. As the worker recognizes this and gives credit for it, the mother will find that the worker is not there to criticize her but to help her realize that she is trying to be a good mother for Jeremy. The worker will help the mother see that the interaction between her and Jeremy is normal and that his behavior is typical and not a sign of disrespect for her. Reconsidering her narrow definition of respectful behavior, this mother may recognize that a broader view is possible. The next step is for the mother to find other ways to reinforce what she already taught Jeremy: to show respect for her even when he does not want something from her. Such a transfer of learning from one situation to another is much easier to accomplish than trying to teach Jeremy a totally new skill. This will make the mother's job less frustrating; Jeremy simply needs to be reminded of what he is capable of doing, not punished for being a child.

There are other, more complicated situations where the parent's unrealistic expectations lead to unnecessarily harsh punishments or unreasonable demands that frustrate both parent and child. Rather than making referrals for counseling that the client is probably not prepared to follow through on, you can offer very timely and useful tips for the parent right on the spot, when they are most likely to be received and implemented. Clearly this is not the solution to everything, but perhaps it is enough to prevent another referral for investigation.

WHAT ELSE?

This question elicits the client's hidden resources. When you want to encourage a client's participation in devising her own solutions and enhance her self-esteem in such a way that she can see that she has lots of good ideas, use this simple but effective question frequently. Unless you ask "What else?," the client might not know about her own resources and hidden strengths. Be sure to give the client sufficient time to think about your question and think things through. You might very well be the first person ever to have elicited her opinions, wishes, and successes. The following dialogue took place between a 19-year-old mother of two who had been badly abused by her boyfriend who "broke my child's leg." Eventually the children were placed in a foster home. The mother talked about how scared she was of her boyfriend, who still stalked her, threatened to kill her, and "jumped on" her even a year and half after she broke up with him. The worker was amazed that she was able to break up with her boyfriend when she was still so scared of him.

Worker: Wow, how did you manage to get him out of your house?
Mother: I just stayed away from him.
Worker: I am sure it wasn't easy for you to do that.
Mother: No, it wasn't.
Worker: So you stayed away from him. What else did you do?
Mother: I got a restraining order.
Worker: How was that helpful?
Mother: It helped a while but then he kept coming back.
Worker: I am still wondering how you got him out of your house and kept him out.
Mother: My father told me to put everything in God's hands and He will take care of me.
Worker: So, that was helpful. What else did you do to keep him out of your house?
Mother: My father told me, "Don't be scared. Just leave it in the Lord's hands." And He will make a way for that person to leave me

alone. Not physically or mentally, but he'll just make a way for that man to leave me alone. And that way, every time he sees me he won't harm or hurt me.

Worker: So what else has been helpful?

Mother: I go to a group, we meet twice a week. We talk about abusive men and stuff like that.

Notice how the mother reveals more and more information about her attempts at breaking away from the abusive relationship that has done so much damage to her, her children, and her future. The more the worker asks "What else has been helpful?" the more the worker learns that the mother has done a number of things, that she has many resources, and that she is not as isolated as many women are. This additional information gives us a better picture of how resourceful this young mother is.

Variations on this question are limitless. Here are some examples.

- What else do you need to do so that your mother will help you clean up the house?
- How else will you make sure that you continue to "hold your tongue" so that your daughter will feel safe with you?
- Where else can you use this approach you just described?
- Who else will notice that you are becoming calmer? Becoming kinder?
- Who else will benefit from your learning to control your temper?
- What else do you need to do to make sure that you will not drink and drive?

WAYS TO OFFER INFORMATION ON CHILD-REARING AND CHILD DEVELOPMENT

During a case consultation a young and inexperienced worker reported that she came across a family with two teenage girls whose mother complained bitterly that the girls never helped with the household chores. The worker proudly reported that she told the mother to charge the girls room and board since they are living with her and, until they reach age 18, they are minors; she said to the mother that they are living under her roof, not the other way around. The worker's pride came from the fact that the mother told the worker such an idea had never occurred to her.

Such an idea might indeed work, and it is truly believable that this mother had never thought about such an idea on her own. So, we asked the worker, "What did the girls do in response to your comment that they should be made to pay room and board?" The worker reported that the girls just laughed and thought it was funny and went back to whatever they were doing.

Certainly the information is useful and valuable, and there are lots of parents who make such rules work, but we believe that information is only valuable and useful when the receiver of the information has a way of implementing the plan and making it work. There are lots of good ideas, but if we have no realistic or practical way to make them work they are useless. So, how do we disseminate information in such a way that clients can use it?

1. Do not talk down to your client. Respect her good intentions and point out other areas of success she has had (for example, raising such a well-behaved child, good student, good listener). Ask her how she might apply these to the current situation.
2. Has the client found that what she has been doing is working, that is, producing the kind of results she wants from the child? If the answer is "no" or "only for a short while," is the client interested in learning about some other methods that might work a little bit better with children like hers? (When you ask this, you are saying that she is not an ignorant mother, only that certain children require a slightly different approach.)
3. What kind of advice has the client been given by friends, neighbors, and family members about what she could try to get better results? (We know everybody is eager to help out.)
4. What does she think might work instead of the advice she did not follow?
5. What has she heard, read, or learned from TV programs that talk about what to do with children like hers?
6. What did the client's mother do when she was growing up that seemed to have helped, both for the parent and the child? How could she adapt it with her own child?
7. Would she be interested in some recent ideas that seem to work with lots of children like hers?
8. Present your ideas not as a panacea, but as suggestions that might work and that other parents have reported seem to work.

"I Don't Know Yet"

There are many things about family life, child development, and relationships between children and parents that we do know. There are also many things that we don't know yet in the CPS field. Although there are new studies coming out everyday, there are many things that we personally have not kept up with or even have doubts about. Not many of these studies provide definitive answers about any of the questions or doubts we might have, and of course we always have more to learn. Being able to admit this takes a great deal of discipline, maturity, and professional integrity, as well as a sense of humility. Being honest with your client is a mark of your respect for him or her as a person. We also find that it is reassuring to clients when we acknowledge our shortcomings; we come across as more human. It is important to always add "yet." It is very different from saying, "I don't know," which closes the door. Get in the habit of saying this when it is appropriate because what is important is not that you need to be an expert but that you know when you need more help.

OTHER CONVERSATIONAL SKILLS

Maintain the Client's Dignity

In a famous song, Mary Poppins teaches the children in her care that "a spoonful of sugar makes the medicine go down." Similarly, a common folk wisdom says, "honey attracts more bees than vinegar." You will accomplish more and help clients change easier and faster when you work with them in a respectful manner instead of lecturing them or trying to force good information down their throats against their wishes. In other words, the more we help clients maintain their dignity and respect their role as competent caretakers, the easier it is for the client to behave in a competent, responsible manner. This has a ripple effect on the children; when the mother feels she is treated with respect and dignity, she will know how to treat her children with respect and dignity.

Find Out What Happened Next

From time to time we come across a parent or caretaker who seems to feel extreme contempt or dislike for a particular child (it tends to be one child who is singled out in the family). These parents use exceedingly harsh language when talking about the child, such as, "Jimmy is from hell" or "He is an evil child." It is very difficult to be sympathetic toward the adult and not to take the side of the child. We are already disposed toward children to begin with, and if we begin to see a caretaker as an abusive person, it is easy for us to betray our inner feelings and opinions.

Taking a child's side often backfires for the child, making things worse rather than better. This issue often comes up in our consultation work with schools. Children, especially teenagers, will report conflicts with their parents that may have resulted in slapping the child or kicking the child out of the home. Since most school personnel (teachers, nurses, counselors, social workers) are more familiar with the child than with the parents, it is easy for them to take the child's biased report of the confrontation as what actually happened. Unless the school or day care personnel use a very skilled and tactful approach, they could worsen the situation for the child. Parents have been known to pull their child out of the school, transfer him or her to another school, move to another school district, or even move out of state.

It is a good idea to interview the child as well as the adult, and it is required by law. Questions such as "Then what did you do?" "What happened next?" "What came after that?" "What usually comes after that?" track the pattern of interaction. Deciphering the predictable patterns around issues such as curfews, boyfriends/girlfriends, or even around bedtime routines of young children helps you to better assess what is abusive and what is not, what seems to be the cultural norm of a family, and whether a one-time event has been misunderstood.

However, there is no question that some children are extremely difficult to raise and some have a way of provoking or the ability to zero-in on parents' and caretakers' sensitive or vulnerable points. Obtaining a good picture of an interactional sequence will help you avoid prematurely judging the parent/child relationship.

Imagine a Different Future with "Suppose . . . "

Whenever you feel stuck, not knowing what the solution to a difficult situation might be, rather than feeling overwhelmed, use questions that begin with "suppose" to develop an alternative future. This word is especially useful when you come across a situation where it appears as if there is no solution, such as when a client feels helpless because his family has never been supportive. A single parent, Betty, in her rage at her daughter for doing her "teenage thing" (such as acting like she knows it all, wanting to have the last word, always wanting things done her way instead of accommodating to the family's needs), lashed out at her daughter, coming close to physically assaulting her. After meeting with the daughter, Michele, and establishing that she was not physically harmed, but frightened at the intensity of Betty's rage at her, the worker met with Betty. Betty was angry at the world and her ex-husband, and felt herself stretched to the max from the stress of coping with life. She was also angry at her 74-year-old mother, who had never been supportive of her, but who always only made demands on her time. Rather than trying to educate or confront Betty for blaming others for her current life situation—her ex-husband for disappearing after the divorce, Michele for blaming her for the divorce, her "unsupportive" mother for not being able to get her own life together—the worker decided to pursue a different route. Having sorted out with Betty that right now she was more angry at her daughter than her mother, the worker needed to make sure that Betty was not going to lash out at her daughter again. Betty explained that if her daughter had "a little better attitude" toward her, maybe she could live with her fluctuating moods, her selfishness, even her mouthiness.

Worker: So, this better attitude on your daughter's part—it seems very important to you. Just suppose . . . just suppose your daughter had a little better attitude, what would change between the two of you, do you think?

Betty: Then I would feel like she is not talking down at me, that she is not treating me like I'm her servant or something. She needs to pull her weight, too. After all she is 16 and has to learn that life is not handing her a bowl of cherries, you know?

Worker: Of course. Sounds like your life is pretty tough and you are carrying lots of burden all alone. So, suppose Michele had a little better attitude, what would change between the two of you?

Betty: Then at least I would feel like I am not pulling all this weight by myself, that I have someone on my side for a change.

Worker: Okay. Of course the burden gets to be too much sometimes. Explain to me again what difference it would make when Michele has a better attitude?

Betty: I don't expect her to be my mother; that's not what I mean. I just want Michele to understand that I am doing the best I can. Maybe her lipping would stop, maybe she would say, "Thanks, Mom," once in a while, just to show me that she appreciates how hard I am working all the time to keep us going.

Because of the worker's persistence with Betty, she began to sort out her anger and what made her lash out at her daughter. What began as a demand that Michele have a better attitude, which is difficult to measure as a concrete indicator of successful outcome, turned out to be a reasonable expectation for appreciation and acknowledgment from a 16-year-old. Betty probably did not know this until the worker helped her by repeatedly coming back to her original demand (better attitude) from Michele. The worker helped Betty sort out her vague feelings of frustration by using "suppose" questions that invited Betty to look at the solution picture, rather than the deficit picture of what Michele was not doing. Ultimately, it turns out that what Betty needed to keep going with her burden of supporting her family was manageable and realistic.

Frequently Ask, "What Have You Thought about Doing?"

Often, clients are faced with impossible dilemmas, such as "Shall I stay with my boyfriend who is abusive to me and to my child or shall I live a miserable life alone for the rest of my life, without anyone caring about me?" "How can I go to work and be a good mother to my three kids?" "How can I stick it out with my drug treatment and get my kids back from the foster home when they cry and hang onto my legs whenever the visit is over? I feel like just saying the hell with it!" "Should I let my mother meddle in my life and make me feel small or should I stand up to her and lose her support?" "Staying with my boyfriend means it will be so much harder to get off drugs! But I'm afraid to throw him out because he threatened to make a false report to the child welfare. I can't bear to lose my kids."

We met a worker who told us about her frustration at not knowing what to do. She was working with a very motivated young mother who was going to school to improve her chances of getting a well-paying job so that she could make a better life for herself and her children. The worker had to tell this mother that as part of the welfare reform program she was in she would have to go to work full-time. This was non-negotiable because it was state law. When the mother asked the worker in an agitated voice, "What do you want me to do?" the worker found herself unable to answer and panicked at the demands the young mother was making on her.

We were very touched by the worker's sensitivity to this young mother's dilemma and her eagerness to relieve the pressure the young mother felt. However, the important point is to see the young mother—or any client in this kind of tight spot—as strong and capable of making decisions on her own. Our job is to agonize with them and help them arrive at critical decisions that they can live with, not to make suggestions for them to follow. How do we do this?

First, give your client the recognition that indeed she is in a tight squeeze and it would be difficult for anyone to make a decision when the options are so limited: "Wow, that's a tough situation you are in and it is a difficult decision to make." Then, after an appropriate pause, ask calmly, "So, what have you thought about doing?" and wait for an answer, allowing her lots of time to weigh various options. More than likely your client will answer, "Gee, I don't know what to do."

Wait a little while longer without saying anything. Usually the client will come up with options and slowly talk herself into one of them. This question is a wonderful way to convey to the client that he or she has the capacity to sort things out and come up with a fitting answer. After all, it is the client's future life and only she knows what is right for her.

In some situations, there is a strong temptation to tell clients what to do because the solution seems so obvious and the client seems so lost. Why not give him an easy and fast answer? Clearly he has enough troubles already. But true empowerment to make choices that are right for the client comes from the client, not from our thoughtful and help-ful answers. Imagine that you have been agonizing for days or weeks about what to do with a relationship that is not going well for you. As soon as you describe the problem to a trusting friend, your friend immediately comes up with the solution to break up the rela-tionship. How would you feel? Sheepish? Foolish? Dumb? Resentful? Exactly! When the problem is so serious, do not offer an easy, simple, obvious answer. It makes one feel foolish to have agonized so much when the answer is so clear. In addition, it is also difficult to imple-ment a solution that someone else comes up with—you decide that it can't be that simple. Worse yet, you decide that this friend does not quite comprehend the complexity of the problem and dismiss the sug-gestion.

More important, even though initially it appears that life is limited to "either this or that," we know that there are many gray areas between such simple black and white choices. Perhaps your client can do both, not all of it at once, but begin with one part, wait for the results, and then try the second option and see what happens next. Or perhaps the client can do a little bit of both options. Frequently, until we get to the first small steps, we are not able to anticipate the large steps ahead. Scaling questions are useful here. Begin modestly and plot each next small step, one at a time. Follow each step with, "What do you think will work next?" This is true collaboration.

Remember that Parents are the Experts

Imagine your supervisor saying to you, "Since you know your client best, what do you think will be the best course of action at this time?" What would be your reaction to your supervisor? Your immediate thought might be, " Well, my supervisor trusts me (or my judgment). I like that. Now, that we have established that I have good judgment about my client, I will need to come up with a good decision on this case." Your working relationship with your supervisor would change, and your perception of yourself as a person with good judgment would become more established, if it was not there before. In other words, your supervisor would become a consultant to you, instead of telling you what to do.

Similarly, parents are experts on their own children, not the doctors, nurses, teachers, or even social workers. We are simply utilizing this reality, helping the parents or caretakers to make the best possible decision that they believe is in the best interest of the child and themselves. Notice the softening stance parents will take when you start consulting them on what would be best for their children. Say, "Since you know (love) your child best . . . " Not surprisingly, when given this kind of credit, most parents indeed decide on the best course for their children, and when it is their own idea, the investment to follow up is greater.

Case Example

Ruth, a very concerned mother, showed up at a CPS office without an appointment and wanted to see a "social worker on duty" immediately because she was so upset about what happened to her 13-year-old Josh that morning. What happened? He was "molested" by his good friend, Tom, age 15. Ruth and Tom's mother are good friends and they watch each other's children when one has to work late or go out of town because of family illness or other emergencies. Ruth worked late last night and had decided to take Josh to Tom's house so that the boys could get their sleep without having to wake them up in the middle of the night. Josh woke his mother up early this morning and said, "I've been touched." He further elaborated that "he had his hands in my pants."

"Where is Tom now?" the worker asked. He ran away from home and as of this morning, nobody knows where he is, and of course his mother is frantically trying to find him, worried about how scared he must be. Ruth relates that she taught her son the difference between a "good touch" and "bad touch." Now she is worried that Josh might develop lifelong problems but she does not want her son in counseling because she used to work as a clerk at a community mental health center and knows "what can happen to kids like Josh." In spite of what Tom did to Josh, Ruth says that she will remain good friends with Tom's mother because they had gone through "thick and thin" together when both were having some tough times during divorces and subsequent relationships with men.

How would you talk to this mother? You might want to stop reading at this point and organize your thoughts about what you might say to her. The following is an outline of how we might have proceeded. See how this compares with your own ideas.

1. We would give the mother credit for coming in on her own and let her know that she obviously did the right thing in reporting.
2. We would compliment her on teaching her son the difference between "good touch and bad touch" and on the fact that Josh volunteered this information immediately after the incident. This is an indication that she has a good relationship with Josh. She obviously worked very hard over the years to build this kind of relationship with her son, despite some difficult times.
3. We would recognize that Ruth clearly wants to remain good friends with Tom's mother, so she is not only a good friend but also a very loyal person who values good friendship. Obviously she is a good role model for Josh; he can see that adults know how to work out important relationships through difficult times.
4. We would say to Ruth, "You have a good sense of what is good for Josh and what you do not want Josh to go through; you know your son very well. So, what do you think would be the best for Josh?
5. When we approach the subject of calling the police to investigate exactly what happened by talking to both boys separately, we would let the mother know we are confident that the outcome will be good for both Josh and Tom.

Imagine the relief this mother would feel, knowing that she has lots of influence in making sure that her child is protected and that she did the right thing by approaching the CPS office herself, instead of waiting for someone to "come and investigate." Imagine how Ruth might respond to your questions. Imagine Ruth's relief at hearing your positive approach and that you will listen to her ideas and that she will fully participate in deciding the best course for her son. Even though this is not likely to be an open case, taking a little time to talk to this mother and reassure her in this manner would go a long way in how Josh and his friend Tom would benefit. When the mother is reassured, she will approach Josh in a much more confident manner, thus conveying to Josh that his reporting to her was the right thing to do and that his friendship with Tom does not have to be destroyed as a result of this episode. You certainly would not want to spend time convincing Ruth that not all mental health centers operate the same way, that children benefit from counseling, and so on, which would take much more time and energy with doubtful outcome.

INTERVIEWING A CHILD

It is crucial that workers have the most up-to-date information about how children's language develops and how their interactions with the interviewer influence the content of the interview. We can reasonably expect that the protocols for child interview will undergo further changes and that most states will revise and update their interview protocols (Michigan Governor's Task Force, 1997). Workers need to be skilled at incorporating the latest information on how children's language develops into interviewing strategies and techniques. Since children are easily influenced by the environmental forces, it is vitally important that we keep in mind the wider contextual issues when interviewing a child.

The initial (investigation) phase of an interview with a child generally occurs in schools, usually during school hours. The idea is that if we interview a child without the parent's coaching, we are more likely to obtain accurate information. Discovery of hard and fast "truth" is fairly difficult; young children are very much influenced by their interactions with others and their desire to please and get along with adults around them. Leading questions are particularly influential and therefore we need to be extremely careful not to use them. Information on forensic interviewing is now readily available and many workers are being trained in age-appropriate interviewing techniques for children. Here we limit our discussion to cases where allegations of abuse and neglect have been made, since sexual abuse investigation has been thoroughly studied and researched (Ney, 1995; Poole & Lamb, 1998; Sternberg et al., 1997; Yuille, Hunter, & Zaparnuik, 1993). Such forensic interviewing techniques can easily apply to cases where no sexual abuse allegation is involved.

Setting

Most initial interviews with children take place in the school. This requires particular sensitivity on the worker's part. For example, when a CPS worker requests an interview with a student named Billy Stanton, the worker usually goes to the school office. With the approval of the principal, the child is sometimes announced on a PA system and transmitted to every classroom in the building. This means every child in school knows that Billy Stanton may be in some sort of trouble; in most schools, when a child's name is called out via public speaker, the announcement draws his classmates' meaningful stares. Everyone in the school knows that Billy must have done something wrong and that he is going to "get it." A more sensitive way of asking Billy to come to the office would be to convey a message to his teacher via the secretary or the nurse. Perhaps a student messenger or helper could give a note to the teacher discreetly in a sealed envelope requesting that Billy come down to the office.

Remember that this interview is usually conducted without the parent's consent or awareness. At times, it is the school principal who calls CPS. Some school boards have adopted the policy of having the principal or another school official sit in on the interview in an effort to support or protect the child as well as protect the school. If that is the case, our preference is that the person representing the school be someone with whom the child is connected emotionally and to whom he or she has access later—a guidance counselor, social worker, nurse, teacher, teacher aide. This person, of course, would need to understand and respect confidentiality issues. It is important that someone from the school be involved in some way in order to help the child process the experience of the interview and to facilitate transition back to "school mode" once the CPS worker leaves. Children are more likely to act out after a CPS interview when no one helps them process, digest, and make sense of the experience.

Building Rapport

For building rapport with children, experienced, competent workers like Will Rea of Cortland County Child Protective Services, New York, use a sketch pad and box of washable markers in order to begin with personal information. Will finds that most children, even those who are taught not to talk to strangers or authority figures, will readily begin to color as he talks to them. He begins by drawing a little caricature of himself, which relaxes the child. Then he draws the child's face, inviting the child to give directions on where and how many eyes to put on the face, what color the hair should be, and other facial features. This not only quickly builds rapport with the child, but also works as an assessment tool to gauge the child's developmental level and ability to name colors, shapes, numbers, letters. Next, he asks the child's help in drawing a rough picture of the outside of a house; then he quickly moves to the interior of the house and asks where the child's family members spend time, sleep, eat, do homework, and so on. Within a matter of minutes, even the very shy child begins to describe his family, who sleeps with whom and in which room, who has just moved in with them, who is visiting, how many dogs and cats, and so on. Will Rea further describes his work in the following manner, "I often ask the child to tell me whether to put a sad or happy face on the stick figures, and gain information about the emotional state of the child, siblings, and caregivers."

Rather than saying to a child, "My job is to help children and their families," he strives to stay neutral, by saying, "I like to listen to what people like and don't like. It's good to hear that someone likes something, and if someone feels bad, mad, or sad, and it's okay to not tell something she does not want to tell. I know lots of ways to help." He also gives the child lots of control and tells a child to give a stop sign by holding up a hand. "If you want to stop for a while, use the bathroom, or just don't want to tell me something, hold up your hand and we will stop for a while. I won't be mad if you do that." It is important to give the child a sense of control over the interview.

Will Rea cautions against promising that the child's life will be better or that he or she will be safe, since workers never really know what placing the child out of home will turn out to be, whether better or worse for the child. When interviewing children, it is best to keep in mind that they tend to have the clearest memories about extremes. They may not remember their fourth physical abuse, but they are likely to remember the first, the most recent, the scariest, the time that happened in a shopping mall, or even when someone intervened for him or her. Children, like adults, tend to remember events in association with some other events, such as it happened on his birthday, when it snowed, or rained, or when the dog got sick, and so on. Therefore, it is better to say, "Did anything funny or happy or scary happen around the same time?" Or they might remember what favorite program was on television when it happened, and so on. Children, like adults, may also use slang, such as wee-wee, ding-dong, and number one and number two. Try to match their language instead of asking the child to change the word to something more acceptable.

Will Rea emphasizes ending the interview with a child with a "three wishes" question: "If you had three wishes, and no one knew you wished them, what would they be?" He hears some amazing wishes from children, not always about themselves, but wishes such as, "I wish my daddy wouldn't hit mommy" and others equally touching regarding their concerns for others. It is important to end the interview with thanks and praise for talking to the worker, whether the interview was productive or not. Will recommends ending the interview with neutral topics such as favorite television show, activities, pets, food and so on. He further suggests that you ask the child, "Is it okay if I tell your mommy you are real smart and have nice manners?" This helps to alleviate the child's anxiety and forestalls such questions as, "Are you going to tell mommy I talked to you?" This kind of debriefing at the end of the interview helps the child make the transition back into his or her usual routines.

According to Will, the elements of successful interviewing with a child are:

- Interdisciplinary teamwork—coordinating legal, mental health, victim assistance, law enforcement agencies, and school. Often the CPS worker can become the central person for these various players from different disciplines, coordinating and updating information.
- Keep the tone neutral—do not express shock, sympathy, or anger until you are back in your office, with your supportive colleagues.
- Express interest but make no promises. Once a child is betrayed, he or she may take a long time to trust someone again.
- When your emotional toll gets too heavy, let your supervisor or another supportive person know about it.
- When anyone on a interdisciplinary team does a good job, write a "thank you" note. Many people will appreciate your going out of your way to notice their exceptional work. Most people will notice occasional appreciation and remember you. This is your way of advocating for your future clients.

We are learning a great deal from the field of linguistics, most importantly that children's language development is not a miniature model of adults'; it develops much differently than we once thought. We now understand that reality is created and altered through talking. This new understanding of how language works is a double-edged sword; that is, while language is an easily accessible tool when our purpose is to create change, it is also difficult to establish truth and facts through language alone when interviewing children.

A 7-year-old child told her teacher that her mother had hit her on the neck with a hairbrush. A slight bruise was visible. A few minutes into the conversation with the investigator, the following dialogue took place.

Worker: So tell me again. You said your mother hit you in the neck with your hairbrush. Where did this happen—in the bathroom, in your room, or in the kitchen?

Child: In the kitchen. My mom hit me for no reason.

Worker: How many times did she hit you on the neck—once, twice, or many times?

Child: Many times. She hit me many times.

Worker: Tell me again, where did she hit you—on the arm, your head, or on the neck?

Child: On the neck. Then my brother came into the bathroom and he
    fooled around and my mom yelled at him.

Depending on the age of the child, this simple exchange can be
interpreted in many different ways. However, it should be fairly easy
to figure out that this 7-year-old child seems to respond to the last
words the interviewer uses. Many studies indicate that this is quite
normal with children: Children tend to mimic and pick up the last
words of the interviewer and bring in unrelated material. Some children
are swayed by repeated exposure to the same information, either
through repeated leading questions or through conversations over-
heard. Poole and Lindsay (1996) found that children err in reporting
events not because their memories are bad, but because their memories
are so good. They mix up topics and freely bring in unrelated material
because of three major mechanisms at work: limited understanding of
language, limited understanding of the interview process, and memory
source monitoring errors.

Good interview practice also includes a little time to debrief at the
end of the interview, even if you have decided that the allegations
have no merit. Without this, the children tend to become very disori-
ented and either act out or become very withdrawn. This can happen
even with debriefing, but it usually helps to ease his or her transition
back to the classroom.

Balance Positives and Negatives

Although it is easy to focus immediately on the complaint that
prompted your visit to the school, the interview will be much more
productive if you first make some small talk with the child. Jokes
about the room, about your mistakes on the way over to the school,
or something you did that made you look foolish, for example, can
break the ice. Complimenting the child on her pretty beads or pins or
his "fast sneakers" and asking about who takes such good care of him
or her that he or she looks so neat today is one possibility. Another
good way to get started is to ask about his favorite class and what he
is best at in school. Asking about his favorite music or the name of his
favorite teddy bear can help build rapport. Be sure to ask the child
about what he likes best about his weekly visit with his dad, what he
doesn't like about it; what is good about, and what is not good about
it; what makes him happy and unhappy during the visits, and so
on. These are some examples that you can adapt to fit the child's
circumstances. Investigative interviews need not be limited to what is

negative, disliked, and uncomfortable. When you balance the positive and the negative, you are more likely to get accurate information.

Explain to the child the purpose of the visit, using neutral and nonlegalistic language. Avoid professional jargon at all costs. Talk to the child at eye level and use simple words. "Billy, my name is Mary Smith and I am from Lake County Social Service. I try to help children and their families. You haven't done anything wrong that I know of. You are not in any trouble with me. I don't work for the school." Then you can gradually introduce the rules of the interview and that he or she can say "I don't know" anytime during the talk. Explain the purpose of your interview by starting out with, for example, "Billy, I want to tell you that there are people who care about you. Tell me about people who care about you." Allow the child to list those who care about him, including best friends, teddy bears, and other secret friends. "And I want to make sure that you are safe and do not have to worry about things that grown-ups should take care of. Is it okay if I ask you some questions about your visits with your dad?" You can repeat the same questions about living with mom (Grandma, Uncle Joe, foster parent, etc.) in order to make a balance.

All children have a strong sense of loyalty and commitment to their parents or caretakers. Be sensitive to this sense of loyalty by staying away from asking questions that may demean or criticize the parent or caretaker or that are disrespectful of the adults they live with. Remember that at the end of the interview the child must go home to the parent about whom he or she may have said something negative to a stranger. You can imagine the child's awkward and uncomfortable position of feeling that he or she may have betrayed his or her parent. It is not difficult to imagine how this might create a negative interaction between the child and the parent, without the parent realizing what might be going on. You can also imagine how this may unwittingly trigger the child to act out. Of course if there were any sort of abuse or neglect going on, the child might feel relieved to realize that help is on the way. Even so, the child will feel some ambivalence about the interview. Sensing vaguely that he might cause his parent harm is a heavy burden for a young child to bear, even if the child ultimately benefits from it. The child is already in a vulnerable position of not being able to do the right thing whatever he tries.

Young children are not able to see that people are more complex than just being "all good" or "all bad." Given the choice between "good" and "bad," most young children, even those with parents who abuse or neglect them, are more likely to see parents as good rather than bad. It is not in the child's best interest to try to help him see his parents as "bad," even if the facts seem to point in that direction.

Although you may see some goodness in the parent, it does not necessarily mean that child will be safe staying with that parent. It is best when CPS can acknowledge and validate what the child sees as "good" in her parent and at the same time explain steps that must be taken to keep the child safe because of the "not-good" sides of the parent.

However difficult this situation is for you at the time, and until further research shows us a better way to handle this interview protocol, our only suggestion is to be thoughtful and gentle with the child, allowing the child sufficient time to say good things about both parents and showing your good faith effort at believing and trusting the child. We are increasingly aware that young children are greatly influenced by the adults around them. When adults are alarmed, the child's anxiety increases and when the adults are comfortable around the child, so is the child. Therefore, it is important to use neutral language when talking to a child and to use lots of relationship questions to get some idea of the child's perception of what important adults would say about what the child just said.

In Table 5.1 we have summarized the useful questions outlined in this chapter. This can be used as a guideline until these questions become second nature.

Table 5.1

LEAD-IN QUESTIONS IN SOLUTION-BUILDING

What, Where, and How
(Avoid using "Why" questions.)

What does _____ expect to come out of your coming to this meeting?

What part do you agree with and what part do you disagree with?

What tells you that you should rank yourself at 5 today?

What difference will it make with your drinking when you move up from 5 to maybe 5.5?

What have you done instead of drinking at a time like this?

What difference do you want your parenting class to make with your child?

What would your daughter say that she likes the most about your being sober?

What would she say is different about you when you are clean?

(continued)

Table 5.1

Continued

How do you know it will work with your daughter?

How did you manage to get out of bed this morning?

How does your mother (best friend) think parenting class will be helpful for you?

How will you make sure that your child is safe in the future?

Who is the first person to recognize that you are becoming calmer?

Where is the best place for you to gain control of yourself?

Where in the house do you feel relaxed the most?

Questions Framed in Tentative Language
(It is collaborative and consensus-building.)

Could it be that you really want what is best for your children?

It appears that you really want to be a good parent and to do what is best for your children, would you agree?

Perhaps you really know inside that you really don't want to do drugs as much as you do?

It appears that you really want what is best for your family, even though this is very hard for you?

Suppose, just suppose, you had more money—what difference would it make for you?

Suppose your husband were still alive, what would you be doing then that you are not doing right now?

I wonder what you really were like in those days when you were more independent?

Could it be that you really want to make sure that your child is safe?

Relationship Questions

What would your mother (best friend, etc.) say would be best for you?

How will your best friend know that miracle happened and your problem is solved?

Who among your friends will be the first to recognize that you stopped drinking?

(continued)

Table 5.1

Continued

How could he/she tell without your saying so?

What would he do then?

What would your children say about how they can tell that you love them?

What would your children say they like most about your being calmer?

What would they say about how that is helpful to them?

I realize that your children are too young to talk, but just suppose that they have the words to tell me. Suppose I asked your daughter what she likes about you being sober, what do you suppose she would tell me?

What do you suppose she will tell me that she is like when she knows you are sober?

What would she say is different between you and her when she believes you are sober?

What would your boyfriend say it would take for him to take you back?

What would he say about how determined you are not to take him back this time?

Questions about Client's Personal Meaning and Language
(Always pick up the client's exact words and use them to formulate your next questions, except, of course, impolite language.)

You are clear about not cleaning up the toilet. What does it mean to you? What about it that is so important to you?

Let me understand this clearly. So, what does it mean for you to follow through with this?

I am a bit confused. So, what about drinking too much (hitting your child, losing your temper) is helpful to you?

Say that again—what difference would it make for you to (drink too much, lose your temper, sleep all day, etc.)?

(continued)

Table 5.1

Continued

Future-Oriented Questions

So, when you no longer have to hit your child "upside the head," what will you do instead?

So when you can remember to say your "serenity prayer," what will you be doing differently?

Suppose you do "stay cool," what would your children say how helpful it is to them?

When you are in "God's grace," how would your daughter say she can tell that?

Chapter 6

Investigation as Intervention and Prevention

EVEN THOUGH REMOVAL OF CHILDREN FROM NEGLECTFUL AND ABUSIVE parents occurs in only 10% of all the cases investigated by CPS, the common perception of the public, legislators, health professionals, policy-makers, and workers themselves is that CPS is synonymous with scooping up young children from the rat-infested housing or brutal abuse by their parents to a safe haven. The challenge for CPS workers is to discern and make judgment calls in the other 90% of cases—those that are called by various names, including unsubstantiated, denied, closed, assessed, and so on. This chapter addresses this difficult challenge. It is divided into two parts: repeated investigation cases, those which are not high profile media cases, and those that are commonly believed to be "difficult," special problem cases for most workers.

REINVESTIGATION CASES

Administrators, supervisors, frontline workers, and policy-makers consider reinvestigation cases as the most difficult, baffling, costly, and frustrating part of CPS work. These cases are often lumped together as "chronic cases." Reinvestigation means that a family is visited more than once by a CPS worker for possible neglect and abuse. Each time the level of evidence and concern is not severe enough to keep the case open, so it is closed or "denied." It is easy to imagine the frustration of the families and workers involved in such situations. We have heard many workers groan and sigh when assigned a reinvestigation case; repeating the same questions and procedures with the same family is tedious work.

Since there are no statistics available on this category of cases, it is difficult to know the length of time between phone calls that trigger repeat visits. It seems to range from two to three months or even five to six months. Some experienced workers classify these cases in the following categories: 30% are related to family disputes, such as divorcing or divorced parents using CPS to continue their battles (that is, non-CPS cases); 20% involve parent and adolescent conflicts on discipline issues, curfews, boy/girlfriends; another 20% involve personal grudges against family members, former friends, and neighbors; and the others defy categorization and "fall between cracks." The latter group cannot be neatly packaged into a category of services, and agencies do not have the funding to customize services. Many families do not quite qualify for any outreach programs such as in-home treatment services, and they are not likely to follow up on referrals to community-based service. They are not usually referred to "ongoing" services either, because there is no identifiable neglect or abuse.

From an administrative perspective, reinvestigation cases are cause for legitimate concern. According to a recent report (Packard, 1998), a single investigation visit by a worker costs $813. Five visits to the same family costs $4,065. Certainly this money can be spent better for different services that will have a longer-lasting and beneficial influence on the family.

Not only is the financial cost enormous but the human cost to workers and families is also inordinate. Workers feel that they are going through a repetitive, unproductive cycle, which lowers morale. Families feel intruded upon, that the visits are annoying, and that the workers are, as one mother described, "pesty" and "stick their noses where they don't belong."

CPS is mandated to investigate all cases when there is a reasonable cause to be concerned, in other words, when we don't know for sure that a child is safe. Those cases could go either way: A visit is required to substantiate or deny (close) the case. You know these cases: The house is filthy enough, yet habitable; the parenting skills certainly could improve yet the parents have not harmed the child in any tangible or documentable ways; the mother admits to using drugs and alcohol, but the children seem to be functioning at an acceptable level and she is doing an okay job of ensuring their safety. We can make a long list of "what if" situations that cause us to worry and lose sleep. Workers and supervisors often call these "chronic neglect" cases, and there seems to be little we can do to make things better.

Many supervisors and workers feel weary about these cases. One supervisor told us that she makes sure that assignment of such cases is rotated among workers so that one worker is not continually stuck

with monotonous, repetitive work. This is one of many possibl
to deal with repeat investigation cases. We would prefer that the a
decide to support workers by providing training and other he
that these reinvestigation cases would not be so monotonous or repetitive. One of the most important ingredients in CPS work is building
positive client-worker relationships that will facilitate the protection
of the children and their parents. Some agencies seem to take for
granted that multiple referrals are standard and acceptable. But let's
look at this problem through another lens.

A Fresh View: Investigation as Prevention

What if we saw investigation not only as an intervention tool but also
as a prevention tool? What if we saw these cases as opportunities for
laying the first brick of a new building—the foundation, so to speak?
As workers and clients began to build a different future, imagine the
change in attitudes! Rather than accepting these re-referrals and repeated investigations as a given and thinking there was nothing to be
done about agency rules, we would find a great deal of room in which
workers, supervisors, and administrators could maneuver.

We have already emphasized that within the context of CPS investigation we cannot not intervene, that is, just by showing up on a family's
doorstep we are making a statement about the parents' ability to parent,
to take care of their children, often creating a crisis for them. In this
chapter, we focus on the idea that investigation can be a preventive
tool as well. While you are doing an assessment to make sure that the
child is safe, you will find a great deal of room to insert some of
our suggestions and turn the conversation into a preventive effort by
utilizing resources within easy reach of the parent, rather than looking
for resources outside the family.

Looking at What's There

New national and state laws are greatly impacting the way CPS cases
move through the system. While we strongly believe we must, at times,
step back and let clients make decisions on their time, we are aware
that new national laws (ASFA, 1997) and state legislation are enforcing
time limitations on decision-making in child welfare cases, especially
those where there is serious risk to a child. The federal law requires
states to move children more rapidly into permanent homes by speed-
ing court response and, when necessary, terminating parental rights
and promoting adoptions. In the past the luxury of time allowed families to move more slowly to make necessary changes. In the following
sections we suggest that some families will not be able to move quickly,

even though the potential is there. In an ideal world, we could enact the following suggestions without the pressure of time constraints. While we acknowledge the demands of these new laws, we believe there is still room to trust the process that families will, in their own ways, determine the course of action for their children, even if it is not carried out as quickly or thoroughly as we would like it to be.

Keeping in mind the legal demands, let's look at reinvestigation cases from a fresh perspective and capitalize on what is there, instead of agonizing over what is not. This will require us to adjust the lenses through which we look at our clients. First, about looking at what is there. Parents or caretakers who are successfully navigating, even marginally, the maze of parenting or coping with the harsh realities of life are doing something right. However inadequate their care may seem, at least they are not abusing or neglecting their children to an extent that you need to consider immediate removal of the children. Quite the opposite at times! In fact, they are doing a reasonably good job of making a home for their children, in spite of the number of obstacles they face, such as mental or physical illness, chronic depression, economic hardship, substance abuse, repeated breakdown of the beat-up car, unreliable source of support or child care, an ongoing cycle of job-hopping or unemployment, and a myriad of other pressures and difficulties in coping and managing an ordinary, everyday life. Look for extraordinary, heroic courage rather than a lack of adequate resources or competent parenting skills—you'll find a small seed that could potentially germinate and bloom with the right amount of care. It is not a beautiful, blooming flower yet, but the potential is there. Finding this small potential is the beginning step. Keep in mind that a seed may lie dormant for a long time before it germinates. It is possible that you may never get to see the flowers bloom. Likewise, someday, when the client is ready for a change or when circumstances alter so that she can put her life together, she will make use of whatever guidance you have offered in the past. We have to trust this process; it may take a long time and we have no way of knowing what makes things finally come together.

Below is a list of suggestions that you can implement as soon as you determine that the case is likely to be a single visit and that you will either refer the case for services or close it. Even if you refer the case to other resources in the community, actually following through with the referral will probably take a while and you can still do the following without jeopardizing the referral process.

1.   As soon as it becomes clear to you that there is no ground for substantiating neglect or abuse, immediately shift gears and ask

the parent solution-building questions such as: "Your little girl is so friendly (or she has such a beautiful smile)—you must have done a good job of encouraging her sunny side to shine. How do you do that?" "How do you manage to do so much when your life is obviously very difficult?" "What keeps you going day in and day out?" "Boy, you really must care about your son (daughter). I can see in his eyes how much he loves you and how important you are to him."

2. Look for the client's successes, however small, and then acknowledge them. Observe the mother wiping the child's nose with a tissue; exchanging a smile with her child, with a twinkle in her eyes; or the young child wrapping himself around his mother's leg when you first meet her and the mother patting the top of the child's head, as if to reassure him that this stranger is harmless. The parent will remember your comment that she must love the child very much and you can see that they have such a warm relationship. This is probably the first time the parent ever heard such kind assessment. We have seen many mothers break into tears when their deep love for their child was acknowledged.

3. Bring in others' perceptions of her whenever you can, using "relationship questions" (see chapter 5). Ask how other important persons in her life understand how she keeps hanging in there when her life is difficult. It is possible that nobody in her life has ever asked about her ability to cope in difficult circumstances; therefore, the client might seem confused or at a loss for words. Be patient and give her lots of time to sort out her answer. Use coping questions (chapter 5) to follow up on her description of what keeps her going.

4. Even if the client has no immediate answer, do not assume that it was a wasted question or that it went over the client's head and she was not bright enough to understand. Clients have reported months or years later how they often think about what a worker said and how much they were touched by it.

5. As you are winding down the interview and getting ready to leave, casually ask, "So, what do you suppose it will take for you to keep going at this level?" Listen to her answers, some may amaze you.

6. Ask, "What kind of help do you need to stay at this level?" Use scaling questions (chapter 5) to assess the parent's confidence level, then follow up with strategies for raising her confidence just a little bit.

7. Ask, "Suppose you stayed at this level for a month or so. What will be different with your family? What will be different with the children? What would they say?"

Even if you do not go any further than this, you have already made a significant difference for this client for the following reasons:

- The client is much more aware of what she is doing right, and that she knows how to do it, and thus is able to repeat those successful behaviors.
- Once given this kind of awareness, she is more likely to look for other things that she is doing right, such as keeping the house clean, feeding the children a good meal on time, being more thoughtful of the child's needs, and listening to their wishes and desires.
- As this continues, the mother is much more likely to expand her thinking and remind herself to pay attention to her successes with the child. Such awareness seems to make a positive difference and is likely to lead to a positive interaction with the child.
- We are aware of the importance of the mother's positive feelings about herself and their effect on the child. When the mother is positive, the whole family seems to be positive and, of course, vice versa.

Deciding to Make a Referral and Close the Case

As we mentioned previously, offering unsolicited suggestions or advice to clients amounts to a waste of energy. There are many reasons for this:

- It is difficult for the client to believe that someone who has not lived his or her life could come up with the answers so quickly.
- The client does not feel that he or she has the energy to take on a new task.
- The advice does not fit the client's state of mind.
- The client thinks it will take an enormous amount of work to get started.
- The client has other things on his or her mind, other worries, and does not want to add to the burden.

When we offer suggestions or advice, we raise our own expectations for the client, that is, we expect the client to follow through on our good ideas. When this does not occur, for any of the above reasons, we begin to be irritated and annoyed with the client, which fosters a negative interaction. And for a host of other reasons that we cannot know, clients are not likely to act on the suggestion unless they are ready to do so. What pushes the client into action is beyond our control; all we can do is to take advantage of what we see—but it is clear that when the client is ready to take steps, she or he can make significant progress rather quickly.

When the idea of possible good resources in the community comes to mind, do not rush to offer suggestions so that you can get to the next home visit case or emergency. Take a few minutes and do the following:

- Ask yourself how much the problem that prompted the phone call to CPS is upsetting the client. You can discern this by the client's affect and the words she uses to describe the event.
- Ask the client what she has thought of doing about the problem.
- Does the client have some idea about how to handle the problem when it comes up again? If she or he does, ask for details. If the planned solution sounds reasonable, you might want to indicate that it is a good plan and ask how she came up with such a good plan. Ask about ideas on how to follow up. If the client's ideas sound reasonable, and she is confident she will follow through on the plan, then close the case. If her idea seems somewhat unrealistic or that it will create more troubles, ask for more details.
- Use questions like, "So, how will that be helpful?" or "How long do you think it will last?"
- If the client concedes that it might not last very long, or that she has no idea about what to do, then the client will listen willingly to your suggestions. You might indicate that "other people in your situation have done this, this, and that" and wait for her response to see whether she is receptive to the idea.
- If the client indicates that she is interested in further information, leave the information, asking her to let you know how it goes.
- If the client is hesitant, then you might want to leave your business card with information on community resources, indicating that "they might be able to help you with this kind of problem/concern."

Always be prepared to give specific referrals, with names, phone numbers, brochures, and other pertinent information that will help organize the client's understanding of what to expect. Often clients are unaware of resources that can be helpful to them or have heard inaccurate rumors or reports about someone's negative experience.

When It Is a Repeat Investigation

Families involved in repeat-investigation cases are usually known to CPS. If you are a new worker in your area, most of your colleagues will know about them, either because they have personally investigated the same family or because the family name is well known to the agency. Any worker who has been on the job for 5, 10, or 15 years in the same county gets to know many of these repeat-investigation cases. We have met some workers who knew the last boyfriend the mother had and how many times the police were called to the family home because of complaints from neighbors about disturbing the peace or about the children. Many veteran workers also know families personally, especially if they live and work in the same small, rural county, where everyone shops at the same grocery store, goes to the same church, and the children go to the same schools. Certain clients are known as the "town drunk" or "black sheep"; everyone knows that so-and-so has had three husbands and a family reputation as "bad seed."

The most common reaction to a repeat-investigation visit is dismay: "Not again!" followed by an expression of frustration. "I know everything I need to know about the Smith family" or "That family never changes!" Remember that this repeat visit is equally, if not more, frustrating to the family, who has to sit through another ordeal. Statistics indicate that you are very likely to make repeat visits to the same family many times in your career. So, rather than seeing this second, third, fourth, or fifth visit as "more of the same," you need to think differently this time.

If This Reinvestigation Is a Brand New Case for You

Take a few minutes and review the previous investigation record. It is probably one of those "dispute cases" that does not belong to CPS, but the conflict with the family, neighbor, or friend is not solved. Perhaps the phone call was triggered by environmental issues, such as heat, electricity, or water being turned off, which indeed may pose a risk; or the filth in the house is such that it has finally triggered the attention and ire of neighbors; or one of the children missed one too many days of school; or the school "has had it" with the parent's inability (or unwillingness) to get the child immunized and cannot wait one day longer. Here is what you can do.

Think of your investigation as a follow-up meeting. Think of your visit as a follow-up to the previous investigation visits. Think of each subsequent repeat visit as third, fourth, fifth meetings, and so on. Even though this visit is your first to this family, think of yourself as part of a relay or tag team. It makes very little difference to the client who you are or which agency you come from; all the workers from various social service or health care agencies seem to blur together and they cannot, nor do they want to, distinguish you from some other worker.

As a way of bridging with some other worker's previous visit, and in order to keep friendly conversation going, spend a few minutes asking the client, for example, how he or she keeps the house in reasonable order and manages to help the children do well both in school and socially while working long hours, or comment on your observation of how well the children listen and follow directions. Reinforce the client's successes with much support and validation of his or her hard work and good intentions to be a good parent.

Ask what it would take to keep successful parenting (or management) going. This is truly where the preventive work begins. By highlighting even the smallest success, such as a tidy bedroom or a clean bathroom, you are helping the parent make the next step of a successful transition to better parenting. Very likely, no one has ever told the parent she is doing a good job of keeping one part of the house clean or neat, and she has probably never told herself that either. Therefore, whenever you see a small success, we suggest that you ask the client questions, rather than handing out praises; praises from strangers are difficult for many clients to accept, since they do not feel terribly confident about themselves.

Focus on what they want (goal). "What needs to be different in your life so that you don't have to put up with our agency coming and asking you all these questions?" Defining the client's goal is important; it is the first step the client takes toward change. When the goal is generated by the client, it is more likely to be accomplished. For most clients, your visit is not something they asked or wished for, and so it is particularly crucial to find out what is important to them. Agree with what the client wants as a valid beginning stage, and then discuss how achieving that goal will make his or her life better.

Find out who is important in the client's life. Instead of assuming that all children are important, all family members are supportive of the client, and so on, ask and listen carefully to what she says about who is important to her. Then accept that person as the most reasonable and logical one to value, often using her exact words. For some clients, it does make a difference to call a grandmother a granny or gram, grandmama, or old lady. For some clients, argument is not the same as fighting, and is different from discussing, for example. When you can approximate the words clients use, you will connect with them quickly and efficiently, thus establishing a positive relationship. You can refer back to this important person repeatedly. For example, we once worked with a mother whose first child, named Nakisha, died soon after birth due to a birth defect. In her grief and sorrow, the mother kept ruminating about Nakisha's death. When the mother became pregnant again, she still kept thinking about her dead child and neglected her prenatal care. She was referred to grief work group, individual counseling, and numerous support groups with no results. The public health nurse became increasingly concerned about the mother's inability to bond with the fetus, even though the mother was visibly getting bigger. When I (IKB) met the mother, she was sad and tearful, and kept ruminating about what might have been done to save the baby, while talking about Nakisha in present tense, as if she were still alive. Her husband, family, and friends were getting frustrated with her because she behaved as if none of them existed and repeatedly rejected their advice and suggestions.

I decided to use this dead daughter as an important resource for the mother and to talk to the mother as if her dead infant were still alive and able to give mother suggestions. I said, "I realize that Nakisha must be in heaven and looking down on you and must have lots of things to say to you." Mother agreed that surely Nakisha is in heaven because she was such a perfect child and must be sitting on the right side of God. "So, since she is a child with a heart of gold, what do you suppose she would say to you about how she would like you to live your life?" "What do you suppose Nakisha would tell you would be good for you to do?" "What do you suppose she would tell you about how she wants you to take care of her little sister who is about to be sent to earth and live with you?" "What about her daddy; how would she like to see her mommy and daddy get along?" The result was a dramatic turnaround in the mother's view of herself and her family.

Create a detailed safety plan with the client. The more detailed, concrete, and behavioral the client's safety plan, the more likely it will succeed. Be sure the child is included in this safety plan. When the client makes sweeping statements, such as, "I ain't never gonna hit that child again" or "I know better now than to get drunk while the kids are running around and believe me I will never do it again. I learned my lesson and I know what can happen to me and my kids if I get drunk again," we know he or she really "means it" at the time. However, unless the client has concrete, detailed ideas on how to implement his or her good intention, such sweeping statements are not very useful. The following dialogue gives some suggestions on how to make the plan more concrete and how to include the child.

Mother: I sure learned my lesson this time. I will never drink again when the little ones are around, that's for sure. I know what could happen.
Worker: I am glad to hear that, and that you are going to make the changes for your children's sake as well as yours. Everybody knows how difficult it is to do. Can you explain to me how you are going to fight the temptation to drink again? You know you

will be tempted. (*The worker normalizes the craving the client is likely to face and helps her make plans to deal with it.*)

Mother: I've been thinking about not drinking on and off for some time now and I really can see that it's not good for me and or my kids.

Worker: So, tell me again, what will you do differently when the craving first hits you? (*Holds the client responsible for change and planning the solution step by step.*) How will you know that it is the craving for drink and not something else? (*Draws on the client's expertise on problems related to drinking.*)

Mother: Oh, I know it well because I have fought it before and I used to win. (*The client spontaneously offers information about exceptions.*)

Worker: Oh, you have? When was that?

Mother: Oh, about six months ago. I stayed away from drinking for about three months.

Worker: That's impressive (*with genuine surprise*). How did you do that?

Mother: I went to church in those days. It really helped to go to church because I was so busy and helping other people made me think about how blessed I was that I had something to give. I kept busy and had peace of mind.

Worker: So, what were you doing different with Travis when you were busy, felt blessed, and had peace of mind? (*The worker uses the client's exact words and involves the child in this solution picture.*)

Mother: He was with me all the time. I used to sing to him when we were walking to church, to the grocery store, and he loved to run around the church and play with other children there. (*We are getting a pretty good picture of how this solution was good for him also.*)

Worker: It sounds like it was a peaceful time for you. So, what do you have to do to have that peace of mind in your life again? (*Immediately moves into the client's plan for implementing her solutions.*)

Mother: First of all, I need to pray a lot to prepare my mind, then I have to call the pastor, then I will just have to go to church starting this Sunday morning. Travis will like that because he'll get to see all his old friends again. (*We are getting a pretty good picture of how Travis will fit into the plan, and it sounds pretty healthy for him also.*)

Worker: So, suppose you do all this. What would be different between you and Travis? (*The worker zeroes in on the solution for Travis, which seems realistic and doable.*)

Asking coping questions and miracle questions (see chapter 5) will help the client describe his or her solutions for avoiding repeat visits.

As the client describes the details of his vision, he begins to implement his solution and take control of the situation—even if the problem was generated by someone other than the client.

Review when life or the relationship was a little bit better. What did the client do to make it better in those days? What would it take to return to the previous level of good relationship? If that is not possible, then what needs to change so that life is more tolerable for the client, the caller, and CPS?

Find out how motivated the client is to not have the repeat visit, perhaps using scaling questions. Follow up with questions such as these:

- What tells you that you are at 3?
- What will you do differently when you move up from 3 to maybe 3.5?
- What will _____ notice different about you when you go up from 3 to 3.5?
- When _____ notices these differences with you what will s/he do differently?
- What will it take to get you started going from 3 to 3.5?
- How sure are you that you can help the CPS to stay away from you?
- Tell me more about how your life will be better when these visits stop.
- What would your children say about how that will improve their life?

These questions not only elicit information on how motivated she or he is to stop the visit, but also provide valuable information on what the client might actually be able to do to improve his or her life in such a way that you both can see it. Of course, any improvement ultimately benefits the children.

Look for exceptions, even in those "iffy" or uncertain cases. The uncertain cases are the most stressful to deal with. Instead of viewing them as agonizing, problematic, or a waste of time and energy, remember that your agonizing about this case and not being certain about your decision-making are indications about you and your client. How is that? CPS work is not comprised of simple black-white judgment calls; there are no easy and fast answers when it comes to human life and a child's future. We want all our decisions to be safe and wise, that is, safe for the child and good for the family. Therefore, we applaud you for your struggle to find solutions to keep these families together.

We also believe that your struggle speaks volumes to your client. If it were a clear-cut case of abuse or neglect, you would know what steps to take immediately. Make sure, using all your investigative skills, that the child is safe. Of course, if there is a clear indication of risk for the child, you need to take immediate steps to either reduce or remove the danger and risk. However, your not being able to make such a decision means that there is a hidden treasure somewhere and your job is to find it, polish it, and hold it up to the sun so that it will shine. These are, again, the small exceptions to problems and the potential source of success. Clients have told us what a difference it made when a worker did not immediately take their kids away, but instead took time to see the possibilities. One client said to us, "I thought to myself, everyone can see it, they're going to take my kids—it's gotten this bad. But the worker helped me to pull myself together, thank God."

Keep in mind that since you (usually) have 30 days to complete your investigation and make a decision, you can always return for a second look. Listen and observe in a way that is unbiased. During the second and third visits, you may want to spend some time talking to the parent about his or her plan of action to remedy the problem you saw, for example, the dirty house, the garbage on the floor, missing doors in the bedrooms. But more importantly, comment on and enhance whatever small signs of safety, good parenting, and love for the child you see that can be nurtured, enlarged, and made to grow.

Be sure changes are sustainable. When you notice small changes that make it possible for you to close the case one more time, make sure that the family has other infrastructures in place to maintain the changes. Does the client have the ability to pay the utility bills? Is there a reliable child care arrangement? Is there a plan to keep the toilet working, the house clean, etc.? Without such foundations, this family is likely to come to the attention of CPS again.

If This Is Not a New Case for You

When you are faced with a repeat investigation, the first question to ask is, "Has anything changed since the last visit three months ago?" Of course, there are situations that call for immediate action. When you can safely rule out immediate danger but the situation again falls on the margin and you are not able to substantiate neglect or abuse, consider it as a second, third, fourth, or fifth meeting, rather than repeating the first investigation five times. That is, think of ways to build on whatever existing safety strategies are already shown by the family. When there are no significant changes and the family circumstances have not deteriorated, something is working for the parent. Look for evidence of small successes in the parent and find out what has been working, in detail, since the last visit.

If there are positive changes, such as the mother is now working or in job training, has reconciled with her partner, is drinking less, looks less tired, is coping better with life, or the children are healthier, doing better in school, the following questions are useful:

- How did you do it?
- What (or who) has been most helpful?
- I wonder how you did that?
- How did you know it would work?
- What else did you do right?

Engaging clients in self-complimenting talk helps them to recognize their own resources and successes. Sometimes, a small change in a client's perception of herself changes the way she deals with those around her. The manifestation of a change in attitude can be significant.

If there are negative changes, ask about the safety plan. While you are conducting a safety check, be sure to give credit to the caretaker, the child, or anyone involved in having maintained some level of safety for the child. Always give credit to the caretakers/parents before you give recognition to the child. Remember, when clients feel validated as good parents by professionals who must know about such things, their interaction with their children is more likely to be positive. (Of course, if the parent still needs to improve on certain areas, such as getting a medical checkup for a child, cleaning up a dirty house, making sure she gets medical care herself, and so on, then you will need to modify your comments to fit the circumstances.)

The following questions validate parent/caretaker while involving him or her in finding solutions.

- How did you cope when things were tough?
- What helped you get through such a bad time?
- Considering all that happened to you during the last four months, how is it that you are managing as well as you are without any help from anyone?
- What do you think needs to be different so that your life will be little bit better?
- What would it take for you to go back to the level of managing you were at before?

When such questions are asked, clients realize that they were once in a better position; this reminder of their previous success is very helpful and gives them hope.

Whenever you feel discouraged about the case, scaling questions can be very useful. Ask the client to estimate his or her current level of functioning. Then ask what he or she needs to do to *maintain* that level. If the client becomes a little bit more optimistic, ask scaling questions to assess his or her confidence. Also ask relationship questions: What would significant others in the client's life (spouse, child, friend, family member, child's teacher, church friend) say he or she is doing right? When you are skeptical of the client's high rating of confidence, ask:

- What tells you that you are at 7?
- What would _____ (best friend, etc.) say about how confident you are, on the same scale?
- What would _____ say you will be like when you move up one point?

Comparing the client's perceptions with a significant other's and your own of where the client is on the confidence scale will determine your next step.

Present the case to your consultation team, supervisor, manager, or other respected member of your unit. Before presenting your case, ask yourself the following questions:

- Suppose the client was really honest with herself. What would she say she wants for herself, for her children, and for her life?
- What would she say I am doing that is helpful?
- What would she say I am doing that is most helpful? least helpful?
- On a scale of 1 (lowest) to 10 (highest), how helpful would she say I have been?
- What would she say I can do to raise it one point higher?

Ask yourself the following questions to determine the format that would best suit your needs:

- Do I want to talk to the group of my team members, supervisor alone, supervisor plus trusted colleagues, or just my best colleague friend?
- Do I want to talk first, lay out what I know about the case, then ask questions?
- Do I want to do an oral presentation along with written questions or do I want everything to be oral?
- Do I want to include the outcome of this discussion in case record?

Once you answer these, then you can proceed with the following questions:

- What else do I need to know (see) about this parent (family) so that I can make a good decision?
- What will let me know that the children in this family are safe? What is my assessment of the safety for the children on a scale of 0 to 10?
- What are the available options for cases such as this?
- How can I help this client so that she will follow through on her promise?
- At what point on the scale can I close the case? What will tell me that the child is safer than before?

If the Family Situation Is Worse

Again, we want to remind you that the percentage of cases where the situation worsens is quite low. Situations usually remain static or show improvement in family functioning. When your home visit reveals that nothing seems to have changed for the better, even a little bit (the children are still marginally cared for, the house is dirty, the head lice issue has not been dealt with, the mother seems too lethargic to even care about the family situation, etc.), or worse yet, the condition seems to have deteriorated, then you will need to see this as serious risk to the children.

If you judge that there is a marginal risk to the child, you need to let the parent/caretaker know about your concerns and back them up with what you have observed and heard. You may need to repeat that you are "concerned about your child's safety." Involve the parent in finding solutions and planning realistic strategies: "I can see that you love your daughter very much and I am sure you want her to be safe; so what do you think you need to do to make sure she is safe?" Ask for details of the plan—the more detailed the better. Using scaling questions (see chapter 5), assess the level of safety the parent feels she can provide. If the answer she gives you is not convincing or realistic enough, you will need to reassess whether you need to place this case at a higher level of risk.

When conditions in the home have deteriorated to the point that you are seriously concerned about the safety of the children, you may have to consider removal (see chapter 9). Even then, we continue to collaborate and involve the client as much as we can.

Be honest and straightforward with the client. Do not interpret the situation from a moral high ground, but do explain your concerns to the client in an open and honest manner. Also, do not wait until the situation reaches a crisis point because making a hasty decision in the midst of crisis is not helpful to the children. The best time to make a good decision is before the crisis. Do not threaten; always move in the direction of solving problems the children face. Maintain your composure, stay calm, and keep your emotions in check. Be straightforward about your concerns and solicit the client's ideas on what to do, as the following dialogue illustrates:

Worker: Sandra, we have met several times now and discussed the things we are concerned about, such as the sharp objects, like clothes hangers, laying around that are dangerous to the children; the children's diaper rash; the dirty house, which is unsafe for your young children. It seems like things are getting worse rather than better as we both have hoped for. Obviously, there are so many things going on in your life that perhaps you have no energy to even think about what is in the best interests of your children. What do you think?

Sandra: I really mean to take care of all that stuff but I don't know what to do. I am so upset all the time with my boyfriend who has been cheating on me. If I mention to him that I think he is cheating, he just gets mad and wants to break up. I don't want to lose him. I cry all the time and I don't know what to do.

Worker: I can see that you are having difficulty deciding between your boyfriend and your children. So, what are some of your ideas on what to do? Your children cannot wait for you to figure out what to do about Brian. Based on what you told me about him, it may take a few more years for him to grow up and be able to take care of you in the way you deserve to be taken care of. And I am sure you will feel worse if your children get hurt or sick or something happens to them. Any ideas on what you want to do first? It's tough being a parent, isn't it?

Although the temptation to tell Sandra what to do is great, it is almost always predictable what will happen when you do it. Eliciting the client's ideas works best because it engages her in the development of her own solution.

If the Family Is Frustrated

If you find the client angry, uncooperative, and frustrated with repeated visits, try to take the position that the client is justified in viewing your visit as intrusive, because certainly somebody made a grave mistake. Rather than responding to his or her open criticism by defending yourself, the agency, and the previous worker, listen carefully for the client's underlying message of desperation and frustration and then address it. Rather than giving into the temptation to label the client as "resistant," "uncooperative," "in denial," "wrong-headed," and so on, try to see that the client's frustration is quite normal and legitimate under the circumstances. As one wise worker suggested, think about how you would want to be treated and do not personalize the client's anger. Remember that this is not the same as condoning the client's frustration. For additional information on talking with angry and hostile clients, see chapter 4.

Throughout the meeting, you need to remain courteous. As you point out some things that are going well with the family, watch your client soften his or her stance toward you and see the anger subside. It is always useful to look for the underlying positive motivation and good intentions behind the mask of anger. Detecting such emotions, which are often hidden from the clients themselves, is sometimes called "reframing." Some ways to positively reframe anger include:

- The client is protecting the family's privacy.
- The client is asserting his right to protect his family.
- The client has intense feelings and is honest enough to express them up front.
- The client has a good sense of boundaries and privacy.

We met a very competent worker in a small rural area who told us about her experience with a client who had a volatile temper and foul mouth. Because of the agency's previous experience with the client, the CPS supervisor requested that the sheriff accompany the worker to investigate the latest report. When the sheriff approached the mother, she poured out a stream of bad language and threatening gestures with such intensity that he withdrew without attempting to subdue or talk to her. When another experienced worker heard about this standoff, she volunteered to talk to the mother since there was a young child inside the house. When we asked that worker later what she did differently from the sheriff, she paused for a long time and then said that she never thought of the mother as threatening or scary but as amusing and funny. Therefore, the worker was not afraid or defensive and did not feel the need to protect herself from the mother. The worker was allowed inside the house and was able to make sure that the young daughter was safe and well. This episode illustrates how different perceptions of the same situation can cause different reactions and responses to those reactions. This interactional view of clients, even those who are angry and hostile, is helpful because it tells us what to do and what not to do.

Request a case conference. If the family is frustrated, you and your supervisor are probably also frustrated with the family. A case conference can help ease the situation. Invite the parent(s) as well as someone who can advocate for the parent, such as a church minister, best friend, or neighbor. The purpose of this meeting is not to have a showdown on who is right or wrong, but to find the best and safest means possible to keep the family together, in the most collaborative manner possible. If it is not possible to keep the children with the parent, then the range of options can be discussed. We offer the following outline for this meeting.

Someone other than the supervisor or worker should chair the meeting; it could be an administrator who has special skills in dispute management or, ideally, a trained conflict mediator from outside the CPS system who can remain neutral and has the ability to see both sides of the disagreement as valid and reasonable. The chair can open the meeting by mentioning some good things the worker wrote in the record. He or she should state the purpose of the meeting, that is, to find the best ways to make sure that the children are safe and to determine what services might be needed. It should be emphasized that CPS is on the side of the family and wants to see the family stay together, if at all possible. The basic agenda is:

1. What does the family want? What does CPS want?
2. What resources does the family and CPS have to work toward these goals? List exceptions and past successes for the family.
3. What is the best way to achieve these goals? Who will do what, when, and for how long?
4. What are the signs of success?
5. Who will be the monitoring/liaison person?
6. When will the next review be?

It should be further noted that such family conferences are intimidating to many parents, especially if this is their first encounter with the system. We heard a sad story: All the professionals who were participating in a family conference thought that the meeting was going rather well because the parents seemed to agree with the flow of the discussion, until a perceptive participant realized that the paperwork spread out in front of the father was laid upside down. To her shock and horror, there was no mention anywhere in the record about the family that the parents were not able to read! The professionals had to quickly call for a short recess and regroup and decide how to carry on the meeting without embarrassing the parents.

Ongoing Cases and Later Visits

Following the usual brief small talk, all subsequent visits should begin with the question, "What is better, even a little bit, since we last met?" Notice the phrasing. It is very different from "Is anything better?" to which most clients would readily answer, "No." Even when you are this careful, the client will answer in three different ways: "It is a little bit better," "About the same," or "Life is worse." We will address each of these answers and offer suggestions on how you can respond to them.

"It's a Little Bit Better"

When you get this response, you are on a roll! Follow up this answer by asking who, what, when, where, and how questions (see chapter 5). Remember, you want to hear the details from the client; she will be more convinced by her own words and explanations than your logic. When we say details, we mean *meticulous* details. The following is an example of how this kind of conversation can go.

Worker: So tell me, what's been better since my last visit—I guess it was last Thursday?
Client: Oh, it's a little bit better.
Worker: I'm glad to hear that. What's better, even a little bit?
Client: Umm . . . I have been busier. When I get busy, I don't spend so much time thinking about all the terrible things Davey did to me, you know, I can forget about bad stuff and just keep going.
Worker: So, tell me again, what do you think about when you don't think about Davey and all that stuff that he throws at you?
Client: I think about how much I love my kids, how they are growing up, and how funny they are sometimes. You know, when I get busy, I can concentrate on what I have to do, not what happened to me. Then I can pay attention to my kids. Actually it is better for me, too.
Worker: How is that? Say some more about how it is better for you.
Client: So, Davey left me in the middle of the night for another woman. He was going to sneak out with his clothes and stuff. Of course, I was, you know . . . just thought I was going to die. I kept thinking, how could he do this to me after all these years and with two kids, and all the stuff we went through together. I still cry at night after the kids are in bed, but it helps that he doesn't come around.
Worker: (*Getting back to what is better*) So, when you pay attention to your kids, what would the kids say is better for them?

Client: They will say that Mom is more cheerful, paying attention to them—they like that, of course. I can't tell you how much they help me to keep going. I don't know what I would do if I didn't have them. I am thankful that I have my kids.

Worker: Boy, you really love your kids, don't you?

Notice how the worker is able to keep the focus on what is better. It is very common for the client to lapse into talking about how depressed, upset, angry, worn out, and so on, she feels, but your job is not to get bogged down with such talk and to focus on how she is different when she is focusing on her children and keeping busy. You can also follow up with "What else is better?" asking for more details of what else she is doing to make herself feel better. Continue this kind of conversation as long as you can and then ask a scaling question. How confident is she that she will be able to keep thinking about what is good for her children, what is good for herself, and what else she needs to do to keep things going?

Although you may be tempted to become a cheerleader and point out what is right and what is better, it is more beneficial for the client to figure it out for herself. Let her convince you that she discovered her own way to make her life better, which in turn is much more convincing to her. Sometimes, as the saying goes, less is more.

"About the Same"

You are more likely to hear this answer than any other until, perhaps, the third or fourth home visit. When clients answer this way, it is safe to assume that they mean, "Life is going okay, but I was not looking for big changes, and anyway nothing exciting happens around here." Don't become discouraged; instead, pursue the *details*. How? By retracing each day.

Imagine this. Suppose today is Tuesday and we were to ask you, "Say, Bob, how did your last Tuesday go?" You might find yourself stopped in your track, scratching your head in confusion, and saying to yourself, "Tuesday, Tuesday, now what did I do on Tuesday?" You might look up at the ceiling, trying to remember last Tuesday, but nothing seems to stand out in your mind. Why is this? Because unless something extraordinary happened last Tuesday (perhaps it was your birthday, you got a raise, got in a car accident, or some other catastrophe or unusually exciting event happened), you are not likely to remember last Tuesday.

Clients have the same memory lapses. Ask the client about last Tuesday. Next, ask about Wednesday, Thursday, Friday, and so on. You will help the client realize that she had a fairly trouble-free week;

for many clients, this is a success. The ensuing conversation will then explore what the client will need to do to repeat such trouble-free days; this becomes the baseline for the client. At this point, the scaling question comes in very handy (see chapter 5). Do not give up.

Even if the client insists that "nothing is different" or "nothing is better," you can say, "Wow, that's great; that's not easy for most people. How do you keep things the same? It means you are doing something right to keep an even keel. So, how do you do it?"

Persistence is one of the CPS worker's most valuable virtues. Particularly because clients' lives are fraught with difficulties and seemingly insurmountable obstacles, it is important to maintain your optimism when working with them. Whenever you encourage clients to see hope for themselves and their children, to see successes in themselves, you are making a difference.

"Life is Worse"

For many of our clients, life is unpredictable—and indeed, drastic and unexpected events occur far more frequently than they do to us. At these times life is worse; unexpected illness or a slight economic downturn can mean loss of a job ("last hired and first to let go"), the car breaks down once more, one more fight occurs in the family, and emergencies of all sorts strike. Workers in the "ongoing" programs, where cases stay open up to 60 or 90 days, can easily become discouraged when faced with a series of disasters or unfortunate events. Workers become just as vulnerable to discouragement as the family when such events seem continue to happen. What to do?

This is the time to remember the "coping question" and its variations. All is not lost and you will begin to feel hopeful. Assuming you admire the client for having survived such tough situations, ask, "I can see that you have been through some terrible things (or bad news, ordeal, disaster) during last few days. How do you keep going in the face of such terrible events?" You want to remind the client that somehow she managed to survive one more difficulty thrown her way. Indeed, it takes a great deal of courage and stamina to have survived what many clients go through each day. "How did you do it?" It does not take elaborate sentences or words to convey the message that we respect and admire their ability to withstand such terrible emergencies and crises. Sometimes, a simple question does a better job, and this is the most empowering question we can think of. It conveys to clients, "Somehow you *did* it, that is, it's a done deal, and in spite of the ordeal, you survived, got by, and you are still in one piece. Now we are interested in *how*." Listen carefully, with curiosity and admiration for their ingenuity and survival skills.

Next, you want to remind the client that she not only survived the unfortunate event, but somehow managed to prevent its making the rest of her life worse. "How come you are doing as well as you are doing, given what you just went through? Most people who have gone through what you just been through would not be able to maintain their sense of humor like you are doing (or manage to get out of the bed in the morning). How do you do it?"

You are likely to get answers like, "I didn't know I was managing it; I don't feel like I'm doing it," or "I guess I come from a long line of survivors," or "What choice do I have, I just put my head down just keep going." These kinds of answers are truly inspirational and convince us more than ever about the invincibility of the human spirit.

Case Example

When we first met Brenda, she had numerous physical problems and unexplained pain in her body, and she said she was fearful of "everything under the sun," including that she may have been abusive to her children while her memory lapsed. These difficulties made her wonder whether she was losing her mind. She sought help with her physical pain, her tendency to black out, poor memory, and inability to focus. When she eventually ended in a psychotherapist's office, her fears and doubts about her potential abusiveness and various information she provided indicated a strong possibility that she may have been abusive toward her children during her blackouts. Brenda and her therapist arrived at a decision to report herself to the CPS. We learned that she had suffered terrible, multiple physical and sexual abuses from age 8 to 14; the final straw was that she was left for dead wrapped in a blanket in a field when she passed out from being clubbed in the head by her parents. After many years, she still has difficulty with poor memory, still cannot remember at times how she manages to find herself standing outside her door. Yet, when Brenda talks about her two children, she smiles beautifully and it is clear that she takes pleasure in talking about the little things she does with them, such as taking them to the movies or going out for hamburgers or ice cream. Brenda has become accustomed to our asking "How do you cope?" each time we meet, yet she still finds this question useful, even after a couple of years of meeting sporadically. Her current functioning has shown remarkable improvement. She actively interacts with her children, she looks better, and she is even thinking about going to work.

She usually begins the meeting with complaints of how she is not doing well; then, as we review her life between sessions, she comes to the conclusion that her memory is improving on its own. This format gets repeated each time we meet. What is remarkable about Brenda, however, is that her fear of being an unfit mother has been considerably reduced, and it is not even brought up as a concern any longer.

When to Close a Case

It is easy to lose sight of ending a case. How do we know when we have reached the goal of reasonable safety for the child? We recently met a social worker in Germany who told us that she has carried a case for nine years! Astounded, we asked how she will know it's time to close the case. To our surprise and chagrin, she replied that she didn't know and that she has never been able to figure out when would be the right time to say good-bye to this family. It is certainly unlikely that this would happen in this country, but we have seen cases that have been kept open for several years. This is when obtaining an internal consultation, such as case supervision, or an external consulta- tion with someone who is familiar with CPS and child welfare cases would be extremely helpful. Rather than rely on a timeframe, such as 30, 60, or 90 days, as a guideline, know what you are expecting to change or what will be better by keeping your case open. How will one more week, month, and so on increase the safety of the children in the family? Do your skills need boosting?

Although the changing legislation makes such long-term contacts unlikely in the U. S., some families are so used to having social services and systems in their lives that various workers become a part of the family, taking on the role of aunts and uncles to the children. It is possible that, without the ongoing support of social services, many of these families would not function as well they do. At times, the mere presence of a worker can prevent further deterioration of a family. For these cases, a clear focus on the goals and expected outcomes of each contact becomes especially important, so that the client can experience success instead of merely continuing the status quo.

Aside from moving the case along, another primary reason for keep- ing a clear focus on the goals is to help the agency and the client assess progress. We believe that having criteria for successful outcome is particularly important for CPS clients, who desperately need the taste and experience of success in areas that are important to them. The most effective and efficient way to experience success is to use a measure that shows each small incremental movement toward their goal in large block letters. In other words, the success must be something that the client can count, measure, and hold it up so that everyone can clearly see it. Examples might be how many mornings the mother got up, fed the children breakfast, and got them out the door on time for the bus, or how many times she talked to the children in a soft, gentle voice instead of screaming or calling them names.

Why Should I Go to All This Trouble?

You might easily ask this question while saying to yourself that you are so busy and have no time to "waste" on cases that you will either close or refer to some other community service. The reason we want you to take a few more minutes with these reinvestigation cases is that taking a little more time now will likely reduce your having to visit this same family over and over again. Imagine how frustrated the family must be! (We would say that if the family is not upset with you, there is something terribly wrong with the family!) Imagine yourself making the fifth, eighth, or tenth visit to the same family! At times, these repeated investigations happen because the worker thinks, "I have followed the required procedures and there's nothing more I can do." Yet, if he or she were to take one more step with the client, the client might find the beginning of a solution. Ten or fifteen minutes spent now asking about details may save two hours later on.

We are frequently asked how to close a case when the client obviously enjoys, depends on, and has taken the worker into her life, as if a worker were a member of the family. If a client has reached this point of depending on the relationship with the worker, we have to wonder how much the worker may have encouraged such a relationship. When a worker has consistently given credit to the parent for whatever successes she or he may have achieved during the life of the relationship, and consistently asked, "How do you do it?" "What do you need to do next?" and "How did you know it would work?" the relationship is likely to remain mutually respectful and empowering to the client, even if she seems to lack resources. The worker's role is to foster the client's sense of competency, mastery, successes, and pride in his or her accomplishments.

Be sure to use scaling questions periodically to help clients assess and measure their own progress and gauge their accomplishments. For example, ask:

- On a scale of 1 to 10, where 10 stands for how confident you feel that you will keep your temper under control and not lash out at your son, and 1 stands for how shaky you felt about your ability to control your temper when we first got involved with each other, where would you say you are at today?
- Let's suppose 10 stands for how confident both you and CPS feel about your ability to keep your children safe, and 1 stands for how

bad the situation was when we first started working together, where would you say you are at today?

- What would your children say, if they could describe it, about how safe they feel your family life is now?

If there is a gap between your perception and the client's, or between the parent's and the children's measures of safety, you can draw the client's attention to this by gently asking for ideas about ways to narrow the gap. Remember that each visit should make a difference in somebody's life, no matter how small, and make a child's life a little bit better.

Details Matter

We cannot emphasize strongly enough the importance of details! Although they may seem ordinary, mundane, even boring, these details make up our everyday life. Out of the ordinary, something extraordinary stands out. Vague, broad promises like "Don't worry, I will make sure that this will not happen again, I promise" are not good enough. We are sure the client means it and is sincere about his or her intentions, but good intentions without a concrete plan that assures the safety of the child are not worth much. Even the best intentions disappear when faced with dire situations, anger, or frustration. If a client breaks into tears or becomes agitated and angry, do not back off from getting detailed information. Ask who, what, when, where, and how questions until you are satisfied that the parent has viable, realistic plans to do things differently, and that the steps are small enough so that the parent can carry them out in his or her circumstances. Asking behaviorally specific questions is not a sign that we do not trust the client; it serves as a cognitive rehearsal, that is, the more the client repeats his or her plans in detail, the more he or she will be able to implement them. When you ask with curiosity in your voice, incredible naivete in your posture, and a non-expert demeanor, the client does not feel offended. Do not hesitate to revisit the questions repeatedly. Each time you ask, you will be impressed by how many more details the client offers. This will increase your confidence about your assessment of the child's safety.

SPECIAL PROBLEM CASES

In this section we want to address issues that come up repeatedly for discussion in training, supervision, consultations, and case discussions.

It is very confusing to most human service providers that there are so many psychological theories that seem to conflict with each other and ideas or explanations that seem to link cause and effect in numerous different ways. Many veteran workers have even stopped listening or going to training sessions because theories seem to come and go, like teenage fashion. Experienced workers have pointedly asked us whether solution-building is another "flavor of the month" and how long it will last before another "super-duper" magic idea will be peddled to them. We sympathize with these practitioners and understand their frustration. But, despite the frustration and confusion, it would be disastrous if we had only a single explanation for human behavior. A single explanation would mean a single solution to a particular problem, a one-size-fits-all mind-set.

Diversity and complexity open up possibilities for varied solutions to very complex human conditions. It seems, however, that CPS has more questions than answers. It takes a great deal of sophistication to live with uncertainty and the unknown, especially when a child's safety is concerned within the context of modern-day family life. We offer an alternative to the traditional way of looking at complex human problems and sensible and realistic ways to manage them within the context of CPS. Rather than speculating about causes and etiology, we focus on what an average CPS worker can do in his or her daily practice to mitigate serious problems like substance abuse and family violence.

Referral to a specialist can be a solution; yet, as you know, clients don't always follow through or stick with the program. The client often shows up at the specialist's office just to pacify the referring agent, and there is no assurance that the client will complete the program or change as a result of the referral. Most treatment programs that work with mandated or involuntary clients experience high drop-out rates. Making a referral might be useful for documentation purposes, in the event your decision is challenged, but it is not useful for the client unless the client truly believes that following through is partly his or her idea and that he or she sees some potential benefit from it. Therefore, we encourage you to try the solution-building approach, which initiates the process of building on small changes and successes. Being the frontline worker means you already have access to the client; most specialists have to wait for the client to show up in their offices (although the number of outreach programs for women and children is increasing). Your special effort in helping the client make the transition to a treatment program is helpful; more importantly, however, when clients experience small successes with your help, they are making progress toward the life they want and will be more encouraged to follow through on your referral. Consequently, your role as a CPS worker is crucial in making the successful transition to the next level of service and increasing the chances of success.

Substance Abuse

General consensus among service providers, supervisors, administrators, and policy-makers is that up to 70–80% of CPS cases are affected by substance abuse (abuse, dependence, addiction, etc.). Parental alcoholism and drug abuse have especially devastating effects on children and family life because they can be hidden for so long. Since there is much speculation and several possible explanations for why women are drawn to drug and alcohol use, and much has been written on the subject, we will limit our discussion to what to do. For the sake of practicality, in our work we use the term "problematic use" to define drug and alcohol use that creates any kind of problem, whether legal, financial, social, or family relationship, for the client.

Most substance abusers, both men and women, unjustly carry the negative reputation of being devious and sneaky, liars and cheats, and dishonest with friends, family, and treatment providers. This perception comes from ignoring the context of the abuse. For example, you are familiar with how Juanita's family, friends, and other caring people give her lots of pep talks, lecture her about the evils of drinking and drugging and the medical problems they may cause. They tell her she must be strong and develop the will to quit cold turkey; anything less is often believed to be a sign of weakness and not trying hard enough.

This familiar refrain is difficult to hear, even if it is true. Juanita begins to doubt herself, questioning her ability and motivation, and begins to believe she is a weak person. Naturally, she finds it painful to doubt herself and becomes defensive anytime someone mentions her wasted talent and potential. She finds it easier to make a promise, just to get out of a difficult and uncomfortable topic of conversation. Her promises are grandiose and unrealistic: "I will never drink again. I have finally realized what drugs and alcohol are doing to my life and I swear I will quit altogether." Of course, family and friends, wanting her to turn her life around and wanting better things for her, believe that these heart-to-heart talks will produce dramatic change. When Juanita fails to deliver on her promise, her credibility is diminished, and the family tries harder, with more pressure and intensity. This scenario is repeated over and over, and then we have a predictable pattern.

By the time this case comes to your attention for neglect or abuse, it is pretty clear that this pattern has been going on for some time and, therefore, it behooves you not to repeat the same interaction with this mother. Instead of trying to convince her that drugs or alcohol are bad for her or will destroy her children's lives, quietly ask, "Juanita, I can see that life has not been easy for you for quite a while. You sound like the kind of person who has been thinking about all these things going on in your life. So, tell me, you must have a good reason for risking as much as you have been. Can you tell me what some of your good reasons might be?" When you take this posture, that Juanita must indeed have very good reasons for risking so much, you are changing the familiar pattern. This is not the answer to everything, but it is the beginning of looking at her life and her choices in a different way. It shifts the burden of *doing* something about her problem onto her, rather than asking her to constantly feel guilty, shameful, defensive, apologetic, and inadequate. Many people assume that negative feelings motivate people to do better. Perhaps this is true now and then, but generally these negative feelings cause people to be more depressed and unsure, to lose initiative, and to give up on themselves. I am sure you have heard many clients tell you that they have become hopeless, that they feel just worn out and tired, and that they lack the energy to keep trying. Such feelings not only compound their problems but also lead them to give up any vestige of hope for change.

What Does the Parent Want?

When a family that is struggling with substance abuse comes to your attention, it is usually because drug or alcohol use has caused enough problems in their lives to attract attention. This very fact can be useful for building motivation to take steps to address the initial problem. That is, rather than assuming the client agrees with others' concern and assessment that alcohol or drug misuse is problematic, you need to determine what is most important for the client. Therefore, listen carefully to the client for clues about what is important to him or her: Is it, for example, being left alone by CPS, wanting the school to stop bugging her with notes about the children's reports of their family life, keeping the children at home?

Listen for clues about how the client perceives her drinking or drug use. Is the parent most concerned about someone meddling in the family's life or that she uses alcohol and drugs to avoid dealing with life's problems? If the parent indicates that it is the former, you need to agree and normalize her annoyance at the intrusion of others, including yourself, and then proceed to negotiate a goal. When this discussion is handled calmly, respectfully, and collaboratively, frequently the goal of getting rid of all these meddlers includes the client's taking steps to do something about her problematic drinking or drug use so that she will achieve what she believes is good for her and her family.

Once you reach this point, do not push for treatment or abstinence prematurely.

Remember, unless there is an immediate risk to the child you need to proceed at the client's speed to arrive at a reasonable goal. Be calm, follow the client's lead, and steer the conversation toward realistic and doable goals that the client is interested in. At this early stage, your goal is not to drill into the client's head that she has a problem with substance abuse, because she is likely to view such emphasis on her substance abuse as an accusation and condemnation of her as a bad parent; it is better to move slowly toward thinking through how to insure the family's—including the parent's—safety. Building a positive relationship with the parent will make it easier to proceed to the discussion about exceptions. Accusations of harming her children should be held at bay, unless you are confident that you have developed the kind of relationship that shows the client that you care and are trying to help, not to meddle and make her life more difficult.

What Is the Client's Plan?

Rather than trying to convince the client that she has a substance abuse problem (because other people have tried without success), ask her how she plans to follow up on her goals (of getting meddlers out of her life, for example). Listen carefully to her ideas. Pursue her ideas to a logical conclusion without shooting them down. Premature rejection of her ideas is disrespectful and the same as dismissing the client. In spite of the myth that substance abusers are in a fog most of the time, they are often quite sensitive to your reactions and can quickly sense your subtle rejection. Remember, it takes considerable sophistication to separate rejection of a person's ideas from rejection of the person. Many clients have difficulty making this distinction.

Ask about Exceptions

A myth that is prevalent in substance abuse treatment is that the substance, drug or alcohol, takes over the individual, whose only alternative is to give in to it. Many clients have bought this notion and at times use it to avoid taking responsibility for solutions. A homeless drug addict indignantly explained his situation this way: "What do you expect me to do? I'm a drug addict, for God's sake. There is nothing I can do about it." Therefore, asking about exceptions is a powerful way to help clients without demeaning them. This approach helps clients become aware of their own ability to control the substance.

In a casual, conversational tone, ask about the times the client could have used drugs or could have gotten drunk but somehow decided not to. Perhaps by some coincidence the client was able to walk away, do something else, or decide against using drugs or alcohol for only a day or even a half-day, but this golden nugget becomes the first building block for a clean life. Continue your questioning with a posture of curiosity, naivete, and amazement. At first, your client may think that you are trying to trick him or, since he has not heard this kind of questioning before, he is likely to miss your question. Do not be misled by your client's confusion; hang in there with a gentle persistence. Follow up with more questions about the details of exceptions. Even if you do not proceed further than this, this kind of discussion is likely to leave a profound impression on the client and force him to reflect on his small success, perhaps for the first time in a long while.

You can return to the topic of exceptions again and again during your follow-up visits. This information can become a road map for the client to start charting what he needs to do more of to build on this success strategy. At this point, perhaps you and the client can discuss whether he is willing to weigh the next level of help and explore some options: AA, residential programs, intensive outpatient treatment programs, for example. Of course, the selection of options depends on what realistic services are available in the community—and how to pay for it.

Relapses

Relapses are the most frustrating, discouraging, and frightening parts of the process of recovery. Yet, they are normal. When clients believe that the only success is total abstinence, then it is easy to believe that any failure to remain totally clean for the rest of one's life is an absolute failure. Quitting "cold turkey" for the rest of one's life is not what normally happens. No wonder many clients become discouraged, even suicidal at times, and tell us that they are tired and ready to toss in the towel. Client relapses also trigger a sense of failure for treatment providers. The typical reaction is, "Oh, no, not her again!" followed by dread, anger, and frustration.

An "either/or" approach to problematic use of substance is not helpful or realistic in most clients' lives. Abstinence is achieved through trial and error and, as they say, it is the process, not the "end goal," that counts. A practical approach is to view each relapse as "two steps forward, and one step back," that is, to celebrate two days of sobriety and learn from the one step back. One mother explained, "Keep your head down and just keep going until you get there." Each step forward, however small and slow, is a movement toward a long-term success, which is certainly an improvement in the quality of life for the family.

Rather than dwelling on failure, spotlight the client success, that is, how long she has been clean or sober since the last relapse.

1. Instead of saying that she has been sober for "only three months," ask how she stayed sober for "three long months"; find out the details.
2. Do not allow her to dismiss "only three months"; emphasize how difficult it must have been to stay sober that long and ask about every little detail of her successful strategies for staying sober for three months. Also ask how other important people in her life are reacting to her differently now that she is making progress.
3. Make a big deal of her small successes; turn ordinary accomplishments into extraordinary successes, because they are the foundation of future successes.
4. Ask her how she stopped herself from drinking or drugging more. How did she stop herself from doing more when she did? Again, do not be dismissed by her talk of failure, but insist on finding out every little detail of her success. What internal or external cues did she respond to? How did she decide not to dismiss these cues? Accepting support and help from family is a very good idea. It is commonly known that people with supportive families do better at recovery.
5. Find out how her way back from relapse affected her children: How did they respond to her getting sober again? What did they like about her being sober again? It is important to help the mother repeatedly connect her recovery and relapse to her children so that she can see that she has tremendous influence on her children's life.
6. Discuss what she learned from this relapse and how she will integrate it into her life.
7. Scale her confidence on maintaining a steady course toward her goal.
8. At any point along the way, you can negotiate with her what she wants her next step to look like. Consult with her on some of her ideas on about to achieve the next step.
9. Use scaling questions to help the client chart her own progress toward her goal, detailing plans for each step toward how she wants her life to be, what she needs to do to get there, and how she will know that she got there.
10. Remember that these are difficult questions to answer. You need to help her sort things out, weigh her options, and make choices. It is important for her to take the time to shape her future.

Women and Substance Abuse

Many women report that their first introduction to drugs or alcohol was through their boyfriends or partners, usually in a social context, and that what keeps them using drugs is the mistaken notion that continued use with their partner or supporting their partner's use will preserve their relationship. Many women who prostitute for drugs use the money not only for their own drugs, but also to support their partner's drug habit. We have also seen numerous drug-abusing men living with mothers who were receiving TANF (Temporary Assistance for Needy Families) money; many experienced CPS workers know that these mothers are often prime targets of drug-abusing men who exploit their TANF payments or force their women to prostitute for them. Not surprisingly, then, women's motivation for quitting drugs is often related to the importance they give their relationship with their children or their male partners.

Women value relationships; their socialization has been very much oriented toward cultivating and maintaining relationships, worrying about what other people think, and sacrificing their own personal needs for their children's and partner's. Yet, women substance abusers are often treated as if their recovery process is the same as men's. The traditional alcohol and drug treatment programs in this country and in Europe are primarily developed from long-term experience of treating male, chronic alcoholics who ended up in the gutter. Thus, the treatment models are characterized by a confrontational, hard-hitting approach to self-scrutiny and admission of loss of control as the first step toward recovery. It makes sense that the recovery process for men begins with an emphasis on learning to exercise self-care, to be assertive, and to express oneself. Because the aftereffects of male substance abuse are often destructive not only to themselves but also to the community and society, such as violence against others, increased criminal behaviors, and drunk driving accidents, substance abuse by men is much more visible and noticeable to the society than that by women.

Women's substance abuse is often hidden from the public view for much longer time than men's. In fact, in Japan women alcoholics are called "kitchen drinkers" because their problems and the social and familial consequences are hidden from view. Only in recent years have the very different physiological and psychological paths of men's and women's substance use and abuse been recognized. Effective treatment must take women's unique needs and process of recovery into consideration, instead of treating them as if they were smaller, milder versions of men.

Our clinical impression is that women begin treatment with different motivations from men and choose different pathways to recovery. Many women report that what motivated them finally to seek treatment was the loss or the threat of losing their children and family. This "wake-up call" was the first step in their recovery process. Not surprisingly, many mothers report that for a long time their substance abuse was hidden from those around them because they would make sure that they waited until the children were in bed before they began their drinking or drug use.

Many mothers also report that their "waking up" came because of their children's begging and pleading with them not to drink or use drugs, not because they were arrested or caught prostituting. Most mothers' aspirations and dreams are related to their children's future and how much they want their children's future to be better than theirs. Thus, we believe that "making a better future for one's children" is a great motivator. We use what matters to women, that is, relationships with their children, to motivate them to begin and maintain their recovery processes. We suggest that you ask the following relationship questions to evaluate, motivate, and maintain their recovery processes:

- What do you suppose your children would say that you are like when you are sober (clean)?
- How do you suppose your daughter would say your sobriety affects her?
- What kind of mother would she say you are when you are not drinking?
- What would she say is different between the two of you when you are not drinking?
- What do you suppose your family (best friend) would say they like about your sober self?
- What would your husband (boyfriend, partner) say is different in your family when you are sober?
- What would your family say was the longest you've been sober? How would they say you've done it? What kind of help do you need from your family so that you can do it again?
- What would finally convince your family that you really will change this time?
- When your children are finally convinced that you will stay sober this time, what will be different with them?

Referral to Treatment

Many CPS workers heave a sigh of relief when the client admits substance abuse as a longstanding problem, or when the client finally requests information about treatment. The immediate reflex is to refer clients to treatment and turn the case over to the experts, who will take care of the problem. Before you decide to do the same, we suggest that you consider the following points, since it is not the *program* that will solve the substance abuse problem but the client's investment in making the program work for her. While getting the client into treatment is important, good preparation for success in treatment is likely to decrease your frustration with the client later on. The most difficult aspect of substance abuse treatment is not stopping alcohol or drug use; it is managing the relapses and setbacks that are considered failures by the program and the client. Repeated failures at treatment only decrease client motivation, confidence, and hope, thus diminishing self-confidence and expectation of success. There is nothing more demoralizing than to fail one more time. Most CPS clients cannot afford another failure; they need to appreciate every little successful step to know that they are moving forward. In order to increase the chances of success this time, we suggest that, before rushing to make a referral, you ask the following questions:

- How long has she been struggling with this problem, and what has worked for her?
- What has been the longest period of time when she has been able to either cut down on drinking or avoid using drugs at all on her own? Ask for the details of how she was able to do it (what, when, where, how, who).
- What did she learn from this period of success about her substance use and abuse?
- What was most helpful in accomplishing her goal of cutting down or abstaining?
- How confident is she that she can do it again? What are the details of her plan?
- Does she want to do it alone or with help? What kind of help did she seek in the past? What worked the best? Who was most helpful? What will increase her chances of success this time?
- What needs to be different this time to increase her chances of success?

Realistic Solutions

The most common reason why women have difficulty taking advantage of treatment services is because they do not have access to them. Therefore, be sure to consider how she will get to the treatment program, who will watch the children while she is there, how she will get the money to pay for methadone, and so on. Will such services restrict rather than expand her life? The most frequently mentioned problems for women accessing treatment are transportation and child care. If following through on the referrals becomes almost a full-time job for the client, then she has been set up for failure. For example, immediately after having her two children removed and placed in her parent's custody, Janet was eager to follow all the worker's recommendations and even asked for more. But Janet lost her driver's license because of the latest in a number of drunk driving charges, for which she also had to pay a fine of several hundred dollars; that made it impossible for her to see her psychotherapist whose office was 30 miles away. She agreed to participate in AA and substance abuse treatment with outpatient aftercare program. Her husband, Brad, also had several drunk driving tickets and lost his driver's license. He needed to go to his substance abuse treatment program as well as a program to reinstate his driving privilege; he also agreed to attend AA and expressed his sincere desire to follow through with all of the aftercare recommendations. Because of their intense fights in front of their children, they asked for marriage counseling. And of course both Janet and Brad agreed to visit their children at the grandparents' home every weekend. They both held full-time jobs, and they had no means of transportation in a small rural community. Janet's job in a nursing home was described as extremely stressful, and Brad needed lots of overtime work in order to pay for all the fines, damages, and therapy sessions. In the midst of all this, Janet attempted suicide by overdosing on pills and was hospitalized for three days. In this case, all the additional "help" offered to and accepted by the couple added to their already high stress level.

I (IKB) met a mother of four who was much older-looking than her 26 years and who was at risk of "losing her children to CPS" because of her chronic alcohol abuse. Alarmed by the seriousness of the threat, she finally acknowledged that her own efforts to stop drinking were not working and agreed to go on Antabuse. This required that she have a complete medical examination and then attend group sessions at the county hospital where she received her daily dose of Antabuse. The group session was scheduled at 3:30 P.M., which was the worst time for her, because that was when her older children came home from school. While she was taking a public bus with the two younger children in tow, the older two would be home without adult supervision. She knew that she would never make the meetings, which of course meant she was disqualified for Antabuse. There were similar issues with the methadone program. Methadone is administered daily, only at certified drug treatment facilities, such as county hospitals. Such programs restrict clients' lives; for example, they cannot go out of town for funerals, family events, or to celebrate a grandmother's 80th birthday, even if they can afford such travels. Just piling on the resources is not the answer: Clients must have a realistic plan to access them on a sustained basis; otherwise, we are setting them up to fail again.

Family Violence

Domestic violence is not about parental spats or mutual fighting. It is a pattern of learned behavior that includes physical, sexual, and psychological attacks as well as economic coercion that adults use against their intimate partners. Domestic violence can have a tremendous impact on children even if they are not physically harmed. Many children who live in homes with domestic violence may experience difficulties at school, with friends, and in their relationship with their parents. Emotional, developmental, and psychological problems in children can often be traced to exposure to repeated, serious domestic violence. Loud and violent fighting between parents (and/or other caretakers) is very scary for children and adolescents. Often, the children are threatened and warned not to talk about the fights in the family. They are told that it is nobody's business. Young children often carry a heavy burden; many even feel they have caused the fights. They try to protect their parents from each other or shield their younger siblings and as a result may be harmed themselves. As public awareness increases about domestic violence, with most states enacting laws criminalizing domestic violence, new partnerships are being forged between law enforcement and CPS around this critical issue. In many states, mandatory arrest laws are in effect, and the requests for personal protection or orders are becoming more frequent. Many states are writing CPS policies that help CPS workers deal with this critical issue. Cross training between domestic violence, and CPS is becoming more frequent (Findlater & Kelly, 1999), enabling workers from both fields to learn how the problems tend to overlap and how to effectively address both domestic violence and child and family safety. The following example illustrates one effective approach to working with domestic violence cases.

Six-year-old Linda called 911 when her parents were in the midst of a serious fight. Hearing the noise in the background, the 911 operator kept the child on the phone as the police and CPS drove to the home. The 6-year-old conveyed several pieces of useful information: There was no gun in the home; the father "always hits Mommy when he's drunk"; and she, Linda, was really worried about her two sisters, ages 4 and 1, and her mother. She said that when the 4-year-old had tried to help Mom, Dad threw her to the floor. In the background the mother was screaming to Linda to hang up the phone, but she did not. When the police arrived, the father was arrested for assault and taken to jail for 24 hours. The CPS worker found an embarrassed and beaten mother who was angry with her 6-year-old for calling the police. The CPS worker could have temporarily removed the crying and obviously distraught children, but it was clear to her that they were traumatized enough by the situation and did not want to be separated from their mother. Instead, the worker asked the mother if she felt safe and what she needed to do to keep her children safe. Instead of telling her that the children were being harmed, the worker asked the mother how she kept the children safe during such episodes. The mother, breaking into sobs, detailed how she regularly tried to keep the focus on her during their fights to keep the father from hurting the children. The worker then used solution-building strategies to help the mother develop a safety plan for her children and herself. The worker also complimented the mother for teaching Linda how to use 911. She gave her information on personal protection orders, the name of a family advocate who could assist her in obtaining help, and numbers for local domestic violence programs, but did not push her to contact them.

Although at first glance it would have been possible to justify the removal of the children because of the violence, what the 6-year-old made clear was that her Mom needed help and that was what she wanted—not removal from home. It was also clear to the CPS worker that there was a strong bond between the mother and her children.

While domestic violence is a very complicated issue, workers need support and training on the issues and dynamics of domestic violence in order to respond appropriately. Here are a few suggestions that may be useful:

1. Because there is such a high incidence of domestic violence in CPS cases, it is important that you routinely assess or screen for it. Always ask the mother if she feels safe.
2. In cases where domestic violence is suspected or acknowledged, try to interview the mother alone, without the perpetrator. Ask about her safety plan. "How have you been able to keep yourself and your children safe in the past?" List what worked and what did not work. This not only puts the mother in the role of expert on her situation, but also lets her teach the worker about her unique situation.
3. Do not share information gathered from interviewing the mother with the perpetrator without her permission.
4. Ask the mother how she copes and who she can count on to help her.
5. Find out what kind of help she needs. Do not assume you know what might help her. It is possible, despite your sincere offer of help, that she does not feel safe or confident that the violence will not escalate. Many women in domestic violence situations have created strategies for enhancing the maximum safety for their chil-

dren. These are usually very competent behaviors, which are frequently misunderstood and misinterpreted by well-meaning family members, friends, or even CPS workers. In fact, many women in domestic violence shelters feel that CPS workers do not understand domestic violence issues and present a threat because of their power to remove children. Notice again that the worker who responded to the 911 call from Linda heard the child ask for help, not removal.

6. Ask for consultation from local domestic violence programs on cases where domestic violence is evident. CPS can also become a valuable resource for the shelter workers.

Misunderstandings about Abusive Men

Words such as "antisocial personality" and "violent" are often used to describe men who exhibit abusive behaviors. There is also much speculation about what makes these men so violent and abusive to their weaker partners. It is beyond the scope of this book to address these concerns and therefore we will limit our discussion to what to do and how to deal with these men. We have also met many workers who are intimidated and become fearful for their own physical safety when faced with men who have abused their partners. When the worker is fearful of the client, he is likely to sense that fear and respond in kind, thus triggering a chain of events that may indeed confirm the worker's fear that he is someone to be scared of. Abusive men's bad reputations, as difficult people to work with, stem in part from our own mishandling of the encounters with them. Contrary to common perception, physical abuse is often very controlled and targeted; it is seldom random, out-of-control behavior. Abusers tend to break only what the victim values, not their own valuable possessions; their violence is often very targeted and limited to certain persons or certain area of the body.

Notice how the abusive behavior is often directed only at the man's wife or girlfriend, and not toward his boss, sister, mother, or coworkers. All relationships are fraught with the risk of lost tempers and frustration with each other, yet these abusive men do not target their bosses or coworkers or lash out at them as often as they do their partners.

What this tells us is that, contrary to the popular myth, these men are very much in control of their behaviors, and if they can control themselves with their boss or coworkers, they certainly are capable of controlling their behavior with the partner and even with you. One exception may be when the person is under the influence of drugs or alcohol to such an extent that his judgment is severely impaired. In that situation, you need to take safety precautions and leave the scene as soon as possible (see chapter 4). Some innovative treatment programs empower these men to gain control of their behavior quickly and effectively (Sebold & Uken, 1996, 1999). Sebold and Uken have documented an impressive outcome of 14% recidivism five years after treatment and 90% completion rate with just eight sessions spread out over four to five months. Their program works consistently with client goals. The group sessions set the tone of respect for clients, who are asked what they want changed in their lives and held accountable for those stated goals in concrete, behavioral, measurable terms. They have successfully used scaling questions not only to assess progress but also to enable clients themselves to assess their level of success and determine what they need to do to maintain that success and move forward.

Contrary to frequent, unsolicited advice, most abused women do not wish to leave the relationship. They only want the violence to stop. It is a disservice to encourage the woman to leave her partner unless it is her own wish to discuss leaving with you. The most respectful service we can provide is to ask her what she wants, listen to her safety plans for herself and her children, and provide services as needed and requested, rather than imposing a solution on her. Just because one aspect of her life is not functioning well does not mean that she does not function well overall. Your respectful approach and willingness to listen to her may be a very new and yet very needed experience for her.

Crises and Emergencies

Inevitably, we run into emergency situations. So do our clients. An emergency or crisis occurs when an out-of-the-ordinary, totally unexpected event occurs in one's life, for which the person is unprepared. When resources are limited, emergencies and crises tend to proliferate and take over one's life. The lack of readily available transportation can magnify the emotional intensity of the situation. And yet, one person's crisis may not be another person's crisis; what a worker may consider an emergency may not be felt as such by the client—or vice versa. For example, a mother called CPS and threatened that, unless they came over to her house and did something to control her daughter right that minute, her daughter would be carried out in a body bag. Everybody flew into action and immediately dispatched two workers to the family home, and alerted the police department. When the breathless workers arrived at the client's home less than 20 minutes later, the mother who made the phone call and the daughter were talking together, still excited but in no visible crisis.

Following are some suggestions for you to keep in mind as you proceed to resolve crises and emergencies.

- Most important, stay calm. Having confidence that you will somehow find solutions will help you to stay calm. Keep your voice soft and use ordinary, everyday language.
- If this is the first such encounter for you but probably not for the family, ask the client (or children) about the last time similar events happened.
- Find out what was done that was helpful, even a little bit: the who, what, when, and how of a past solution to a crisis.
- Ask if the same solution would work this time. Can the same person help again? What would it take for that person to help this time? How can the client ask the same person again? Who can he or she contact: Family members? Neighbors? Friends? Who can take over now?
- If there is no available person or no prior experience of solving this crisis, then proceed to find out what small thing needs to happen first. Does the family need medical help, food, heat, or electricity in the house?
- If older children are involved, they may be familiar with useful resources in the current situation; enlist their help.
- Always keep in mind that the least disruptive, least intrusive measures should be tried first.

Mentally Ill Parents

It is extremely frightening and scary for children when parents show symptoms of mental illness, such as paranoia, hearing voices, crying and refusing to get out of bed, or behaving in an unpredictable manner. This is unnerving for adults, so you can imagine how difficult it must be for young children and adolescents. Yet, mental illness in parents is not always a threat to their children's safety; an exception would be a parent's history of having been violent toward family members. Nor does a parent's mental illness mean that the child is likely to be mentally ill. We have met people who grew up with very disturbed parents who have become competent and successful parents.

Mental illness is not an "all or nothing" phenomenon; a person who hears voices can be very lucid and clearheaded much of the time. People with thought disorders who hear voices telling them, for example, to "Hang yourself in the tree" or "You are the devil and deserve to die" do not always do what the voices tell them. It is good idea to keep in mind that thought disorder is not called behavior disorder—it is the thinking that is disturbed. Contrary to sensational news stories in the media, outbursts of violence by those with such labels are rare. We have found that people with schizophrenia can function reasonably well when they live in a structured setting, take their medication, and have family support. Generally, a combination of medication and psychotherapy is effective and may be helpful in controlling the symptoms. At other times, life's stressors add to the severity of the symptoms. Mentally ill clients want the same things in their everyday lives as other people—to get along with family, have bills paid, live in a nice place, have a satisfying job, and so on. It is important to respect their wishes and work with them, making referrals when appropriate.

A psychiatric evaluation is necessary and may be useful to make an assessment, even though a medical diagnosis does not always tell you what you need to know to determine when and how to keep the children safe. Clients with a long history of mental illness have probably had numerous, sometimes negative, encounters with mental health professionals. They may adamantly refuse another evaluation, but you may need to insist on it for appropriate purposes, such as to insure the safety of the child and to help the mentally ill parent find out what kind of medication might help. Again, when you deal with these clients in a calm, caring, humane manner, they are more likely to respond to you in positive manner.

Assess the risk to the child by looking at the child's social support and family environment. Is there a supportive adult around the child? Is the parent nurturing when lucid? Is the child upset or comfortable? How does the child experience the parent's mental illness: Does it seem natural to the child or is he or she upset about the parent's "odd" or "strange" behavior? Most importantly, is there a supportive extended family member, church network, neighbor, or friend who is available to pinch-hit when needed? You should also discuss with the parent what steps she is taking to insure that the family life goes on normally. Look for exceptions to the problem. The exceptions to their mentally ill behaviors restore hope in children, as well as the other family members. Coercion, forceful demands, confrontations, and threats do not work, but only exacerbate already difficult situations. Stay calm and, by all means, go slowly.

Medication

Many mentally ill clients have been prescribed medication, and generally medication does help. However, some patients are often very reluctant to take their medications, usually because they are not comfortable with the side effects or they do not understand what the medication is designed to do for them. Many physicians and nurses are so busy that either they do not or cannot take the time to explain in simple words what the medication is designed to do and what patients can expect from the medication or what kind of side effects are to be expected. Whenever you find that a client has been prescribed medication, be sure to ask or find out whether he or she is *taking the medication properly* or whether the dosage needs to be adjusted. Having medication on hand does not mean that the client is taking it regularly.

If you find that your client is not taking medication, gently ask what he or she is doing instead that seems to help. Unlike the stereotype of mentally ill people as "out of it," crazy, not knowing where they are, and so on, most are quite oriented toward reality and fairly able to engage in rather clearheaded conversation, especially in positive interactions with those who care about them. It is helpful for you and others around this person to be calm and gentle and to engage him or her in as normal a conversation as possible. The more isolated the client is, the more symptomatic he or she becomes; thus, a supportive family or social atmosphere is crucial to successful treatment.

Find out what they are doing to help the medication work for them, such as eating healthy, exercising regularly, avoiding alcohol and drugs, learning to breathe properly and use relaxation techniques to stay calm, and finding ways to take pleasure in small things in life. Support these healthy activities while encouraging clients to take control of their medication use, rather than seeing themselves as passive beneficiaries of doctors' orders.

Difficult Children

Every parent knows that all children and especially adolescents are different and have unique personalities, quirks, and needs. A big challenge of parenting is to accept children as they are and encourage them to develop their uniqueness. When parents are able to accommodate their child's special needs, we usually see good parenting practice. However, some children are difficult to raise. For example, it is very difficult to remain calm and consistently loving with a very colicky baby who screams and cries all the time, even when the parents are well functioning and have a variety of supportive resources. We once knew a mother whose baby screamed for the first nine months of his life, adding to extreme stresses the mother was already experiencing.

A colleague of ours told us about an amazing grandmother she met while working in New York City some years ago in a program for drug-affected infants and the adults who were raising them. The grandmother was raising a "cocaine-baby" who was a toddler when our colleague met her. The child was restless, constantly agitated, into everything, and difficult to discipline, which tired the grandmother. When asked how she was coping with raising a difficult child who required her around-the-clock attention, she explained that she had accidentally discovered a way to give herself little breaks throughout the day. One day she happened to have a blue bath towel folded into a little cushion on the floor of her living room and she asked the little boy to sit on the towel. To her amazement, he was able to sit quietly for a couple of minutes, as if he were catching his breath. This perceptive grandmother remembered this chance event and had been repeating it ever since. As the little boy got older, the length of time the child could sit still on the cushion increased and she realized that this calmed him down as well. He had become so attached to the blue towel that when she had to wash it he lingered by the washing machine and dryer so that he could sit on it as soon as it was clean (Judith Schaffer, personal communication, 1994).

When interviewing a mother of a difficult child, use solution-building questions and techniques (see chapter 5) to look for parental coping strategies. Ask who has helped and what seems to work, even a little bit. Get the parents to use those exceptions to the problem as a model for building longer problem-free periods.

Depressed Mothers

Women are more prone to depression than men, and there is no consensus on why this is so. Many workers report that their biggest concern is mothers who are depressed. Here are some suggestions that you might find useful.

1. Normalize the mother's depression. For example, any mother of five little ones demanding constant attention would probably think about running away. She feels she will never get enough rest and is always tired. Of course, when one is physically tired, one is more likely to feel depressed and irritable. It is normal for a mother to feel that she is buried in diapers, dirty dishes, and endless repetitive work that never quite ends; that's her reality and it might go on for some years yet.

2. Ask her how she copes, even for a short while. Listen to her describe how difficult her life is, how her relationship with a partner is not going well, that he is not helpful, demands that she act like they do not have children, that she be able to go out of town at the drop of a hat, and so on. Her coping strategies are her strengths and resources. Find out about them in detail. Remind her that if

she gets up in the morning to feed her children, she is doing something successful. Find ways to build on this small success.

3. Find out who has been most helpful to her in the past and how she can get that person to help her again, even sporadically.

4. Ask her if something has happened recently to worsen her situation. It is possible she might be going through a difficult life-change event, such as the loss of an important grandmother, a breakup with a partner, or some unexpected illness.

5. Ask her what kind of help she needs in order to get back on the right track, to make her life a bit easier. Listen to her carefully and do not assume that you know better what she needs. Do not proceed to tell her what to do or make suggestions to her that she may not be ready to hear. If she says, for example, that staying in bed and not getting up all day is helpful to her, instead of telling her that you may have to place her children in a safer environment, ask her, "What about staying in bed all day is helpful to you?" and listen to her answers. She might have very good ideas.

6. While you are trying to provide what she needs to get a little bit of respite care, a small break, and time to be alone, listen to her answers to "What keeps her going, without giving up, as many other mothers would feel like doing?" Her response can be a powerful tool for you to use. Answers to this questions will surprise and inspire you.

7. Instead of rushing in with all sorts of ideas to help ease her depression, listen to her carefully and give credence to her view of life. Do not try to hasten her out of her depression. It is a complex problem and may require both medical and psychological treatment. Ask about her willingness to consider medication as a way to "begin to feel better." You and the client should determine together what might be the right decision for her.

8. Clients should not be pushed into making big decisions. This is not the time to leave a husband, move out of town, or make some other life-altering change.

Mothers with a History of Sexual or Physical Abuse

A woman with a history of physical or sexual abuse may have difficulty with certain issues in life. Such abuse can leave lasting emotional and physical scars that require healing. However, we want to caution you not to automatically assume that a mother with a history of sexual or physical abuse must be suffering from serious mental or physical disability. Not only is this kind of assumption generally incorrect, but it may result in your seeing the woman as a victim and, without realizing it, treating her as a handicapped person.

Asking miracle questions and other goal-directed questions will help you focus on her needs and wants. Allan Wade (1997) advocates that, rather than seeing a woman who has been violated, either physically or sexually, as a victim of brutality, find out how she fights back every day. Goffman (1961) studied insane asylum and prison inmates and discovered the "small acts of living" that they performed to fight back, such as pretending to swallow medication while a nurse was watching, only to spit the pills out into a toilet when the nurse left, pretending to be crazy in order to make the staff leave them alone, and many others. Many women who have suffered physical and sexual abuse also report having responded to the abusers with personal small acts of asserting themselves. One young woman reported that, whenever her mother would come home drunk and beat her up with no apparent reason, she was so enraged at the unfairness of her mother's act that she refused to cry or show her mother that she felt pain. But of course she cried herself to sleep many nights. Some clients report hiding their younger siblings whenever their father came home drunk in order to protect them from his abuse. They took the beating in their siblings' place, drawing the abuser's ire by refusing to answer in a polite manner, deliberately messing things up, and defying him in numerous other ways. These "small acts" are compelling evidence for the client that she did not passively accept the abuse or violation of her integrity. Assuming that even the victim of the most brutal sexual and physical abuse has withstood it and somehow survived it with enough courage to go on to school, get married, have children, raise children, hold responsible jobs, go to work every day, and even help others in need, is empowering. Helping a client who has been abused to realize the inner strength she had even as a child is a very powerful way to enable her to recognize her own resources and existing abilities.

The fact that she suffered a traumatic past is not what matters; rather, the meaning she attaches to her history determines her self-perception. Once a woman sees that she fought back rather than passively accepting abuse and assault, she changes a view of herself, from the role of a victim to a fighter who stood up for injustice, in her own way. Once a mother recognizes this new view of herself, she will change the way she deals with her children. She will become more confident of herself and in her ideas. She will become a role model to her children, who will take on their mother's competence and strengths and begin to view themselves as successful people.

Chapter 7

Case Closure:
How Good Is Good Enough?

MOST CPS CASES BEGIN WITH A GREAT FLURRY OF ACTIVITY, WITH CLEARLY spelled-out procedures and regulations and paperwork governing every step of the opening of a case. For example, all investigation must be completed within 30 days (sometimes 21 days), or those reported for possible abuse or neglect must be contacted within 24 hours of the initial report to CPS. Once the case enters the CPS system, however, the criteria for leaving the system are not so clear. This is the biggest complaint parents have about CPS. They feel that the workers continue to raise the bar toward some unknown standard they can scarcely comprehend, much less attain. We believe that clear termination criteria should be determined as the case is opened, so that families know what is required of them. In practice, however, cases are often closed because they are referred out to some other service or by default, that is, through actions other than those initiated by CPS.

We suggest that you keep the following questions in mind as you open the case:

1. How will you know that your work with a family has been helpful?
2. How will you know that your presence in the family's life has been useful and that the family is better off now than before CPS involvement?
3. How will you know that the family members have reached the point where they feel capable of going on without you?
4. How will you know that the family members have reached the point where they can conduct their own lives without you and the child will be safe?

Your clients are likely to be asking similar questions, even when their involvement with CPS is brief.

The decision to close the case must be based on the philosophical view that the power to change lies with the family. When a family is the recipient of long-term social services, the implied message is that they are unable to make good decisions on their own and therefore must rely on outside help to carry out even the most routine tasks such as taking care of young children without endangering their welfare. We accept that everyone needs helping hands from time to time to navigate the complexities and complications of modern day life, but sometimes extended help is too much. Maintaining clients in long-term services conveys that we do not think that they will be able to get by without us. So that we do not lose sight of our goals, we need to ask from the first day of contact:

1. How will this family's life be better because I am here?
2. How does one more day, one more week of keeping the case open help this family?
3. What do I expect will be different with this family after one more day of service?

CPS'S GOAL-DRIVEN RELATIONSHIP WITH CLIENTS

Social welfare services are purposeful and goal-directed and must show measurable outcomes of its activities. We begin our professional relationships with termination in mind. It is easy to forget this nature of our work when we are faced with an unending series of crises. This "emergency" atmosphere of CPS makes it difficult to catch our breath and step back from the endless "fires" we must put out. The logical question is, after the fire is put out, how will we know that we can walk away from the scene? Or will we need to not only put out the fire but also restore the kitchen, buy a new stove, new pots and pans, new dishes and tableware, and then teach the family to cook more nutritious food? It is a difficult question to answer. It is helpful for CPS workers to also ask: What is the specific behavior that is putting this child at risk *right now*—not in the future. What do I need to see this family accomplish to know that it was a good thing that I was in their life during this crisis?

How Good Is Good Enough: Evaluating Family Progress

This sounds like a straightforward, simple question, but it is really very complicated and not so easy to answer. CPS has been increasingly criticized for its tendency to raise the bar on what constitutes an accept-able level of parenting and child care once a family enters the system. A client we met described her encounter with the worker who took her two boys, aged 4 and 10. Self-described as "big mouthed" for speaking what's on her mind, Andrea explained her frustration with the system since her children were taken from her because she did not have family or relatives to care for them while she was incarcerated for a few days. Eight months later, she was "butting heads" with her social worker, who was "piling up on me one unreasonable demand after another." With a rather puzzled expression on her face, and anger and frustration in her voice, she said, "Let's say they have taken the children from your home because you have an untidy house, a poor house setting. Then they find out that your husband beats you and you drink a little too much—which have nothing to do with keeping a clean house. But they keep your children. You have to work on every area of your life before the children will be placed back in your house." Andrea was complaining that she is expected to be the perfect parent—which nobody can be.

Thorpe (1994) makes a careful distinction between a caretaker's child-maltreatment behavior and his or her "particular moral charac-ter." For example, the statement "She is an alcoholic" carries a very different meaning than "She is an alcoholic mother." Notice how the behavioral characterization, an alcoholic, can slide into the moral char-acterization of the latter statement. An "alcoholic mother" paints a much worse picture of this mother's moral character. When someone is described this way, her other behavioral or moral standards or conduct completely disappear. We are left with the stark image of a mother who is irresponsible, uncaring, selfish, "in denial," and who resists any attempts to help her. The side of her that is caring, responsible, faithful, loyal, overwhelmed with life, among many other qualities, disappears from our view. We believe this slide into moral characterization causes the "bar to be raised."

This is a common complaint from parents once they have had the children removed from their care. Little attention is given to the untold human cost to children, who are fearful they will never see their parents or siblings or their friends at school. We once heard a prosecutor say, "What's three months to a child?" Three months can be a lifetime to a child. No doubt the worker has very good reasons for delaying the return of Andrea's children, but unless those reasons are explained in such a way that the client understands them, the worker will seem unreasonable and obstructionist.

This concern comes across very clearly in a Jackson County, Michi-gan, FIA focus group study of child welfare clients. Very thoughtful

CPS staff and administrators decided to survey the customers of their services and invited a random group of former CPS clients to give their opinion on what and how questions should be phrased in the customer satisfaction survey (Gonzales, Case, & Keggerreis, 1999). They were provided with transportation, child care, and food and met over several evenings to formulate questions to accurately reflect the administration's intentions and the philosophy behind the CPS delivery. All the professional staff were struck by the customers' willingness to thoughtfully study the phrasing of each question. The authors of this questionnaire were moved as they listened to the participants describe their personal experiences with CPS. The survey questions listed in Table 7.1 show how important it is for clients to be treated with respect. They want us to listen to their ideas. They want helpful and needed services delivered in a timely fashion and input into shaping their future.

Many clients believe that decisions on whether to remove the children, when the children will come home, what they are "forced" to do before their children will be returned, and when workers will make surprise visits to their home are all made willy-nilly, on a whim, with

Table 7.1

JACKSON COUNTY SURVEY OF CPS CLIENTS

Please answer the following general questions about your experience with FIA and the staff. Circle the number that best fits how you feel. 5 means you strongly agree. 1 means you strongly disagree.

1.	*I was treated with respect.*	5	4	3	2	1
2.	*My calls were answered promptly.*	5	4	3	2	1
3.	*The appointment times were convenient for me.*	5	4	3	2	1
4.	*The worker was on time for the appointment.*	5	4	3	2	1
5.	*The worker listened to me.*	5	4	3	2	1
6.	*I had a role in directing my services.*	5	4	3	2	1
7.	*I received the services I needed.*	5	4	3	2	1
8.	*I received services that were helpful to my family.*	5	4	3	2	1
9.	*I received services within a reasonable time frame.*	5	4	3	2	1
10.	*I felt that my opinion counted.*	5	4	3	2	1

no understandable logic or explanation behind them. This kind of misperception greatly contributes to adversarial, coercive, and nonproductive encounters, causing a battle of wills between equally caring people. As in Andrea's case, the victims of these profound misunderstandings are the children, who are helpless to control their lives.

Workers frequently comment, "I explained to Jane so many times but she refuses to hear what I have to say." This explanation is not good enough: Being a professional means being willing to take the burden of finding ways and acquiring the necessary skills to help clients understand us correctly. Of course, clients must find ways to work with us, but the major burden is on us, not them. We must also keep in mind the power difference and how that power is used. Quite contrary to how most workers view their jobs, as having very little impact on the client, workers have tremendous power and influence over clients. A visit from a worker, even though the parent was not at home when the worker came to visit, can cause the parent to clean up the house, wash the children, and send the child off to school the next morning. A business card left at the door with a note to call the worker at their convenience can trigger a chain reaction of positive activities (Don MacLean, Shiawassee County, Michigan, FIA, personal communication, 1999).

In addition, as we have mentioned before, family members need to know that they are working toward a goal that they have set themselves. As experts of their own situation, they often know exactly what and how they will change to achieve their goal. Here are two examples. In the first, Martha, a Chinese-American colleague of ours, was working with a Vietnamese mother who was overwhelmed with problems caused by a language barrier, cultural differences, and poverty. The mother's husband drank and would lose his temper and become abusive toward her and the children. When Martha showed up one day, the mother was distraught and in the midst of an acute crisis, trying to decide what to do about her family situation. Martha herself had very little clue about what would be the most prudent, legal, and helpful thing she could do, so she asked the mother, "What can I do that will be useful to you today?" Without missing a beat, the mother said, "I go church. You go church. You hold baby. I pray." Being a Buddhist, it never occurred to Martha that praying might be helpful to this Catholic mother. Martha immediately understood that the mother needed to go to church and pray and was asking her to go with her and hold the baby. Not knowing what else to do, Martha agreed. This intervention eventually led to talking to the priest, who not only spoke Vietnamese but was also able to help both Martha and the mother. Martha's client knew precisely what her goal was and what she needed to do to achieve it. Martha, in turn, knew that the family situation would improve because she was there to help that day.

In the second example, an early-childhood intervention team in Albuquerque was determined to work respectfully with their clients and with their clients' goals. Maria "lost" two older children to CPS some years ago and she had lost contact with them. When her newborn baby was delivered drug-affected, she was immediately referred to a team of early-childhood intervention specialists working under the direction of a very sensitive and thoughtful pediatrician, Dr. Andrew Hsi (Hsi, Cunningham, & Bouchard, personal communication, 1997). The team learned that the mother had been a multiple drug abuser who prostituted to support her drug habit. Her most burning wish was to keep this baby because, as she pleaded with CPS and Dr. Hsi, she felt this baby would give her a reason to get her life together. The team decided to work with Maria and teach her how to raise her baby and save her life.

It quickly became apparent that Maria did not even know how to hold her baby in her arms while feeding him. Instead, she would place the baby on his back on the couch, prop him up with pillows and diapers, and stick the bottle into the baby's mouth while she sat next to him and watched TV. The team realized that they faced a big challenge in trying to teach Maria about the importance of holding the baby in her arms for emotional bonding, while respecting her role as a mother.

The team arrived at a strategy that worked. Rather than lecturing her about the baby's needs or the importance of holding a baby, they decided to give the baby a voice of his own. During home visits and regularly scheduled infant screenings at the clinic, the professionals involved would speak for the baby whenever Maria touched him. When someone saw Maria changing her baby's diaper, they would come over to her and coo to the baby, saying things like, "I can see you like that very much, Miguel. When your mama touches you, it feels good, doesn't it?" "I can tell you like having your mommy touching your face. Oh, look how much he likes your finger on his face." "Look at him; he really likes it when you hold him in your arms." "What a happy baby he is today—no wonder, he likes your holding him when he takes his bottle. My, what a happy baby he is." "I can tell it makes him so happy: Look at him smile." These repetitive comments reminded Maria that her baby loved her touching, holding, cuddling him. In the process, Maria learned about her baby's emerging personality and how to pay attention and respond to his needs, all of which were new to her. When I (IKB) met Maria and Miguel, at the time a 7-month-old bundle of joy, Maria showed off a highchair she had picked up from a rummage sale and reminded me that "my baby likes to be touched and when I play with him, then he is easier to handle." She had finally become an expert on her baby. Then we discussed how well she was doing on methadone.

CRITERIA FOR SUCCESS: WELL-FORMED GOALS

Well-formed goals are determined by the worker and client together. The client's investment in the goal means that he or she is more likely to put some energy into implementing it, and is thus more likely to create a change. Good goals are small steps that the client can take immediately, perhaps even as soon as today or tomorrow. Even though clients' problems are generally huge, it is unproductive to proceed with a big goal. What your client needs, more than anything else right now, is a quick taste of success to show him or her that progress can be made. The following example from an ongoing case illustrates the process of forming "good" goals.

Mrs. Evans, a handicapped grandmother in a wheelchair, was raising her three grandchildren, boys aged 12 and 11 and a girl aged 9, in a small trailer home on the outskirts of a medium-sized city. The case came to the attention of CPS when the grandmother called to ask for help, saying that she was ready to put the kids into a foster home because she felt she could no longer care for them. Mrs. Evans sounded desperate, and it was decided that indeed she needed some assistance immediately since the children were at risk of being placed out of home. Mrs. Evans's main complaints were that she could not control the children from her wheelchair because obviously the children moved faster than she could. She didn't know how to discipline them, especially the two boys, who were sneaking out to the city at night on their bicycles, breaking the curfew. This occurred more often on weekends than on weekdays. Mrs. Evans worried about their coming home in the dark on a country road with no streetlights, and the boys had no night reflectors on their bicycles or clothing. She was more alarmed since a recent accident in which a drunk driver hit someone walking on the road near her home. The children got along nicely with each other; overall, they did not present a major problem for Mrs. Evans. Mrs. Evans was quite competent in carrying out her daily chores, cooking, washing, and other housekeeping activities from the wheelchair. There were no known relatives or friends in the area and the family did not belong to a church. Contact with the children's mother and father was almost nonexistent, since the mother abandoned her children and moved south when the children were young. Although the boys could clean their rooms better, help out with the housekeeping chores, and do better in school, these were not the major concerns. One problem immediately noted was that Mrs. Evans tended to yell at the children, which they ignored.

Where do we go from here? First, think about strengths and resources. Although it may seem like there are very few resources available between Mrs. Evans and her three grandchildren, this is not the case. Despite Mrs. Evans's making noises about placing the children in a foster home, it was quite apparent that she had a great deal of hope for her grandchildren. She believed that they could do better; she had faith in their future and in their ability to make it in life. This goodwill toward the boys would go a long way. There were many indications that Mrs. Evans was not finished with them and had not given up on them. This was a very good beginning; it is possible to support and build on such goodwill. Even if removal of the boys was the ultimate answer, it would have been too big a change to entertain at this initial point. Following is an assessment of the strengths and resources in this family.

1. The grandmother, in spite of her handicap, agreed to raise the children some years ago. This is an indication of her commitment to her grandchildren. She does not regard her being wheelchair-bound as enough of a handicap to deter her from raising three children by herself. This strong commitment to the children needs to be explored more, with a view of how to capitalize on this.

2. The children are doing reasonably well in school. The grandmother reported no serious complaints from the school about their behavior and the children are going to school every day and performing average academic work. Mrs. Evans did not impress us as a caretaker who reads a great deal, which means that the children are somehow making it in school without adult supervision or help with homework. Apparently they are not mixed up with a bad crowd of friends. What draws the children to school every day? How do the children do this? This area also needs to be explored to find out more about what the children are best at in school, what they excel in, and what their interests are.

3. Mrs. Evans reported that, even though "there are moments," the children get along quite well with each other. How does this happen? Who taught them to get along with each other? Was it Mrs. Evans? Somehow she provided the children with a supportive atmosphere. What else do the children know how to do well?

Once you have established this information, you can proceed to finding out what the goals are. What seems like a reasonable outcome that the family and CPS can achieve together? Mrs. Evans's goal of wanting to make sure that the boys are safe is a reasonable goal to work toward. Most workers would support this goal; when it is achieved, it will lead to the family's getting along better and it will be good for the children. Mrs. Evans will have less reason to yell at the boys and will thus become calmer. When she is calmer, the boys will be less likely to run away from her and more likely to do things together.

Positive Goals

The negotiation for a goal must not begin with the goal of stopping the boys from running into the city. If you begin with this negative action, you are more likely to think in terms of restricting the boys from going into town in the dark. Not only did Mrs. Evans's attempt at this fail, but it also is a poor goal because it is difficult to measure and recognize when the boys *stop* sneaking out. A good goal indicates the presence of some other behavior, that is, the boys will do something else instead of "not running away." It could be, "The boys will make arrangements with someone for transportation to a movie," or "They will bring their friends home on Friday evening," or "They will rent a video after school on Friday and watch it together." When any one of these is being done, Mrs. Evans will know that the boys are safe and she does not have to worry about them.

Small Goals

Again, the goals must be small enough to start right away. Perhaps the best modest goal is to maintain the boys' good behaviors: going to school every day, getting along with each other, being respectful of their grandmother, and whatever else they are currently doing that Mrs. Evans believes they should continue. This certainly is likely to be successful for them, since this is something they already are doing. Once this is solidly established, then we can add some more to this list.

Concrete, Behavioral, and Realistic Goals

Goals should not be stated in vague terms, like, "They will have better attitudes" or "He will be less mad and yell less." Even though these are very worthy goals, they are too vague and subjective, that is, only Mrs. Evans will know when the boys have a "better attitude" or that she is less mad. It is not clear how the boys will know when their grandmother thinks their attitude is "better." The following dialogue is an example of how you can translate this vague goal into a concrete, behavioral, and realistic goal.

Worker: Sounds like a very good idea, that the boys learn to have a better attitude. Suppose they get this better attitude, what will they be doing specifically to make you think to yourself, "Hey, I think the boys are beginning to have a better attitude"? What will you see that will make you say that?

Mrs. E: Gee, I don't know, I'm usually so busy yelling at them, but I suppose I will see them pick up their own dishes after eating, clean up after themselves, maybe even help me with chores, like taking out the garbage and sweeping the front porch, the floor, without my yelling to remind them.

Worker: Yes, I can imagine that would be a big help. So, you have an idea that they know how to do that—picking up after themselves, taking out the garbage, and things like that.

Mrs. E: Yes, of course they know how to do these things. I taught them, you know. They didn't learn from their mother, so I had to teach them to have better manners, you know, so they know all about it.

Worker: So, you want the boys to remember all those good things you taught them?

Mrs. E: That's not asking for much.

Worker: Of course it is reasonable.

From this conversation, it is easy to see that Mrs. Evans has a definite set of behaviors in mind that will indicate to her that the children have a better attitude. Now you can easily move into a discussion about the most recent times when the boys actually picked up after themselves, and so on. Such exceptions will firmly establish the boys as competent and able to take care of themselves and Mrs. Evans can be complimented on having taught the boys this important skill. Imagine the boys listening in on this conversation and how it will affect them.

Goals That Include a Solution Rather Than an Absence of a Problem

Most workers and clients are good at describing goals as the absence of a negative behavior, such as, "Mother will not scream at her children" or "I wish Brian would stop whining about everything, he drives me crazy." Whenever you hear comments made out of frustration, immediately ask questions, such as, "What do you want Brian to do *instead* of whining?" "What is he like *when he doesn't whine*?" "How do you know he can tell you what he wants *instead* of whining?" When you and the parent are clear about the desired behavior, it is easier to figure out what steps are needed to move in that direction. In the case with Mrs. Evans, the worker negotiated with her exactly what the boys would be doing, instead of what they wouldn't be doing, that would indicate their attitudes were better.

Meaningful Goals

The goal must be negotiated in such a way that the client feels what is important to him or her is respected. Not only is this a respectful way to work, but it is also pragmatic and realistic. Since clients have minds of their own and often see CPS as "meddling busybodies," it is important that your work be guided by what the client values.

It was clear to the worker in Mrs. Evans's case that her concern about Mrs. Evans's yelling at the boys was not Mrs. Evans's priority; she wanted to feel like she had some control over the boys' behavior. The worker's concern for the safety of the boys had some promise as a goal, that is, this was something in which Mrs. Evans was also invested. It seemed clear that when Mrs. Evans felt the boys were respectful of her, her urge to yell at them would disappear on its own, and when she felt the boys were safe, she would probably be calmer with them.

Client Goals: Tailoring Solutions

Rather than insisting on following a program regiment, such as eight weeks of parenting classes, substance abuse treatment, money management classes, and so on, think of these as tools to be used toward a goal. That is, if the court has ordered a mother to attend substance abuse treatment, for example, and if the goal is offered as such, the client will likely misunderstand what the court is interested in. The court does not simply want the mother to show up bodily in these programs; signing and showing up do not mean that she will avoid drugs—only her abstinence will. You need to make this clear when you talk to clients about program goals.

- So, suppose you go to this substance abuse treatment that the judge says you must do, how does this treatment fit into how you want your life to be?
- Now that you have made up your mind about wanting to stop doing drugs, how will you take advantage of this program that you will start next week?
- By going to the parenting class, what are you hoping will change in the way you handle your daughter's whining?

Sometimes program goals are not suitable for a client. This was the case with Mrs. Evans. Getting her out of the house to go to parenting classes to learn more effective strategies of raising her grandchildren would not have made any sense to her at this point. She was not asking and wondering about her parenting skills, nor did she have any doubts about her ability to parent. Her thinking was focused on, "If only the boys were a little bit better behaved." Had the worker pressed the issue of parenting classes or meeting with other grandparents with similar circumstances and problems, Mrs. Evans would most likely have felt insulted or offended and coerced into something she did not see the need to "waste" her energy on. The worker wisely stayed away from that issue for the time being and concentrated on what the client saw as the pressing event.

WORKING WITH IMPORTANT OTHERS IN A CLIENT'S LIFE

Clayton and Jeanetta are parents of two small children, now aged 6 and 4. Their problem began soon after the birth of the 4-year-old, Ronnie, whose birth was very difficult for the mother. It appears that Jeanetta began to show psychiatric symptoms such as hearing voices, an inability to get out of bed, and suspicion of her husband, accusing him of having a girlfriend and sneaking off to have sex with the girlfriend. Her depression was so severe that occasionally Jeanetta stayed in bed all day, failing to feed the children. Clayton worked two jobs, trying to pay various doctors and hospital bills, and was not available to support or help out with the children or household chores. Since he did not have a car, Clayton was gone from home for long stretches of time, placing the entire burden on Jeanetta.

Finally recognizing that they were unable to cope with the responsibility of raising the young children, the parents voluntarily requested temporary placement of the children out-of-home when the younger child was 6 months old, and the older one about 2 years old. Because voluntary placement of children is rare, CPS and foster care service workers went out of their way to accommodate the family's needs. Jeanetta entered psychotherapy with a psychiatrist, who promptly placed her on medication while she was in the hospital.

The couple worked hard to have the children returned home, with various services in place, including homemaker services and a visiting treatment team to help Jeanetta manage her young children. Shortly after, however, Clayton lost one of his jobs and began to fall behind financially again. Jeanetta became depressed again and needed to be hospitalized. This eventually resulted in the family's becoming home-less, and the children were placed in foster care again.

While seven different community services had been offered during the four years the family had been in the child welfare system, no professional had ever met Clayton. When we first met the couple together as yet another attempt to have the children returned to them (for the third time), Clayton mentioned that this was the first time he had ever met a social worker. Because Jeanetta had manifested all the outward symptoms of needing help with various issues, including parenting, housekeeping, money management, searching for housing, psychotherapy, counseling, medication management, and so on, all services offered by all the community and child welfare services had been directed at her. Yet, we discovered that Clayton had been the driving force behind keeping the marriage and family together, as well as working toward having the children returned to them.

This case vividly illustrates the importance of including everyone in the client's life as a potential resource for meeting family goals. We applaud the emerging philosophy that emphasizes utilizing family and social network resources. Family group conferences in CPS are being piloted in Michigan, following the general trend in the field (Ban, 1993; Hassal, 1996; Hudson, Morris, Maxwell, & Galaway, 1996; Ryburn & Atherton, 1996).

HOW CLOSE ARE YOU TO ACHIEVING YOUR GOAL?

When you have established clear goals, the tasks and activities that will help move the client toward these goals become very clear. The process of monitoring the changes that the client is making and any positive movement toward the goals are the building blocks. Scaling questions can be used to measure progress. For example, by asking yourself and your client the usual question of "If 10 stands for 'I feel confident that Todd is safe,' and 0 stands for how unsure I was when I first opened the case, where do I stand on safety issues today?" Along the way, also ask yourself: What do I need to see happen in this case to move 1 point higher? Be sure to include, "What would the children in this family say about how safe they feel now after two weeks of my presence in this case?"

SETBACKS AND RELAPSES

The normal process of change occurs one step at a time—or even two steps forward and one step back. This kind of back-and-forth movement is to be expected, especially when clients have a multitude of worries and concerns. People rarely make a change and stay on a straight and narrow path. Yet, many clients view a setback as a failure and become discouraged. This phenomenon is easily seen in the field of substance abuse treatment, where the only measure of success is abstinence.

When there is only a single criterion of success—total abstinence— there is no room for mistakes or failures. Anything less than abstinence is considered a failure, by both the treatment professionals and the client. It is easy to understand why many of your clients with substance abuse problems become easily discouraged. The enormously helpful and very popular twelve-step programs can become problematic when each setback means starting all over, from step one, even though the client may have achieved all the way up to step six before the latest setback. Many chronic alcohol and drug abusers will tell you how tired and hopeless they feel, living in constant fear of failure. Many will succumb to this sense of hopelessness and give up on themselves.

Whether the client's goal is to control his or her temper, clean the house, or stop drinking, it will not be easy to attain. Our job is to assist clients with their goals and keep their hope up, especially when a setback discourages them. Following should be your responses to any form of relapse or setback, whether it is another fight, another failure to clean the house, another runaway episode, or another drink.

1. *Keep your hope.* First of all, do not become discouraged and give up on your client or yourself. Remember that setbacks are part of the learning curve that everybody must experience; recovery is a three-steps-forward, one-step-back process. Quitting cold turkey and staying drug-free, for example, without replacing the drug-using behavior with some other healthy behavior, such as a new hobby, physical activity, involvement with a social network, and so on, is extremely difficult to accomplish. Change takes time.

2. *There is no magic pill.* Life is not a rose garden and there are lots of thorns, but these thorns also help us to appreciate the roses in life. Similarly, the harder the client struggles for success, the sweeter the taste of success; what we earn through hard work is sweeter than what comes to us with little effort.

3. *Ask how the client stopped when he or she did.* Instead of asking what made her lose her temper again, what started the fight, or how he managed to start drinking again, ask how she managed to slap her child only once, not twice; how they managed to end the fight after 30 minutes so that it did not go on for two hours like last time; how he drank for two days but stopped before the third day, and so on. Find out about the details. These questions imply that

clients have the power and ability to control themselves and are able to tune into various cues they receive from their surroundings or from within themselves. Devote a considerable amount of time to these details because they are the clues that the client was wise enough to pay attention to:

- What told you (how did you know) that it was time to _____?
- What was the first small thing you did when you decided to _____?
- In the midst of your anger (drunk/high state, etc.), how did you make yourself listen to your inner voice?

4. *Ask how this setback was different from the last one.* Every setback or relapse is different, especially the small details. Find out what small part was different: Did the client stop sooner? Apologize sooner? Use more positive language? Speak more gently? Find out how the client came to the decision to end the setback. If the differences are positive, find out how he or she will repeat them again.

5. *Each setback is a learning opportunity.* Elicit the client's idea of how he or she will incorporate the new information learned from this setback. How does the client plan to incorporate this new information into his or her life? Again, look for specifics and details.

6. *Review the difference achieving the client's goal will make in his or her life.* Use relationship questions (see chapter 5) for this. Here are some examples:

- What would your children say they will notice different about you when you're not drinking? What would they say they like about that?
- Who will be the first to notice that you are making changes with your temper?
- What would your daughter say she likes the best about your controlling your temper?
- What will your son do differently when he notices these changes in you?

7. *Help the client assess his or her progress.* Once the client has a way to assess his or her own progress (or lack of progress), it is easy to move to the next step. Scaling questions (see chapter 5) are useful, for example:

We have been working together for three months now. You have had many successes and several setbacks. You learned a lot about yourself in the three months since we started. Remem-

ber the numbers question I've often asked you? Where would
you put yourself on a scale of 1 to 10, where 10 stands for your
meeting the goal of being as confident as can be about not losing
your temper, and 1 stands for when we first started to meet
together?

Discuss with the client how she managed to come so far and what
might be the next step she needs to take to move up to the next level
of confidence.

WHEN AND HOW TO SERVICE AND CLOSE THE CASE

Since close to 57% of all CPS cases that receive one investigation visit
from a CPS worker are closed following a single home visit, workers
are already quite experienced in terminating cases. Of these single-
investigation cases, some are referred to community agencies, kept as
ongoing because there is low to moderate risk. When services such as
intensive family preservation are available, cases may be either closed
or kept open to ensure delivery of these services.

Ending child welfare services for families is not always determined
by the consensus of the worker and the client, but by real life circumstances surrounding the case, such as a child's running away, the
mother's marriage to a boyfriend who seems stable, the father's marriage to his paramour of many years, or the family's decision to move
closer—or away from—relatives. Sometimes, families move across
county, state, or school district lines in order to get away from what
they consider CPS "harassment." It is easy for the worker to feel helpless
or out of control when cases close in such an unplanned manner. Yet,
our many years of experience, as well as many studies (Talmon, 1990),
indicate that unplanned termination does not always result in dire
consequences. Even those cases that we believed were "lost" or "misera-
bly failed" because the family disappeared, moved away, or even voluntarily terminated parental rights turn out surprisingly well years
later. Examples too numerous to count have taught us that people are
a great deal more resilient than we give them credit for and that it is
better for the children in the long run when we remember this reality.

Of course, we believe the best possible way to terminate a case is
for you and the client to arrive at a mutually agreed upon goal, one
that is based on behavioral indicators rather than a time deadline.
Client motivation is higher and the rate of change is faster when clients
experience success than when they hold themselves together until the

time is up, which is similar to serving a jail sentence. Each achievement and success are cause for celebration.

LEAVE NO FOOTPRINT

CPS would do well to adopt the Zen saying, "The enlightened one leaves no footprint" for the majority of situations. First we must do no harm to a child or a family, and the child and the family should not be worse off because we were there for a brief period. Second, we must leave the family better off than when they first met us. Instead of being overly "intrusive" in the name of saving the child from maltreatment, we must learn to "leave no footprint," making the family believe that they have accomplished the level of safety all by themselves. When the parent who has been investigated cannot remember that CPS was in her life once upon a time and she is somehow managing her children and her life better, then we will know that we have succeeded. We do not need, or expect, a fanfare.

Chapter 8

Supervision, Consultation, and Ongoing Training

MUCH OF THE CRITICISM OF CPS HAS BEEN DIRECTED AT WORKERS WHO seem to make some poor decisions and are either overly intrusive or not doing enough to prevent extreme abuse or neglect. We believe this criticism is misdirected. Workers do not function in isolation, nor are they indifferent to clients; most of them are committed to their work and care deeply about the safety of the children. Many say they want to make a difference in a child's life. The media's sensational accounts of a child's death or a case of extreme neglect commonly report a statement by a commissioner or agency director that the "worker who is responsible for the mistake must be held accountable" (*The New York Times*, October, 1998). This kind of thinking reinforces the attitude of blaming the worker for the failure of the CPS system—as if the worker *alone* is responsible for the child's unfortunate death. Many social service agencies have decision-making processes that are very linear, so that directors have little direct contact with workers who meet with the families almost daily. Workers frequently do not feel the top bureaucrats understand them or know the difficulties of their work. The workers do believe, however, if a mistake is made with a child they alone will be held accountable. No wonder we have worker retention problems!

We have met several workers who were involved in child-death cases, and they all described their experience as being "hung out to dry on my own" (or some similar metaphor). In addition to mourning the child, years later they continue to torment themselves. They question their decision and spend countless hours reworking the case. Many detailed for us the brutal manner in which review committees, supervisors, colleagues, and attorneys all contributed to the pain they suffered. They reported a loss of confidence in their motives and their ability to make good decisions. They began second-guessing and doubting themselves. One worker had turned angry "at the system" and decided to "just coast along until I collect my pension" and retire. Even 14 years later, one worker we met was still bitter at the lack of support and the "guilty until proven innocent" stance that he had faced from those around him.

We suggest that supervisors, managers, and administrators are key in supporting changes that empower the workers and make the cultural shift from "hung out to dry" to "we are in this together" in order to serve our clients.

RESOURCES WITHIN THE CPS UNIT

Many CPS units have workers with 5, 10, 15, or 20 years of experience. They have told us they find their work rewarding and are content with their jobs and work environment. We recently met a young, newly hired worker who was enthusiastic about her job, saying that she expects to stay with CPS until she retires. If we could only provide these young workers, who are full of energy and desire to change the world, with the tools, support, and supervision to do their jobs well!

Many of the experienced workers know how to navigate the system in such a way that they are comfortable within it and have learned to help clients and make a difference in their lives. Many have a wealth of experience with a variety of cases that any novice CPS worker would be likely to encounter; they know what has and has not worked. When time is set aside within the staff meeting or a separate case consultation format is made available, this wealth of knowledge and experience can be shared in an atmosphere of respectful dialogue, nurturing innovation and skill enhancement. CPS is in a unique position to direct families to preventive services often before serious problems surface. We need to capitalize on this opportunity. Most CPS units can use the stimulation of an experienced individual, who spurs the whole unit to refocus on its mission and learn about making good and wise decisions. A forum where workers can regularly solicit advice, ask about what works, and report successes is an important component of on-the-job training.

The Workers

Together we have personally interviewed and shadowed more than 150 CPS workers and their supervisors in order to learn about their attitudes, values, sense of mission, beliefs about their career, and motivations to come to work everyday. The majority of these workers have excellent reputations among their peers, supervisors, and administrators and are respected by their colleagues. They are dedicated, hardworking, resourceful, deeply caring, highly skilled, and able to make tough decisions under the most difficult circumstances on their own while in the field. Because it is difficult to predict what sort of situations they are likely to come across, they need to be flexible, curious, interested, and most of all, have a sense of humor and not be "full of themselves," as one supervisor described it. We wondered how they described their own work and what made them excellent CPS workers. A common thread emerged. We want to describe below what we have observed.

Don MacLean of Shiawassee Family Independence Agency, Michigan, is an outstanding worker, and as his supervisor describes, he gets "love letters" from his clients, even those whose children he has removed. A rather low-keyed, laid-back, and calm person, with lots of humor at his expense, he describes his style as "polite and respectful." Don says he always asks for permission to enter a client's house, such as, "May I have your permission to see your children and make sure that they are safe?" He rarely gets turned down. In those rare situations when the client refuses to allow him in the door or even talk to him, and he is sure that the children are safe, he leaves his business card and asks the client to call him back, saying, "Would you please give me a call when you are ready to give me permission to look inside your house?" He finds that in cases with dirty house complaints, when the client makes the call and invites him back, the house is cleaned already and his mission has been accomplished. Since a clean and safe house is the goal of CPS, he believes that the client has already met the goal, and he, then, can close the case. He believes that the most important elements he brings to his job are flexibility and willingness to realize what it might be like when clients have the overwhelming feeling that they have no control over what happens to them. He believes his upbringing has a great deal to do with how his own application of CPS philosophy has evolved—that is, being respectful to others, no matter who the other person is. Having his share of hardships in life has also shaped his approach to clients. Losing a job as a steelworker during the '80s taught him a tough lesson—what it feels like to lose control over one's destiny over life, no matter how hard one tries. He tries to remember this lesson each day. His ability to look at the client's life in a broader perspective seems to counter the CPS tendency to be legalistic and incident-focused.

Deborah Reynolds of Kent County, Michigan, FIA is a vivacious, energetic, and outgoing woman who joined CPS after a maternity leave.

Deborah had been a probation and parole officer for 15 years. She told us that working with CPS is very different from working in corrections. In criminal justice work, it was easier to see things in black and white, guilty or not guilty. She also felt that she had more power as an officer. CPS work tends to be gray, ambiguous, and uncertain. She felt she had much less leverage and power to force clients to do things because the problems and solutions were less clear-cut. After trying to figure out how to bridge the differences and adapt herself to CPS work, she came to understand that she had to make some changes. She had to set aside her tendency to tell clients what to do, and instead be quiet and listen to clients, giving them lots of chances to explain how they saw things, since even concerning risk and safety issues there were fewer clear-cut choices and options. While she learned to turn the complaints into goals, the most important thing she learned was to listen to the client. She explained that she does this by calming her own voice, suppressing what she would like to say to clients on an impulse, and just listening.

Don and Deborah are only two of numerous outstanding workers who love their work and are dedicated to making a difference. It is amazing to us that they can practically walk off the street and ask to come into someone's home and be allowed to inspect and look around. The majority of the workers know how to immediately establish a positive relationship with clients, without heavy-handed use of power or threats. What makes them such good workers? When this question is put to them, the most frequently heard answers are: "I try to put myself in their shoes. I keep thinking it could be me facing a CPS investigation; if so, how would I want to be treated?" What better description of their ability to empathize with the client in crisis?

Our informal survey of workers' attitudes toward their jobs showed that the vast majority of them believe they "make a difference in someone's life." Most chose the field because they want to make the world a better place. Their frequently voiced frustrations are related to the vast burden of paperwork and the feeling that completing paperwork is actually more rewarded than doing good work with clients. As one long-time supervisor said many years ago, "The CPS system takes untrained, highly motivated workers who want to change the world and we do not give them the tools or know-how and send them out into the world. We would never do that with our own children, and yet the system does this all the time."

Almost all of the workers report that they learn from the informal peer network they have developed on the job; thus, when they have doubts about a case, or encounter a shocking situation, they turn to each other for support, validating their perception and learning from

208 Building Solutions in Child Protective Services

informal discussions and consultations. This kind of informal learning is necessary and helpful, and yet can be limiting in that old ideas get handed down uncritically. Since it is difficult to challenge what has worked for others for many years, old practices and the ideas behind them are accepted without challenge or innovation.

Management

Promoting Miracles

We contend that top-level administrators would benefit from using the "miracle question" (see chapter 5) with workers, supervisors, managers, and each other. It is a strategy, if used well, that allows persons to verbalize and project a future outcome that is solution-building, not just complaining. It can become a road map or blueprint for how things might be different in the future as the managers work within the agency and support supervisors and workers. A question such as the following could help administrators to listen to aspirations of supervisors and workers about how they can help families better.

> Suppose after work today you go home, spend the evening in your usual manner, such as taking care of your family, having dinner, helping your children with homework, and so on. During the night while you are sleeping, a miracle happens to CPS . . . (pause) and all the problems we have been talking about just now (as a supervisor, worker, or manager) are all solved. That's the miracle part. When you come back to work tomorrow morning, what would be the first thing you would notice that lets you know a miracle has happened?

As the staff formulate answers to the question, they begin to create solutions to the obstacles they feel are in the way of doing a good job. When the miracle question is used effectively, both administrators and supervisors can explore details about more effective practice and service delivery. Workers may say things like, "Our caseloads would be down to 10," "All the families would change," "Paperwork would be reduced," "We could have flexible funds to use on the spot with families," and so on. Often the miracle question helps set the groundwork for renewing enthusiasm and setting goals for change. Using the miracle question is one way to help workers and staff "own" their job.

A good follow-up to the miracle question is, "What would other staff members say is different about you, your work, after the miracle has occurred? What else would be different? What would clients say is different in the way their workers are dealing with them that shows that you are doing an effective job as a manager?"

Asking Staff How You Can Be Helpful To Them

Smart administrators ask staff their opinions, take time to listen to them, accept their ideas as worthwhile, and advocate for them. Asking staff what you can do to make their job better goes a million miles toward building trust and loyalty. Talking *at* staff does not work very well. Be careful though: If you ask, you will need to change, too.

Sharing Information

Giving staff as much information as possible about the organization and about administrative decisions that may affect their professional lives is important and helps build trust between management and staff. If they feel they are in the loop, they will keep administrators in the loop.

When a new director was appointed to the Michigan Social Service Agency in 1997, and because of a simultaneous early retirement offer, about 15% of the social services staff left the agency. All staff were justifiably worried not only about their jobs but also about how the agency itself would be restructured. I (SK) decided to do weekly updates by voice mail or in person with the entire staff. My motto was: "Everything I know—you know." This approach, combined with providing opportunities for staff to ask questions about rumors they had heard, or fears they had, helped quell anxiety somewhat but also helped provide a contained forum for productive listening and diminished the unproductive worries.

As a manager, I suggested to my staff that the best way to demonstrate the importance of their job was through high-quality performance. It is interesting how much grinds to a halt when transitions occur and how such transitions are used as an excuse for work slowdown or stoppage. These frequent meetings helped me to demonstrate the reality that all individuals have control over is what they do in their jobs and how important their efforts are to the organization. Helping staff see how their jobs fit within the larger vision is important. When the staff feel that they are not listened to or asked their opinions, after a while they can easily feel alone and insignificant to the organization.

Patting Ourselves on the Back

It is tempting to pounce when something goes wrong. While that may be necessary at times, it is not really as productive as pouncing on the good. Taking time to notice what someone is doing and going out of one's way to show appreciation, for instance, writing a thank-you note or giving a small token, really helps promote self-confidence and encourages even better productivity. How many times does the CPS staff get positive feedback for good case documentation or the effective handling of a difficult situation?

At a staff meeting recently, I (SK) asked staff to reflect on their activities of the past few months—to think about what specific job-related thing they were most proud of since we had last met. I then asked them to describe it in small groups to their colleagues. The conversation was animated and enthusiastic. There were lots of laughs and sharing. They liked talking about their successes. This experience provided a way for staff to give themselves a well-deserved pat on the back. It also gave the managers information to follow up on with staff.

The following is a team-building exercise that you might want to experiment with in building teams and staying on task. All team meetings begin with the designation of a team leader who will chair the meeting and keep the team focused.

1. Discuss what others on the team have done to improve the working atmosphere in the unit (department, group, team) during the last two weeks. Discuss what talent, skills, and experience each brings to the team. Allow 10 minutes.
2. Discuss what others in the unit (department, group, team) would say each person has done to contribute to the working atmosphere of the team during the last two weeks. Allow 10 minutes.
3. Ask if anyone on the team identifies qualities, skills, talents, and special contributions that have not been mentioned. Allow 5–10 minutes.
4. What needs to happen at the end of this meeting that will make this meeting worthwhile? Miracles? The chair makes sure that the conversation stays on track and focuses on concrete, behavioral, realistic, and doable tasks. Make a list of these on a white board.
5. When was the last time in recent memory the desirable goal happened? Encourage detailed discussion of this exception. Scale the confidence, willingness, ability, and resources to reach this goal by the team.
6. Discuss what the future would look like if this goal were achieved.

The Power of Thank You

Frequent and sincere gestures of thanks are sure signs that you notice the work the staff does, and it lets them know that they should repeat those good behaviors. Recently, a few managers decided to sponsor an hour break with refreshments they provided for the staff. They encouraged staff to mingle, come out of their cubicles, and mix with one another. Seeing managers work together to provide refreshments, to take time to support, and to respect the hard work of the staff goes a long way. These are avenues that break down the lines of hierarchical barriers, as we present ourselves to the staff as humans, with hearts and warmth.

Expecting High-Quality Performance

Mediocre expectations of the staff reap mediocre performance. It is expecting too little. Knowing that you believe and expect high performance from the staff can motivate them. Tools such as annual evaluations to elicit progress toward behaviorally specific performance outcomes and target goals for the future are effective ways to help staff focus on necessary improvements. These suggestions do not take more time; they only use standard evaluations differently. Most staff know what they do well and how they need to improve.

Administrators, middle managers, and supervisors have extraordinary power to change both the tone and operations of the agency. Planning time to regularly meet with the frontline staff on an occasional basis goes a long way toward acknowledging their work and stressing the role of administration in maximizing efforts for good outcomes. For example, when a colleague became the director of a large county agency, he immediately met with his staff and explained his philosophy of how CPS and all of the county FIA staff were to be oriented toward customer services. He had to repeat this message several times during the first year before his staff came to realize that he really meant it. He also took the time to invite customers to attend a focus group and give their feedback on how they felt they had been treated. One customer reported that it was the first time anyone had asked her opinion about anything and that she was proud she had been selected to be asked her ideas. When an administrator takes time to know the work his staff members are doing, it makes a difference. Good administrators provide guidance, support, and vision. Administrators can:

- Lead by embracing, promoting, and inspiring others to have a vision of CPS that is better for families and more rewarding for workers.
- Introduce solution-focused, strength-based operating procedures as the norm.
- Expect that policy, contracts, paperwork and reports, training, evaluation, quality assurances, and service delivery strategies will be solution-focused.

- Meet with CPS frontline workers and CPS customers to listen and learn from case workers' interventions.
- Hold focus groups that ask community members and social services staff to envision a model of CPS-based empowerment for families, as well as solution-building, efficient, and strength-based intervention (see Appendix C).
- Expect that the CPS system can be more solution-focused and efficient and support the staff who can make it so.
- Let the voice of consumers be heard. Promote avenues for regular feedback from CPS customers to be integrated into any action plan. A suggested format for soliciting input is found in Appendix B.

Staff Meetings

A typical staff meeting in an average CPS unit involves one supervisor and the six to eight workers that make up a unit. Large counties may have several CPS units, and, of course, large metropolitan areas may have several geographically organized offices located closer to clients. More innovative CPS units are located in schools, neighborhood centers, medical clinics, multi-service centers, even in police stations. Of course, in a smaller, rural county where a social worker does everything, or where two or three small counties share a single CPS worker, the routine is quite different. But in most semi-urban and urban areas, there are several workers designated to do only CPS work. Some large counties divide up the tasks along the utilitarian purposes: There are workers who only do one home visit to establish whether the situation merits opening the case and offering services, or whether the call was not appropriate for CPS. In such counties, the CPS office is open 24 hours a day, with a heavy volume of work throughout the day and night.

Staff meetings are primarily devoted to informing workers about policy changes, new rules, new services, changes in contracts with private vendors, and new office equipment that will make the workers' job easier, community agency services available to clients, new and added paperwork and/or changes in procedures, and numerous other details. Usually the staff meetings do not focus on current cases or workers' needs. We have even observed a number of counties where there are no staff meetings at all. We were told that staff meetings were eliminated to save time, so staff met only when there was an emergency or crisis. However, we were also told "off the record" that staff meetings had become so contentious that many staff did not show up, so the supervisor decided to eliminate the meetings. Any important information, such as new regulations and policy changes, were passed on to workers through memos and intranet mail. There was almost no room for discussing cases, agonizing over difficult decisions on cases, polling everybody's impressions, or debating the subtleties of making good decisions.

With so little time spent examining the complexities of cases, is it any wonder that workers fall back on black-and-white or right-or-wrong views and tend to reduce complex and complicated human lives into categories and problems to be solved? The subtle nuances and complexity of being a family are lost in this procedure-driven way of making decisions. Staff meetings could be used to share cases in the spirit of mutual learning, challenge each other, prod and tease out the best way to service the child and family, support each other when needed, and applaud each other's small triumphs and successes. Missing such a valuable opportunity to learn from each other in the spirit of collegial inquiry is a disservice to workers and ultimately to clients. There are many creative, talented, and experienced resources within each unit.

Care and Nurture of Workers

When there is a very difficult issue for one or more workers, such as the death of the child or the discovery of unusually brutal neglect or abuse, it causes understandable and predictable adverse emotional and, at times, physical reactions among staff. These stress reactions to traumatic cases are normal and will occur in our line of work. Therefore, it is imperative that the staff carve out a time and place to support each other, cry with each other, and rejoice in the successful mastery of a child receiving the help he or she desperately needs. We believe the care and support of workers are best done in groups and, as most group practitioners will attest, a well-run group can become not only a support net for workers but also a hot bed of innovation and brainstorming. Those who take care of others also need care and support. This is not only an efficient and effective way to retain the staff but also a humane way to take care of those who take care of the most vulnerable. Workers need to feel valued, validated, and appreciated for doing a valuable service for the society's most needy. When workers feel nurtured and taken care of, they may become more sensitive to families in pain and suffering.

For example, in a tragic case a young child was found close to death from prolonged, severe malnutrition and dehydration, and the child eventually died in the hospital. A thoughtful supervisor, recognizing the entire staff's shock and horror, invited the unit for a brown bag lunch and "emergency" meeting. The supervisor opened the meeting with compliments for the worker who had handled the case, detailing the steps the worker had taken, the issues and concerns in the case, and everything she knew about the situation. She invited the staff to ask questions about rumors they might have heard, indicating that she would answer questions as best as she could. The supervisor modeled her care and concern for the worker by using the language of "we" instead of "you" throughout the conversation. Many workers had a chance to disclose for the first time that they had also had a near-tragic experience with a child. They shared how others in the unit were supportive and how they learned to take care of themselves. Workers felt listened to and supported. The conversation eventually turned to what motivated the workers to choose CPS as their life work and the reasons for staying in it.

Case Consultation

Case consultation is an ongoing resource available to workers, as "trouble shooting" when difficulties arise, a situation has no precedence, a case is likely to fall between the cracks, and when numerous other unique situations arise. It should be viewed as an ongoing and regularly scheduled teaching and staff development tool. Sometimes, it is valuable to hire an outside consultant who is familiar with CPS cases and who also has sufficient clinical skills to offer helpful suggestions. Many CPS clients have mental health issues, substance abuse problems, domestic violence troubles, and a host of other social, legal, medical, and financial problems. Experts in each of each of these fields provide technical assistance and consultation to help workers learn how to respond better in the future when similar situations arise.

Case Consultation Format

The following outline will give shape to the consultation, so that it will be focused and goal-driven, remain collaborative with the worker and the client, and allow all present to share their expertise. Emphasize that the purpose of using the outline is to focus the meeting and thus maximize the use of time, as well as to encourage sharing of expertise.

1. Briefly describe the family and what brought the family to the attention of CPS. What are the safety issues that need to be addressed immediately?
2. What does the family want? What does CPS want? What are ways to reconcile the differences, if any?
3. What resources are there in the family and CPS to achieve this goal(s)?

4. What would the family say you have done to date that's been most helpful to them?
5. List exceptions to the problem and past successes for the family.
6. What is the level of risk, from 1 to 10? What are some ways to lower the risk in this family? What would it look like when the risk was lowered?
7. What are the signs of success for this family? How has the family done this?
8. What would the worker say about how close the family is to being safe? Who will do what, when, where, and how to get to the next level of safety? How long will it take to get to the next level of safety?
9. When and how will we know it's time to close the case?

Below are some suggested guidelines for the peer consultation. Adapt them to fit your unique setting and staff needs. Clear guidelines will reinforce the collaborative nature and purpose of the meeting. Using humor is always helpful and providing food, coffee, and tea helps to promote camaraderie. Encourage staff to bring jokes and humorous stories; laughing at ourselves helps to break the ice. It may be necessary to build comfort and friendship. You may need to remind the staff of the rules from time to time until the pattern becomes established—use a friendly, humorous manner. It takes time, but it will be worth it in the long run.

• Ask the staff to pair up in twos and spend the next two minutes discussing with their partner what happened this morning that made them want to say, "Hey, life is pretty good!" What did they see or do that made them feel lucky or good? What did someone else do for them? Stop the discussion when the time is up and note how nice it is to see everyone discussing the good things in their lives.
• Use the consultation outline and stay focused on answering the questions. Gently refocus if someone strays from the agenda.
• Never allow a conversation or question to begin with "why." Have the questioner rephrase it by beginning with "how come" or ask another question instead.
• Feel free to interrupt and refocus if someone becomes critical of others. Do not allow the criticism and defense to continue.
• Monitor the flow of conversation. The purpose of the meeting is to learn and weigh the options, not to go through with them. Therefore, limit the debate and steer the conversation toward use-

ful, productive ideas that build curiosity and critical thinking in a learning atmosphere.
- Be sure to comment on positive ideas and encourage staff cooperation and supportive interactions in a subtle and nonpatronizing manner.
- Always demonstrate a respectful, collegial relationship with your staff during the meeting
- The discussion may produce several possible solutions; do not rush to form a consensus on a single idea. This teaches the staff that there are many different paths to the same destination.
- Remember that the purpose of all these discussions is to provide higher-quality services to clients and protection to families.

SUPERVISION: "LEADING FROM ONE STEP BEHIND"

Not surprisingly, many supervisors still believe in the myth of "supervision," that is, the supervisor has the superior vision and is the sole source of knowledge and skills. Of course, we recognize that there is a need to hold someone responsible for the task at hand, but there is room to be flexible and nurture workers via supervision. It is easy to lose track of our mission in our large bureaucratic system—one that is not known for encouraging excellence or creativity. Yet, we have met some creative, dedicated, and compassionate workers, supervisors, and administrators who willingly go out of their way to serve the needy in the true spirit of civil service. Therefore, we know that it can be done and that workers can be allowed to aspire to reach excellence in the child welfare system. We want to suggest some practical ways to become such supervisors and encourage personnel departments to revise position descriptions to include hallmarks of this new paradigm of supervision.

Supervisors are middle managers. They often report feeling squeezed from both ends, that is, from the top and from the bottom, which can be an extremely difficult position to be in. However, once they conceptualize their role as having an influence on both sides, they can begin to see just how much influence they have and then take advantage of that.

I (IKB) have a colleague named Brad who works in a county civil service system as a program manager. Brad works under a director variously described by many in the department as "arrogant." He belittles his staff, yells at and humiliates his subordinates in meetings, and rarely listens to staff input. He has driven many to quit or transfer out of this department; Brad nearly quit many times, but his loyalty to his staff and his love of his job and the area he lives in kept him trying "one more time" for many years. When we were talking about his terrible work situation, I casually asked Brad what his boss would say he wants from Brad and his other staff, had I a chance to ask him. Brad didn't know, and we dropped the subject since this was not an official consultation or request for help.

A couple of months after this casual conversation, Brad sent me an e-mail reporting an amazing turnaround that gave him a glimpse of hope for his boss. Brad related that during one particularly difficult meeting, instead of responding to his boss in his usual manner, he wrote "listen" on the top of his notepad and kept looking at his writing. Otherwise, the meeting went pretty much like all the others he had attended with his boss. To his shock and surprise, his boss approached him later in the day and said, "Thanks for listening to my ideas, Brad." Brad was quite sure that this was the first time his boss ever thanked anybody for anything. Now Brad is convinced that "listening" to his boss's ideas and complaints is the key to improving their working relationship. By the way, Brad is also convinced that, although he will never like his boss, he can work with him.

New Approach to Supervision

We want to propose a new paradigm of supervision. Traditional supervision mirrors the traditional approach to relapse prevention: Supervisors must always be on the lookout for a potential mistake and prevent it from happening; and if it happens they must correct it and control the damage. It is easy to link workers' learning their jobs under this kind of mistake-driven approach to supervision to their working in a similar fashion with their clients. The new paradigm of supervision begins with the assumption that the worker has some degree of competence and the supervisor's function is to highlight, shape, and help the worker become aware of his or her inner resources and what life experience he or she brings to the job. Thus, the worker's decision to utilize these strengths is deliberate and sustained. Our conception of supervision is to "lead from one step behind," a term proposed by Cantwell (Cantwell & Holmes, 1994). We like this position of "leading," that is, as supervisors we teach, evaluate, and reinforce from a position of one-step behind, instead of standing in front of the worker and pulling her in a certain direction. We have a different process in mind.

In other words, the new paradigm of supervision relies on reducing or minimizing the hierarchical differences between supervisor and supervisee. Based on our understanding that people tend to relate better and feel more supported when the supervisory relationship is more egalitarian than hierarchical, we offer some useful techniques for developing this type of relationship. Such a collaborative stance is often reflected in the language you use, your voice tone and inflection, and the general posture of working together. In Table 8.1 we list questions supervisors can use to express a collaborative, empowering approach to supervision. Our list is by no means comprehensive; it merely suggests ways to teach the model by using the model.

Language and Posture of Supervision

Like CPS work, supervision is carried out in the context of language, our most useful tool. The primary position we take as a supervisor is that of collaborating with our workers in order to facilitate their competence and success so that they in turn will deal with their clients in a collaborative, respectful manner, who will then treat their children in a respectful, responsible manner and thus keep them safe. The by-product of supervision is change: A novice, inexperienced worker becomes a thoughtful worker who practices a respectful and empowering approach to insuring safety for clients.

Questions as Curiosity in Action

Asking questions rather than telling workers what to do encourages self-observation, which leads to discovery and understanding of their own strengths and areas that need improvement. Questioning teaches workers to be curious about themselves and promotes self-monitoring, a powerful tool for individuals who generally operate independently in the field already. As workers become used to this approach to learning, they will teach their clients to use the same questioning techniques with their children.

Keep in mind that workers' competence does not develop all at once; it grows slowly, over time, in ordinary, everyday activities. Be sure to recognize the successes in the mundane details of workers' days, and you will find that the ordinary will become extraordinary.

We contend that when workers lose curiosity and fascination with their clients, they become bored with their job and take things for granted. Discovering something new about a client or watching a client change for the better is no longer exciting. Thus, one of the important tasks of a supervisor is to instill curiosity, wonder, and amazement, which will sustain a worker through tough times. Adopting a "not-knowing" position (Anderson & Goolishian, 1992) and using solution language rather than problem language open up workers to possibility and options.

Table 8.1

QUESTIONS SUPERVISORS CAN USE WITH WORKERS

Connecting with the Client

What one thing would the client say you did that was most helpful?

What do you suppose she appreciated most about what you did?

What would she/he say is most important to her at this time of her life?

What do you suppose it means to her that she might lose her child?

Where did you get the idea that just listening to her would calm her down?

How did you manage to stay calm?

You obtained lots of useful information this time. How did you do it?

What do you suppose she was so upset about?

What Does the Client Want?

If she could tell you calmly, what would she say is most important to her right now?

What do you suppose it means to her that CPS is involved in her life?

What do you suppose she was so upset about? Any other ideas?

How could you find out what the client wants? Anything else?

What would the children say is most important to them right now?

What difference it would make for them?

What would the mother's best friend (partner, etc.) say she needs right now?

Safety Assessment and Concerns

Knowing what you know about this family so far, how would you assess the level of safety? (scaling question)

How would the mother assess the level of safety? The children? Others?

What would raise the level of safety 1 point higher for this family?

How would you make sure you listen to her idea about how to insure the safety of her children?

What is your assessment of how realistic her ideas are?

At what number would you feel comfortable enough to close the case?

Use a Conversational Style

Treat your meetings as mutual learning experiences, rather than opportunities for you to impart knowledge. Use tentative language such as "I wonder . . . what made the mother decide to calm down with you?" "Could it be that the mother is trying to figure out for herself whether to leave the boyfriend?" "Do you suppose the mother does not really know what to do?" Avoid "why" questions because they are often taken as blaming or accusing and will encourage a defensive posture in the supervisee. Instead, substitute "how come?" Here are some examples:

- I wonder what will work with someone like Mrs. Smith?
- It sure is a tough case, isn't it? I'm not sure about . . .
- How come you say the older sister can't take care of her siblings?
- Maybe you need to look it up and see what we did last time that seems to have worked.
- I'm not sure what your thoughts were about this. Can you explain them to me one more time?
- What do you suppose the mother would say she was thinking when she decided to leave the house at four in the morning?

Although it is understood that a supervisor has more knowledge and the power to make decisions and judgment calls and to influence staff, remember that it is his or her posture and conduct with workers that garner respect—not a position or title.

Take the Worker's Perspective

It is important to see everything from the worker's, rather than from the supervisor's, perspective. Any coaching or suggestions that you offer must make sense to the worker; otherwise she will not integrate them into practice. The worker may comply in the short-term but will not learn critical thinking. For example, a 19-year-old oldest sibling was adamant about wanting to keep her four siblings with her instead of separating them into various foster homes. A novice worker, Sandy, was very uneasy with the young woman's decision. The young woman had "never had a childhood," as she had been the primary caretaker since she was 8 years old because her mother was a long-term drug addict and was now disabled from a cocaine-induced heart attack. Sandy felt that the young woman would be better off having her youth back, rather than being burdened with raising her siblings. The supervisor wanted Sandy to consider all aspects of this case, even though she believed that the client had to follow her own desires and that the young children deserved to have a stable home with their sister. Instead of pressing her point of view, the supervisor carefully asked Sandy's perspective on this:

Supervisor: So, tell me, Sandy, how do you propose you will convince this young woman that it will be in her best interest to agree to place her siblings in foster homes?

Worker: I don't know what will convince her, but I think she shouldn't sacrifice her young life to raise her siblings.

Supervisor: So, what do you suppose you could say that will convince her?

Worker: I don't think she will be convinced because somehow she seems to think that keeping her siblings is so important. But I know she couldn't keep it up.

Supervisor: Maybe not, or perhaps she might pull it off. So, what do you think is best for the siblings? What would the children say?

Worker: Of course they want to stay together. I imagine they are not going to be happy going to foster homes. I guess the guardian ad litem will support their wishes.

Supervisor: So, how will you follow up on this?

Taking the worker's perspective can be good troubleshooting. Frequently workers want the supervisor to validate and support whatever they believe is a good decision. With some experienced workers, it is important to trust and support their intuition about a case and explore their perspectives in more depth. They should be taken seriously, as the following dialogue shows:

Worker: I really don't know what to do with this Jackson case. Any suggestions? I keep going to their house and of course they are never home.

Supervisor: I am curious, Ken—you've had cases like this before and you've handled them wonderfully. What's different about this Jackson family case that makes you wonder what to do?

Worker: I don't know, something is different about this case, something isn't quite right.

Supervisor: Say some more about what's different about this case.

Worker: Something about the previous records on this family, numerous complaints with no substantiation, nothing definite . . . but I have this feeling that there must be something going on, but I don't know how to handle it.

Supervisor: It sounds serious. Let's talk about this a little bit more . . .

Conversations like this can be an important learning process for the supervisor as well as the worker. The issues workers confront might be related to diverse and unfamiliar cultural, religious, and personal beliefs and child-rearing practices. For example, a worker was extremely upset with a family in which three women and each of their children lived with a man who fathered all the children. A total of 16 children and four adults lived in relative harmony and the children were well taken care of. The worker noted and was impressed by how all three mothers organized the records related to each child and had a file on each—including immunizations, and medical, school, and even baptismal records. Even though the worker was initially upset by the fact of four adults living in a polygamous household, the supervisor helped her separate the moral and religious issues from the concerns of CPS.

Techniques for Effective Supervisors

Following are our suggestions to help supervisors incorporate workable supervision into their practice.

1. *Use positive speech* such as agreeing, offering, praising, and sympathizing:

   - This family will be tough to handle for anybody.
   - It sure is a tough case, isn't it?
   - How did you survive an interview with 14 people in the family?
   - Considering how complicated the case is, you sure got all the relevant data. I'm impressed.

2. *Imply advice* rather than give it:

   - Would it be possible to go back for more details about . . . ?
   - How she was able to get her child to the doctor's office is fascinating. It might be helpful for us to learn about her resourcefulness.
   - Suppose you offered the mother a suggestion. I wonder what she might do with it. Any ideas about that, given how she thinks you are out to harm her?

3. *Focus advice* on the client rather than on the worker.
   - I would have given her a lot more useful information on . . .
   - I imagine the child wanted to talk to you about his school activities . . .
   - It sounds like the mother really appreciated what you did when you brought that up . . .

4. *Mitigate advice* by avoiding "should" or "must":

   - It would be helpful to go for . . .
   - You could still go for more information about the father of the child . . .
   - I wonder what would happen if you asked her how long she has been . . .
   - I don't see what harm just asking the mother about . . . would cause . . .

5. *Avoid giving directives* while drawing attention; replace potential directives with observations:

   - The interesting thing is that the client sees it as helpful . . .
   - I wonder how she was able to get out of that abusive relationship?
   - It is interesting how she was able to control herself enough to . . .
   - How do you suppose she will explain this to herself? Any ideas about that?

6. *Provide positive evaluation* of the worker and teach curiosity. Respond to worker's negative self-evaluation with questions, comments, or nonevaluative feedback. Respond to worker's negative self-evaluation with questions, comments, or nonevaluative feedback markers:

   - I agree with you that it was touch-and-go for a while and you hung in there. How did you know that hanging in there was going to help?
   - I agree with you that this is not up to your usual standard of safety assessments. You must have very good reasons for this?
   - I am amazed by how you helped her to come to accept that she needs to go to substance abuse treatment, considering . . .

7. *Model the model, use constructive dialogue* rather than definitive dialogue:

   - Most clients tend to say . . .
   - You could still go for the information we are looking for . . .
   - The client can then say . . .
   - I wonder what it could mean when clients like Mrs. J say something like that?

8. *Use scaling and relationship questions* to teach workers to self-evaluate and to be sensitive to their clients' perception of their work together:

- On a scale of 1 to 10, how safe would you say the family situation is? What do you need to see in this family for you to say they have moved 1 point higher in safety?
- Knowing the Maple School staff as well as you do, what do you suppose they will say they need to see for them to be assured that this mother is doing something about her drug problem?
- You are very familiar with Judge K. What is your guess about how he will react to your report about this mother's petition?
- What do you suppose the mother would say about how confident she is about her ability to convince the judge?
- What about the grandmother? Where would she put her daughter's ability to keep her children safe from her boyfriend?
- What do you suppose she would say about how confident she is that she will stop drinking?
- So, what would this mother say it will take to bridge the gap between you and her?

We recognize that it takes time to learn and become comfortable with this kind of language use in supervision, just as learning a foreign language takes time, sustained effort, and regular practice. However, the pay-off is worth the effort, because this is the beginning of a cultural change. We cannot wait for others to change—they are probably waiting for us to make the first move.

STAFF DEVELOPMENT VS. TRAINING

There is much concern about low worker retention rate and much discussion on how to prevent job turnover and burnout. The majority of CPS and foster care workers complain about the crushing burden of paperwork, ever-increasing caseloads, the lack of recognition from superiors, and low status of the job in society, all of which contribute to burnout and low morale. Almost every training session we have led could easily have turned into a complaining session—certainly an indication that something is wrong with the system. And yet there are many workers who have remained passionate about their work (not necessarily their jobs) after 10, 20, 30 years in the field. How can this be? Curious about this disparity, in 1995 we did an informal, nonscientific study. We made up a questionnaire and asked CPS workers to fill it in anonymously. Following is an excerpt from that survey, where we asked workers to rate several statements on a scale of 1 to 5, with 1 meaning strongly agree and 5 strongly disagree:

1. My job is like a hobby to me.
2. I make a difference in people's lives in my job.
3. I consider my job rather unpleasant.
4. I am often bored with my job.
5. Most of the time I have to force myself to go to work.
6. My supervisor thinks I am competent in my job.
7. My job is just a job, not a career.
8. I want to move up to a more responsible job.
9. My job allows me to do what I went into this profession for.
10. I respect the people I work with.
11. I feel like I am benefiting personally from my work.
12. I like my job better than an average worker does.
13. I am looking for another job.
14. Each day of work seems like it will never end.
15. The only reason I keep my job is because I need money.

Surprisingly, even those who strongly agreed with item 15 (The only reason I keep my job is because I need money) also strongly agreed with item 2 (I make a difference in people's lives in my job). In fact, close to 95% of those who responded to this survey checked 1 (strongly agree) or 2 (agree) on item 2. We came away with the impression that most workers identify with the professional ideal, and this ideal is what originally attracted them to the field and keeps them in CPS, despite numerous obstacles and frustrations they face daily. Even though workers identify with this ideal, we have not done a good job of giving them the necessary tools and support to enable them to feel that they are "making a difference" in a child's life. We believe the solution lies in a new vision of training and career development.

The term "training" is usually thought of as a one-time activity to impart information and perhaps new skills. It is believed that once the information is transferred from the trainer to the trainees, then the task of training is done and there is no further need for training unless the information changes. Rules and regulations are generally written by those who do not put them into practice everyday in every conceivable situation. We propose viewing staff education as "staff development" or "continuing education activities." This implies that developing a competent staff is a lifelong learning process that includes repeated refresher courses to update workers' knowledge and skills to reflect the ever-increasing knowledge about human development and functioning.

Chapter 9

When You Need to Place a Child Out of the Home

WE MET A CPS WORKER IN MICHIGAN WHO DESCRIBED HOW HE WORKED WITH parents so that the father voluntarily "surrendered" his four children personally in the judge's chamber. It took a considerable amount of effort and time to collaborate with the father, who was abusive, physically and verbally, to his children. The father initially objected and disagreed that his behavior was abusive or bad for the children, and the worker, Don McLeon, described the experience as "nip and tuck" in the beginning. Eventually, however, everyone agreed that "surrendering" the children for the time being was best for the children. The father also agreed that he needed some help controlling his anger and learning a gentler way of raising children. The father and Don agreed to meet at 10:00 A.M. at the courthouse, where the father would bring the children before the judge. This was the father's idea.

On the morning of the hearing all the usual participants at such hearings waited to see this unusual scene of a father willingly surrendering his children even though it was not his idea initially. Ten o'clock came; no client and no children. Everyone looked at Don with various expressions, ranging from dismay to disbelief. Knowing that the family did not have a car and had to rely on public transportation, Don pleaded with the judge to give them another 20 minutes. Sure enough, the family of six showed up a few minutes later. The children were all dressed in neat and clean clothes, each carrying a little bag of clothes, shoes, toys, and other belongings. The participants at the hearing were stunned, and Don breathed a sigh of relief.

It is not difficult to imagine that this father would be more willing than most to participate in visitations with the children and to use the time away from the children to learn to control his temper, discipline the children without resorting to abuse, and appreciate that raising children can brings joys as well as sacrifice. We learned that the family was reunited within a short time.

Removing children in an emergency situation and when their safety is in jeopardy is a difficult yet necessary part of every CPS worker's job. Many CPS workers and supervisors tell us that they object to the word "removal" to describe having to place children out of their homes; it reminds them of how we as a society think about children. "Removal" usually connotes something unwanted and undesirable, such as removing a cancerous tumor or garbage from the house. When asked what word they would use instead, one supervisor mentioned "separation," since what we are doing is separating children from their parents (S. Christofferson, personal communication, 1997). Occasionally the term "apprehension" is used, primarily by law enforcement officials and judges. Unable to come up with a more accurate word, we have decided to stick with "removal." Whatever we call it, it is a gut-wrenching aspect of CPS work. We frequently hear from workers how they lose sleep over it, wondering whether they made the right decision.

We have also met many experienced workers who have not only "removed" children but also worked with parents to successfully "terminate" parental rights without incurring their clients' anger. In fact, some workers have reported that a few parents have thanked them for removing the children and terminating their parental rights because of the respect with which they were treated. Some report getting hugs and handshakes at the end of the court hearing from parents who believe the best interests of their children were kept in mind. Removal of a child is commonly believed to be a harrowing, adversarial, and contentious experience, so we wondered: How can it be that some workers experience the opposite? How can application of the same laws and guidelines to similar populations produce such different reactions? The single most important factor may be how one follows the guidelines. When a worker collaborates with the parents and includes them in every step of the decision-making process, they experience the entire process as respectful of them and humane to the children.

Consider this situation. Two CPS workers with similar experience had very different track records of removing children during the first few months of 1998. Both applied the same law, worked in the same postal zone office, used the same "safety assessment" instrument adopted by the State, and had similar tenure of service in CPS. Yet one worker did not remove a single child, while the other removed 34 children. Both were working to insure the safety of children (Van de Kamp, 1998). Why such different outcomes? Even though the general trend in CPS is to be objective, guarding against the individual worker's tendency to use a personal standard to make judgments of neglect or abuse, we are still far from being "objective" and unbiased. It seems that we still rely a great deal on individual workers' discretion, judgment, and interpretation of what insures the safety of children. Such disparity between workers' actions also suggests that decisions about child safety are sometimes made by the worker alone, without collaboration with peers, parents, or caretakers of the child.

Although CPS is sometimes portrayed as the agency that "snatches babies" or "rescues victimized children," in reality such drastic action occurs in only 1 out of 10 investigations that have varying degrees of "substantiation." Yet, a careful look at the paperwork reveals that 90% of the information a worker must gather during investigation assumes that each investigation might lead to eventual removal of the children. In order to reflect the reality that removal of children is not what CPS predominantly does, we decided to place this chapter at the end of the book. It is inevitable that some children will be separated from their parents in order to insure their physical safety. In this chapter we offer some suggestions that will minimize the trauma and perhaps insure a potential long-term integrity of family ties.

CRISIS FOR THE PARENT

In our appropriate preoccupation with children's safety, we often overlook the crisis we create for the parents. Why not take such a crisis and turn it into an advantage for the children and parent? The classic crisis intervention model (Janis, 1969; Parad, 1965) postulates that the time of crisis is the best opportunity for change, as people are most open to possibilities at that time (Whittaker, Kinney, Tracy, & Booth, 1990). Thus, a potential removal can set the stage for changes in some parents. For others, however, it seems to compound the distress and immobilize them, asking for more change than their resources permit. Services can be offered to parents and children simultaneously even when children are removed. We need to ask: What changes are the parents willing to make to increase the chances of getting the children back?

Removal of children is not the end of the problem. It is the beginning of a different set of problems, for both the child and the parent. Why not address this issue immediately? For example, a parent who has a drinking problem will be more likely to admit it and ask for help now than later when she decides how angry she is at CPS. Many parents report that "losing" children to CPS was a "wake-up call" and the beginning of their sobriety process.

I (IKB) was invited to witness a potential removal of a family from their filthy house. The conditions in the home made it unsafe for the children to stay there. Apparently, while searching for a missing adolescent, the police stumbled upon a small bungalow in the working-class neighborhood and noticed a young child. The house smelled so bad that the police had to retreat out to the sidewalk. One of the officers said it was the filthiest house he had ever encountered in his long career. A case record check indicated that the mother had been cited for a dirty house two years earlier. A homemaker service had been provided to help the client clean up the house and the case was closed. We rushed over with a camera to document the degree of filth in the house, in the event it was contested in court.

When we arrived at the address, two policemen were waiting on the sidewalk, with a neatly dressed, heavily made-up young woman who was holding the hand of a little girl of about 5 years who appeared healthy and well taken care of. The mother, Ms. Carson, was surprisingly calm and composed, in view of the neighbors gawking at the police car, an official county government car, and strange people standing on the sidewalk. Ms. Carson seemed to be neither upset nor embarrassed in the least bit; she acted as if she was waiting for a friend, in a calm and friendly demeanor. With the mother in tow, the worker and I went inside and immediately understood the policemen's reaction. I have made numerous home visits at all hours of the day and night and encountered my share of "filthy" houses, but I have never seen a house as dirty and messy as this one. The smell was more than one could possibly tolerate. Garbage was piled high; at places it was difficult to guess how deep it was and I was afraid I would step on something that might make me sick. It appeared they ate lots of fast food. The worker and I looked at each other, and we both knew that immediate removal of human being—or even an animal—would be the proper thing to do. There was no other option. Garbage was several feet deep everywhere, the mold on cat food in a dish was several inches long, and the sink was overflowing with greasy pots, pans, dishes, and everything else you can imagine, while the faucet dripped. As we took pictures for evidence, the worker and I agreed immediately that the family needed to be transferred to a "welfare hotel" and the worker started checking on the availability of rooms at the motel the county used for emergencies such as this.

By the time the worker and I went outside, the police were gone and Ms. Carson blurted out that her mother had offered to help clean the house and in fact had helped her many times before. The worker ignored this comment and proceeded to tell Ms. Carson about her plan to move the family right now. The mother reported that her 6-year-old son would be coming home from school any minute and as soon as he got home, she would be ready to go. I was curious about how her son Bryan would look, whether he would be sickly, with flea bites or even rat bites on his body. He appeared a few minutes later, smiling broadly at his mother and sister outside. He did not ask any questions when told that he could not go inside the house and that his family would have to leave immediately. The worker offered to transport the three of them to the motel, which was not far away.

Imagine what the outcome of this case might have been if the workers were to take some time to talk with the mother as soon as the family was settled into the hotel. If her house was clean enough two years ago, it certainly means she can clean up the house again.

I am still baffled by the fact that the Carson family seemed healthy and the children seemed well cared for. I did not detect any indication that the children may not have been bathed or did not brush their teeth. I wondered how in the world the mother kept the children in clean clothes. There was no evidence in the house, not in the bathroom or in the children's bedroom, that there were clean towels or clothes for them. Where did she keep her makeup, which most women have difficulty keeping together? How did she keep her young children from being infected with so many possible diseases? Imagine the worker asking these questions and many others. How did Ms. Carson clean the house two years ago to such a degree that the department closed the case? What would it take for her to clean up the house again? What it would take to maintain the level of cleanliness of two years ago? What has she learned from her mother's help? What did she learn from the past experience that she can use now? How many days did Ms. Carson estimate it would take for her to clean the house? What would be helpful to get the house into a safe condition? Suppose the worker had asked these and other similar questions immediately after the removal of the children (and the mother) so that the parent could begin to think about what she really wanted to change in her life. We would include questions such as: What was the longest period you kept the house clean last time? What kind of help do you need to get the house safe enough for you and your children? How were you able to keep the house clean last time?

We have discussed holding clients accountable for change. This means taking advantage of these little successes, however small, and getting them to repeat those successes, rather than taking over the tasks ourselves. Insisting that the clients use knowledge and skills they already have leads to true empowerment. If the worker had set out to help Ms. Carson accomplish the cleaning on her own, then we might have seen meaningful change rather than just compliance.

ASSUMPTION OF COMPETENCE

Insuring the safety of the child is a complex, complicated, and uncertain endeavor. Nobody can guarantee the safety of children 100% of the time, despite what the public and politicians would like to believe. Child welfare promises more than can be delivered when they guarantee that all children can be safe all of the time. It is not a simple good parent/bad parent issue but a complex issue of the interplay among overwhelming social, racial, economic, and personal factors. Child neglect and abuse must be considered within the social context (Schorr, 1997); the traditional perspective of individual deficit or personality problems is insufficient. A more hopeful and promising approach is to see the solution as lying in the joint efforts of all segments of the society. It needs to involve teamwork between the parent, CPS, and the community.

There is consensus in the child welfare field that philosophical and political commitment as well as team spirit is needed for more successful and desirable outcomes (Farrow, 1996). Yet, the literature offers very few suggestions on how to turn this vision into reality. Emerging models of family group conferencing are attempting to address this need. It is also clear that it is easier said than done. However, we will try to give you some beginning ideas on how to implement this vision of insuring the safety of children by involving their parents in the safety plan to achieve a true partnership with the clients you serve. We remind you that it will not be accomplished with a policy change or an administrative directive; cultural change will be stimulated by changes in *how* we talk to each other and *how* we do the small, ordinary, and apparently insignificant things we do everyday on a consistent basis. It is said that being a student results in learning; being a teacher results in knowing (G. Rymarchyk, personal communication, 1999). We want our clients to be our teachers so that they can come to know themselves.

Forming a partnership means approaching parents, even those who are indeed unable to give the child the minimum level of needed care, as equal partners. It means informing, consulting with, and soliciting parents' ideas every step of the way, viewing parents as leading forces rather than as passive recipients of our services, and helping parents to create hope for a different future for their family while maintaining their dignity. Like any relationship, forming such a partnership requires work, persistence, and perseverance, and it can be done even when there is never enough time. Following are some helpful ways to form a partnership with a parent if removing the children is necessary.

Unless they are unavailable, include the parents and other family members in all discussions and decisions. You may choose to use family group conferencing. When there are no indications of serious abuse, including family, friends, or members of the faith community who the parent views as supportive can be helpful, especially in creating a safety plan that involves many helpers rather than just the parents. This kind of strategy surrounds a family with others who view family and child safety as a collective responsibility.

If there is no alternative but to remove the children, emphasize that the children are being removed for their safety, not because he or she is a bad parent. It must be clear, though, that apparently harmful behaviors and the inability of the parent to keep the child safe leaves the system no choice. Safety of the child must be a priority. Holding out hope that the child will be returned if the situation improves and behaviors change is helpful, unless it is clear that reunification cannot be accomplished. Parents often describe the removal of their children as "when I lost my children to CPS," the way other parents would say, "I lost my child to cancer," and with similar mixed expressions of sadness, anger, shame, and confusion. However, loss of a child to cancer is very different from loss of a child to "the system," a loss that parents perceive as being forced upon them against their wishes.

"Losing" a child to CPS is a public pronouncement that a parent has failed as a mother or a father. If the initial investigation drags on for weeks, the parent feels she cannot change the course of events. Many parents are too humiliated and embarrassed to make this event any more public than it already is. Even if some parents have the means and resources to contest the removal, the toll on the family is too great for most to bear. Many parents simply do not know what to do and give up on themselves and on their children. Almost all parents want this information kept private, no matter how mistreated they feel. Most clients, who are poor, uneducated, and unable to comprehend the complex bureaucracy of CPS, will certainly have difficulty navigating the system that is investigating them. A young mother described her experience of having her young children taken away by saying, "My kids are all I have." Her sense of failure was devastating. Her hope of "becoming somebody" through motherhood was dismissed in a single stroke; she felt demeaned to an extent that is difficult for most of us to imagine. While CPS must insure child safety, this does not preclude finding better ways to give information, point out what is happening, explain the delays and postponements, etc. Often parents become immobilized by anxiety when they are left in the dark about the process. When they feel mistreated by the system, some parents displace their anger onto their children, lashing out at them and withholding whatever affection they might feel.

The safety assessment should be made jointly with the parents. Unless there is an imminent and clear danger to the children, which is usually an extreme condition of neglect and abuse, the removal should not come as a surprise to the parent. It should be arrived at as the result of a negotiated, jointly assessed process. The parent and the worker can realistically assess the feasibility of the parent's insuring the safety of the children during the investigation period. The worker can assure that parents have knowledge of the consequence of their choices, for example, "If you continue to leave your child alone while you do drugs, I will have no choice but to remove him." When done this way, should a removal be necessary, it is more likely to be cooperative and collaborative in nature with the best interests of the child as the driving force.

One way to be sure your client can salvage her sense of dignity as a parent is for you to put yourself on the parent's side as soon as possible and see things from her perspective, while maintaining your ultimate goal of doing what is in the best interests of the child. This reminds you to be flexible and recognize that there are many different ways to get the outcome you both desire.

The burden of trying to understand each other is mutual; it does not all fall on clients' shoulders. In *The Spirit Catches You and You Fall Down,* Anne Fadiman (1997) gives a perceptive and sensitive account of a tragedy that occurred when Western medicine and the Hmong culture clashed. All those involved in the story wanted to do what was best for Lai Lee, a little girl with serious medical problems (frequent seizures). Yet, the very thoughtful, dedicated, and well-meaning medical practitioners did not know how to listen to the Hmong parents—in fact, they often issued orders and prescriptions without interpreters who could have functioned as "cultural brokers." Out of their repeated frustrations at what they perceived as "medical neglect," they eventually "apprehended" the child and placed her in a foster home, where her condition deteriorated. From the Hmong cultural perspective, a child with seizures has a special connection with the spiritual world. The parents adored and cared for Lai as a special gift from another world. The experts' inability to listen and to learn from the parents, as well as the parents' inability to learn from the experts, resulted in a tragic outcome for the little girl.

The more power you have, the greater difference you can make. We are always surprised to learn that most CPS workers feel that they have little power to shape their practices. Many feel limited and impeded by the enormous pressure to produce mountains of paperwork for the case files. Many feel rule-bound in their practices and kept from doing "social work." Some even report being told that their job is not "social worker" but investigator; that is, they should only dig out facts about child safety and document them. But take a moment to step back and observe what transpires between you and a family you investigate. You will realize not only how much power you hold in your hands but also how much "social work" you can do while staying within the rigid CPS policies, protocols, and rules. You have the power to make a parent feel competent and successful; you also have the power to devastate without saying a word. It is the obligation of those who have more to give more; the more power one has, the more careful we must be in its use. We must use our power wisely and effectively and do our work efficiently and sensitively, without flashing our badges and making raw or veiled threats. We want to make a difference in someone's life, but we must do no harm. Treat those with whom you work as well as you would want and deserve to be treated in the same situation.

Sometimes the best way to insure the safety of the child is to facilitate the mother's or caretaker's getting some respite—time and space to get herself together, collect energy, and establish priorities. While you are negotiating this, continue to build on whatever little evidence you have by reminding the parent that she seems to care about her child and want to do what is good for the child (if this is accurate). You may need to repeat this several times so that the parent is clear about your conviction about her love of her child and fitness as a parent and knows that you are not just trying to appease her. It is because she loves the child that you and the parent need *to think about the most loving thing any parent can do*, that is, ask someone else to parent the child temporarily.

Removal of a child, however, cannot be based on the need for parental respite, unless it is absolutely certain that the child is in peril in the home. Often what happens after a removal is that no further support or help is offered to the parent to effect a successful reunification. The removal then becomes an event of hopelessness rather than a trigger for behavior and environmental change.

Even while you are removing the child from a parent, be sure to keep in mind that *how* you carry out this difficult task makes a big difference in both the child and the parent now—and possibly in the future.

Educate while gathering information. In chapter 4 we discussed how gathering information can serve investigative, preventive, and intervention purposes, all at the same time. Similarly, any professional conversation you have with your clients can have more than one purpose. This dual aspect of conversation means that you can convey lots of educational information about child care and normal child development while learning as much as you can about the client's way of thinking about her world. Here are some examples:

- Most children at that age have nightmares after reading or watching monster stories or movies. Does your son wake up in the middle of the night with nightmares? How do you help him get back to sleep?
- Most young babies like to hear adults cooing and making baby talk. What have you noticed about your baby? How does your baby let you know that he likes it when you talk to him? How do you calm your baby when she is difficult to handle?
- Most young children like to use big muscles when they play, like jumping, running, hitting, pulling, and so on. What about your son, is he like that?
- Many toddlers at your son's age can pull themselves up by hanging onto furniture. Does your Brian do that yet?
- Many mothers have one of those days when they feel like running away from it all (giving away their children). What do you find helps you to cope with those moments?

This kind of questioning imparts information on what the norm is and then teaches the parent to gauge where her child fits within a normal developmental stage, without offending and demeaning her. Such comments also elicit concerns or lack of knowledge the parent may have, which you can then address in your next comment.

Begin with a posture of not knowing. Whenever a drastically new idea is introduced to CPS workers, they quite logically wonder, "Will this new approach violate existing rules?" and "How will this alter the procedures?" We have encountered much skepticism to the notion of taking a "not-knowing" posture with clients. The notion of having to be "on top of everything about the client," as many workers told us, particularly when they show up in court, seems to have reinforced this need to know the minute details of clients' problems over the past years. Perhaps more accurately, most workers believe that the courts demand that they know everything there is to know about a client. Usually this means repeating all the failures and not focusing on how this family has managed to keep itself together for so long. It is easy to understand this skeptical response from workers who have lived in an "only the facts, ma'am" world: A not-knowing stance is the very opposite of the way workers must project themselves when testifying

in courts, dealing with schools, or writing reports and recommendations to the legal system. It seems that most workers have taken their
long years of training to heart and firmly believe that "it is my job to
know everything that's wrong with the parent." Of course, when you
must present a document in court and stand by this document, it only
makes sense to be as accurate and precise as you can, with a great
many details to back you up. However, generally workers are not
taught to document the strengths of the successful behaviors, only
the worst of conditions. This tendency to document the defects so
thoroughly makes it especially important to us to be clear about this
idea of taking a position of not-knowing.

When we suggest taking a not-knowing posture with clients, we do
not mean that we do not know a great deal about human and child
development, what goes into nurturing a child so that he becomes a
healthy and productive member of society, what makes a good family
within our cultural context, or the optimal benefit one gets from living
in a supportive and nurturing environment, and so on. We mean that
when faced with this particular family, parent, or child, it is easy for
us to say, "I don't know what will work best for you and what will
be the best way for you, in your environment, with your background,
how it will work for you and your children." It is beginning with a
clean slate and a genuine respect for this individual and unique family.
For example, because of this willingness to listen to the client's idea
of what would be helpful to him, one CPS worker agreed to accept a
client's invitation and sat down at the client's kitchen table and prayed
with him and the children before driving off with his children to a
temporary placement.

With this posture, we are more likely to assist the client going
through some very tough experiences. Clients will be more willing to
volunteer useful information and form a cooperative working relationship. This will pave the way for collaboration with the parents on
behalf of the children, who are likely to face the enormous challenge
of adapting to the strange environment.

To return to our discussion of removal of children, this not-knowing
posture (Anderson & Goolishan, 1992, and as explained by DeJong &
Berg, 1998) is most useful during the early phases of investigation.
Rather than secretly collecting and gathering information, when clients
can easily spot your subtle shading of language, tone of voice, and other
subtle nuances that betray your suspicion, it is much more productive to
approach most clients at the earliest possible time with a posture of
inviting the client to give you information about herself, her life, and
her children. As many experienced workers tell us, within a very short
time it becomes clear that certain cases are heading in the direction of

removal. Even if you are expecting the case will inevitably reach the court, be honest and up front with the client, without threatening or issuing injunctions. It is very useful to let clients know what may be the likely outcomes of their choices. Most clients are intelligent enough to know that you are not "out to get them" but are working under the legal mandate to assure the safety of his or her child. Statistics show that most removals occur somewhere between four to six weeks after first opening a case. Being as open as possible with clients about their future during this phase of interaction is the most ethical way of working. Solution-building in a collaborative manner with the client means that you will need to bring up the possibility of removal because of abuse or neglect early in the process.

A cooperative, collaborative relationship results in a better quality of information. Even when you are moving in the direction of a removal, you want to maintain a cooperative and collaborative relationship with the client. In her study of drug-addicted mothers and their children, Jiordano (in press) described mothers who were arrested during the night and told to show up in court for the custody hearing for their children the next morning. Somehow they managed to show up, having broken through red tape and other difficulties. When a worker commented on the mothers' desire to have an input into their children's future, their willingness to go through so much trouble in order to be present at the hearing, and their desire to participate in decision-making on what is good for them—signs that they cared about their children—the mothers often either broke into tears or began to talk about how important their children were to them.

Complimenting means seeing beyond the negatives and apparent contradictions, as the workers in Jiordano's study did. Even when a mother has been arrested for drug dealing, prostitution, forgery, and a multitude of other offenses, the worker may still see the positive ways she cares for her children and point this out to her when she needs it the most. The outcome of such conversations is that workers are seen as helpers who still need to gather facts. When there is some element of respect and trust, workers are more likely to obtain full and accurate information. Contrary to a common belief that clients are evasive, deny responsibility for the problem, or blame others for their mistakes, our experience of working with people reputed to be difficult to work with, such as substance-abusing parents, sexual offenders, or physically abusive spouse, is that most people know that what they are doing is wrong, that it is harmful to their children, and that they should not be doing it; in general, they are interested in "confessing their sins." Often they want to change those destructive behaviors and improve the lives of their children and families.

Therefore, always approach clients as if they will be cooperative and want to do what is right and good for their children. By laying out what you heard, observed, or were told by others, you offer clients many possible ways to respond. When clients feel they have options, they do not feel cornered or threatened. Bringing up others' concerns and asking questions in a nonprovocative manner lets the caretaker know that there are others besides you who are concerned about the children's welfare. In the following dialogue, the worker voices concerns but does not accuse the mother.

Worker: Ms. Baylor, I am rather confused. Maybe you could straighten me out. Although I have known you for a short time, many things you say you have done for your children strike me as the kinds of things a conscientious mother would do. But as you know I am here because there are some people who seem to be concerned that your children need to be taken care of better. Any ideas about how to reassure these people that you are doing your best?

The worker asks Ms. Baylor for help in straightening out his confusion. He then establishes his impression that her report of what she has been doing for her children is what most "conscientious mothers" would do. This labeling demands that Ms. Baylor live up to this designation once she agrees with it. The worker then elicits ways to "reassure these people," thus putting her in charge of reassuring others rather than defending against others' accusations. This is a much more empowering and assertive stance than taking a defensive posture.

Ms. B: I can't imagine who would spread a rumor like that about me. I have always tried to do my best to take care of my kids—all four of them—which isn't always easy, you know. They fight all the time and the youngest one wets the bed every night. It is so much work but I can't imagine who would spread such vicious rumors about me. I just mind my own business. Who is telling you such lies?

Even though the worker approached the client very gingerly, she still wants to present herself as a hardworking mother who is overwhelmed with the burden of raising difficult children. The worker does not have the option of responding to the client's demand because of the confidentiality clause; however, observe what happens when the worker sidesteps her requests and validates her difficult life, and then immediately changes the topic to his original question about others' concerns.

Worker: I can tell that you work hard to take care of your children. It's a lot of work, of course. Do you suppose someone might have misunderstood something they saw you do or heard or something like that?

The worker agrees with and validates the client's subjective experience of working hard and trying to be a good parent. He immediately returns to his original topic of "misunderstandings" others have about her parenting.

Ms. B: You know, I do have a temper, I always have, since I was a kid. I really should be more careful with the children. Maybe somebody in the neighborhood saw me yelling at one of the kids. I know calling them names hurts the kids. I almost hit him but somehow I managed to stop myself from going that far.

It may be surprising to you that Ms. Baylor arrived at this conclusion so quickly. However, at some level all clients like Ms. Baylor know that they are doing something they do not feel good about and that what they have attempted to do to remedy the situation is not working. In this exchange, the worker "stayed out of the client's way" and allowed her to arrive at her own conclusion. Now that Ms. Baylor has admitted she has a quick temper ("since I was a kid"), she and the worker can work together to determine what to do about her temper.

When you begin with a tentative question, as the worker did in the above dialogue, you are offering educational information that you and the client can use as a starting point. Notice how the worker set aside the client's demand to know who reported her as unfit mother and yet the client did not argue or insist on answers from the worker. Also notice how the client's tone softened and she became more thoughtful about her parenting skills, almost immediately shifting the topic to herself. It is easy to imagine Ms. Baylor asking for some help with the tough job of raising four children by herself, with her lifelong temper and her tendency to yell at the children. This kind of introspection is very common and it usually happens fairly early in the conversation. This kind of conversation also helps to gather important information about the level of risk and safety concerns.

WHAT ABOUT ANGRY AND HOSTILE CLIENTS?

We are often asked this question during the training and consultation sessions, especially when a removal of children is involved. Many workers seem to view this removal process as invariably ending in extreme confrontation with an adversarial show of force. They rightly worry that clients will walk all over them if they perceive the worker as naive and weak or a pushover, and feel they must maintain a tough exterior in order to let the client know that they know their business and will not be hoodwinked. It is easy to imagine how such a worker will come across to the client, which in turn will perpetuate the worker's self-fulfilling prophecy—and then this same worker will feel justified in maintaining this posture. Before long, the worker is likely to feel burned out; he or she may feel a much higher level of stress on the job than his or her colleagues with similar caseloads and a different attitude.

If your caseload seems to be filled with angry clients who are difficult to work with and you spend much of your energy battling with them, perhaps there is something you can do differently. We suggest discussing it with your supervisor, a consultant, or a trustworthy colleague who seems to enjoy his or her work. Also, read chapter 4, where we discuss angry and hostile clients in more depth.

WHAT ABOUT PARENTS WHO SEE NOTHING WRONG WITH THEIR PARENTING?

We are asked this question from time to time. If you keep asking yourself this question, perhaps this is a good time to stop and review the process. Should your language be more tentative? If your clients are always arguing defensively, could you be on the wrong track? We suggest that you not argue with clients, but turn their response into a question. Notice the differences between the following dialogues.

Worker: Mr. Taylor, do you know that it is against the law to hit your child across the mouth with a closed fist?

Mr. T: What do you mean? Are you telling me that I can't discipline my own kid to make sure that he don't talk back to his parents using swear words? Who says so? Who are you to barge in here and tell me what to do in my own house, with my own kid?

Worker: There are laws now that say that corporal punishment is against the law.

Mr. T: Do they now? What, now the government is going to come to an upstanding citizen's house and look under every bed and make sure I can't discipline my own child who don't know how to behave himself? Is that what you are telling me?

Worker: If we hear any more reports of Andy's being physically pun-
　　　　ished and coming to school with those bruises on his arms and
　　　　back, we may have to take a drastic step.

Mr. T: Is that so? Are you saying you are going to come and yank my
　　　　kid from my house just because I am trying to be a good parent?
　　　　I never heard such a thing! You do that and let's see what happens.

Worker: I am just making sure that your son Andy is safe.

Mr. T: Well, a few bruises on his back is not going to kill him. I grew
　　　　up with a belt now and then, and I don't see any harm in a boy
　　　　growing up with some discipline. I grew up with that and nothing
　　　　bad happened to me—I didn't become a jailbird or nothing.

*A battle of wills and an escalation of threats are not good for the child or the
worker. Notice how the tone of the conversation changes when the worker
uses a different approach with Mr. Taylor.*

Worker: I understand you've been having some difficulty with your
　　　　son Andy lately. Is that right?

*By putting Mr. Taylor's difficulty with Andy as a current, not necessarily
lifelong problem, the worker immediately places herself on his side. "Having
some difficulty with Andy" implies that the problem is between father and
son and this is the kind of difficulty any parent is likely to encounter sometime
in his parenting experience. The tone this sentence conveys is that of a sympathetic CPS worker talking to a father who wants things to be different from
how they are now.*

Mr. T: You're darn right. He's getting a big head and he thinks he
　　　　knows it all, and now that he is hanging out with those tough
　　　　kids, he thinks he can do anything he wants to do, like his no-
　　　　good friends. Their parents are divorced and these kids are raised
　　　　by their mothers who are out in the bar every night and don't
　　　　know what their kids are up to. If Andy thinks he can act like
　　　　those kids he hangs out with, he has more belts coming.

*Observe how quickly the father agrees with the worker. He then implies feeling
unable to control his son, further blaming his son's problem on other kids
who come from bad families. Mr. Taylor even volunteers his theory of social
problems, and in the process he separates himself from the other parents and
tries to establish himself as a very concerned parent.*

Worker: I can see that you really want Andy to grow up right and
　　　　you want to give him the proper guidance.

*The worker validates the preferred view that Mr. Taylor has of himself and
implies that the father wants his son to grow up right, whatever that means*

to Mr. Taylor. She supports Mr. Taylor's view of himself as a good parent, shown by his desire to give Andy "proper guidance."

Mr. T: Of course. Nowadays parents don't care about their kids; they think they are good parents if they just buy them video games and give them a computer.

Mr. Taylor has affirmed his desire to be a good parent. Any future discussion of changes in his approach with Andy can be framed as another way to be a good parent.

Worker: So, you have very strong ideas about being a good parent.

The worker validates one more time that Mr. Taylor wants to be a good parent, without challenging or calling into question whether this is true or not. Observe his responses.

Mr. T: Of course, that's why I try to watch out for his friends, make sure that he does his school work, learns to do chores around the house, gets to bed on time, and not get so wild. I try to do my job right.

Worker: I can see that you really want to make sure that he learns enough discipline. You have done lots of things and have been thinking a lot about how to make this happen.

Mr. T: You're damned right. I figure it's a father's job and he needs a firm hand.

Worker: So, how well are these approaches working, would you say?

Having established that Mr. Taylor has all the good intentions to be a good parent, the worker can challenge him on whether what he is doing with Andy is accomplishing his desired outcome. The worker continues to use a tentative tone.

Mr. T: Well, they are not working very well. Andy is a smart boy but he is using his brains in the wrong way. If he would only think about using his brains in the right way, he could be a brain surgeon.

This is the first hint that Mr. Taylor is acknowledging that his own strong ideas are not producing the desired results. He finally gives credit to his son for having a good brain, thus implying that he needs some other method of discipline to challenge his "smart boy."

Worker: So, how well would you say it is working, I mean, how you've been trying to help Andy go in the right direction?

Still maintaining the tentative posture, and with a stance of curiosity, the worker does not accept Mr. Taylor's answer and revisits the question of how well it is working. It is very important that the worker maintain a posture of curiosity, even though the temptation to lecture the father and point out his mistakes is great.

Mr. T: I must say it's not working very well and that's why I lost it, you know, my temper, the other day when I really let him have it with a belt. I know the belt is not the answer for kids like Andy. You know, the kids are different nowadays.

For the first time, Mr. Taylor feels safe enough to blurt out his mistakes and acknowledge his temper and is now ready to talk about his use of the belt and how badly he feels about his use of force on a smart child like Andy.

Worker: What do you mean, someone like Andy?

Still maintaining his view that Mr. Taylor is the expert on his son, and also to reinforce the philosophy that only Mr. Taylor can change his behavior, the worker asks for more information about Andy.

Mr. T: Well, he is a very stubborn kid, wants to do things his way or no way, and I don't know how to reach him because he is just like me in many ways.

This is the first admission from Mr. Taylor (which took a great deal of courage) that he does not "know how to reach" a child like Andy. It is clear that he identifies strongly with Andy's stubbornness ("he is just like me") and is indirectly asking for help on "how to reach him."

As these dialogues illustrate, two different conversations between the same two people can turn out to be very different in tone and outcome. The effect depends a great deal on what the worker decides to ignore (criticism of other parents) and to focus on, and how she phrases things in such a way that it is easy for Mr. Taylor to acknowledge that his approach is not working and that he needs help in this regard. Of course, it is important for the worker to be sensitive and not intrude on other aspects of his life, such as asking about his childhood or how he was abused by his parents, etc., until he gives clues that he is ready to discuss them. The worker must insure Andy's safety now—not look for causes of a parent's behavior. Often workers try to figure out *why* someone acts the way he or she does (past neglect, abused as a child, etc.) instead of focusing on the necessary, behaviorally specific changes.

The second conversation was more productive because the worker began with the assumption that Mr. Taylor is a caring and concerned parent. The worker addressed Mr. Taylor's fatherly concerns about his son, thus addressing what is important to this father—to find an approach that will direct his smart son to use his good brain in the right direction. Mr. Taylor responded to this stance, eventually voicing his doubts about the way he has been managing Andy. The father finally blurts out that he identifies with Andy and is worried about his future. The worker also learned that he was frustrated with his inability to reach his obviously smart son, and that using the belt was a last-resort effort to find something that would work. By staying calm, listening, and following the father's lead, the worker was able to assess the situation and gather information about what was important to this father, thus avoiding an adversarial confrontation. Even if a worker assesses that the parent is unable or unwilling to raise a child, such information may emerge much sooner when the worker takes a position of sincere curiosity and wanting to see the world from the parent's perspective.

HOLDING NON-OFFENDING PARENTS RESPONSIBLE

When extreme physical or sexual abuse is suspected or alleged, the usual policy is to demand unquestioned cooperation from the non-offending parent immediately. This is particularly so when the medical exam does not fit with the caretaker's description of how the injury might have happened or when the non-offending parent (usually female) refuses to cooperate with the authority or speak against her offending partner right away. The medical team and CPS workers may pressure the non-offending parent to corroborate the medical evidence, especially when a very young, vulnerable child is involved or there is extreme abuse. For obvious reasons the pressure to pinpoint the guilty one becomes extremely urgent when severe injury is reported or a criminal prosecution is a possibility.

We suggest that workers in such situations view the non-offending parent as perhaps holding a key to solving the serious problem rather than as hiding and protecting the guilty partner. As we have learned more about the strategies of non-offending parents, we have become more convinced that non-offending victims are often trying their best to keep the child safe. Taking this view means soliciting and eliciting information in a respectful way so that the non-offending parent wants to participate in finding ways to insure the safety of children. The CPS worker may need to establish a cooperative relationship with the non-offending parent first, and then—at times *only* then—gently move toward a factual account. During this second phase of the interaction, the non-offending parent may provide the information to help the workers assess whether she is capable of making sure that the child will be safe.

Corcoran (1998) asserts that many clinical reports and much of the literature have been quick to infer maternal culpability, especially in sexual abuse cases. The prevailing view of these mothers has been negative, as though they were all alike, despite clinical experiences indicating that the responses of non-offending parents are varied and should not be generalized. Newberger, Gremy, Watermaux, and Newberger (1993) assert that non-offending mothers experience a considerable degree of stress and distress. They also report what most workers have known all along: A child recovers faster and there are short-term and long-term positive effects when the non-offending parent has support and is better adjusted herself. It may be true that mothers who do not believe their child's story of abuse are contributing to the abuse. At the same time, it is our clinical experience that most mothers are tremendously conflicted in their role as central support and nurturer to both the child and the offending partner. Often their social, emotional, and economic support systems are threatened and uprooted before their eyes.

The mother faces difficult choices that should not be taken lightly. She needs to be supported as she tries to sort out a variety of issues: What has been her role in neglecting or being blind to the abuses going on in her environment? How she will respond to the world that is falling apart around her? How quickly she can change her mind-set and behavior so that she can insure the safety of the child? Unless the issues and dynamics are understood, they are subject to misinterpretation. Using "failure to protect" against the non-offending parent is not providing support or care to the child in the long term. We believe that in most cases the offending parent should be held accountable instead of the non-offending parent being inappropriately sanctioned.

A case involving an "uncooperative" mother of a very young child with a severe head injury came to our attention. The child was being treated in an intensive care unit of a children's hospital. Even though it was apparent that the mother was extremely distraught, upset, and pained by her child's precarious medical condition, she refused to answer any questions about how the child was injured. She insisted that she was not in the house at the time of the injury, which was easily corroborated by other factual accounts. The mother spent three days hovering over her child, clearly very worried about the unfolding information concerning the prognosis for recovery. Yet she did not buckle under the tremendous pressure from police, medical personnel, and the hospital staff. The professional staff began to be suspicious and irritated with the mother, insinuating that she might need to be charged and the child removed from her care because of her uncooperative behavior and that she was clearly protecting whoever the abuser was.

A thoughtful and observant CPS worker, realizing that not one family member, friend, or neighbor had visited the mother or the child during the three days since the hospitalization, recognized a pattern of social isolation, consistent with domestic violence. She decided to build a relationship with the mother separate from her role as an informant on the abuser. The worker chose to address the mother as a thoughtful, caring parent, instead of a possible accessory to the abuse. The worker approached the mother and in a calm, soothing, and sympathetic voice asked how she was hanging in there when she must be very worried about her baby. The worker wondered where she got the strength to go through this ordeal, with no apparent support from anyone. She must have been worried sick about her baby.

Hearing this, the mother burst into sobs. She cried for a long time, as if expressing all her worries, anxieties, and fears about her child. Finally, between her tears and sobs, the mother related that her boyfriend is very abusive to her and had threatened to kill her and the baby if she told anyone about how the child was really injured. She further described how she felt caught between a rock and a hard place. She was confused, afraid, and didn't know what to do. This was the small but significant beginning of a cooperative working relationship with the non-offending parent. Serious work with this mother was just beginning. How would she protect herself and then what steps would she need to take to protect her child? Who could she get support from (family, friends, faith community)? What realistic ideas did she have about how to become independent economically? What would she like to see happen to herself and the baby? She began to address these questions while she waited for the medical outcome of her child. Such decisions could not be made quickly, especially when the mother was in a state of shock, fear, and confusion.

A non-offending mother's tentativeness about the fact of abuse is not necessarily an indication that she does not love her child or that she approves of the abuse. Mothers are often heard muttering to themselves, "I can't believe he would do this" or "I don't believe this is happening." As a worker, you can connect with the mother's emotional state, bewilderment, incomprehension, or worries about her child's safety. Ask her how she is coping or who is helpful to her at the time of extreme distress. This may enable the mother to move on to providing useful information.

It is easy to forget, at times, that the non-offending parent is just as upset and worried about her child's injury as we are, if not more so. This is particularly so when the injury is extreme, life-threatening, unusually cruel, and inhumane. The mother of this baby was in a very tough situation, trying to decide on the course of action that would be least harmful for her child and herself. She was also looking ahead, imagining how to have a life without abuse or threat of further abuse. Usually domestic violence programs can provide legal and other needed support and shelter as well. At times, we are so focused on how we would like the outcome to be that we forget about the mother, who is perhaps at a loss as to what might be the best decision to make.

PRESSURE TO BELIEVE THE CHILD'S STORY IMMEDIATELY

The rush to support victims who have been abused by the mother's partner has had, at times, the unanticipated effect of driving a wedge between the mother and older child, just when the child needs the mother's support and help most. It is difficult to make a quick decision to "throw the bum out," especially if the mother-child relationship was strained before the disclosure. It is important for the worker to realize that the mother is in a state of shock. Her life has literally turned upside down overnight. She needs time to re-establish her equilibrium and make plans for the future of the family as well as for herself.

Not all mothers are able to believe the child's story immediately, especially when there has been longstanding conflict between the mother and daughter. Disclosure of such a horrible secret is a terrible reality that many mothers are not willing or ready to accept. Not only does such disclosure place an enormous burden on the mother to solve the problem the daughter is facing, but it also devalues her identity as a mother, a woman, and a partner in a relationship that she might have tried to hang onto. It is a tremendous blow to realize that she may have misjudged her partner, with whom she had hoped to build a long-term relationship. She may begin to question her own judgment and herself: How could I have missed something? Have I been deluding myself about this man, about my daughter? What's wrong with me that my partner is not honest with me, that he could not come and talk to me about this? Where have I failed? It must be my fault. She must sort things out before she can decide what course of action to take. It would be impossible for anybody to come to a fast decision under such circumstances, and it is unreasonable to demand that the mother quickly declare on which side of the fence she will invest her future. Such doubts and uncertainties are compounded when the mother is socially isolated, as most mothers in such dire straits tend to be. It is important to remember that there is life beyond investigation, recrimination, shame, guilt, and punishment. The worker must balance the mother's need to be clear-headed and the demand on her to rise to the occasion and become competent and effective in protecting her child.

THE AFTERMATH OF DISCLOSURE OF SEXUAL ABUSE

Any criminal activity needs to be brought to the attention of law enforcement authorities. Workers usually don't have discretion about whether legal action should be pursued. However, if legal action is not warranted, these steps may be helpful:

1. *Take small steps for the daughter.* In most states, the alleged offender is immediately ordered to separate from the child and a mandate for no contact goes into effect. Do not insist that the mother or the daughter make huge decisions regarding the future quickly. Because of the enormity of the implications and potential problems, everybody feels a great deal of pressure to make decisions immediately. Instead, break everything into small, easily manageable pieces. At times, people do not know what they want to do until they have made a small movement. Being sensitive to this need to slow down the process may prevent making decisions that could compound the problem. The questions below will help you to slow down the process so that you can thoughtfully give control to the daughter or, when the child is young, her mother, every step of the way. The child has felt no control over what happens to her, including the abuse, for a long time; now it is a good time to change such interactions.

Using the following questions will help you decide how best to guide the daughter and, perhaps more important, how to listen to her. They can be adapted to fit the child's age (we focus on teenagers here) and her ability to comprehend the questions. When a young child is involved, a worker can easily adapt these questions for the mother. ("Suppose your child had words to explain how she wants to be taken care of . . . ?") As always, we support and recognize the child's coming forth with information and telling a parent, friend, or someone in school. Then we ask:

- What kind of help do you need right now?
- Is there someone you want to be with tonight? How would that person be helpful to you?
- What about school tomorrow? Do you feel you can handle going to school tomorrow? Do you have a good friend you want to talk to? (Follow up with "How would that be helpful?")
- What about other children in the family—should they be told or not? Who will tell them? What kinds of words would you use to describe what happened? What about the relatives?

2. *Take care of small needs for the mother.* Since the non-offending parent plays a pivotal role in holding their lives together, it is important to involve the mother as soon as possible. When abuse is revealed the non-offending parent is under considerable stress (Newberger et al., 1993); however, when the parent works through her safety plan and makes decisions about the situation, she will be better able to protect her abused and vulnerable child. The following questions may be helpful to support the non-offending parent so that she can in turn support her child, who will need her trust and support for a long time to come.

- What do you need for yourself to cope today?
- Which would be more helpful to you, being alone or talking to someone? If you want to talk to someone, who?
- What are some small things you can do to get through the day? (night?)
- What do you want to tell your child (if the child is interested in talking to the mother) about how you feel about what you found out?
- What do you need to hear (know about) from your daughter? How will that be helpful?
- Since you know your child better than anybody, what are some of your ideas of how best to be helpful to her?

Helping the mother sort out these issues prepares her to actively participate in designing and shaping strategies that would be most helpful to the daughter. At the same time, it is normal for her to be skeptical about the child's disclosure of sexual abuse, because it may mean not only that the mother has been negligent but also that her relationship with the alleged offending adult was dishonest, secretive, and unhealthy.

Whenever abuse is revealed, there are many overwhelming issues for the mother to sort out. She may not be in a stable emotional state, especially if she has few supportive persons in her life. A worker can help the mother sort out what information she needs to begin to believe the child and what difference that is going to make for her.

By establishing a positive relationship with the mother, the worker may be able to obtain assessment information. We believe that a good assessment includes not only a listing of problems but also suggestions for how to proceed (Berg, 1994). A worker may learn that at this point in her life the mother does not have the capacity to change her behavior enough to protect the child. It is always helpful for the worker to see the mother as potentially a part of the problem—and of the solution. When a worker presents both putting the child's needs first and maintaining a relationship with the alleged abuser as viable choices, without pressuring the mother, she may decide to re-examine her relationship with the offender

3. *Take small steps for the family.* Again, if the child's safety is assured for the time being, the important point to remember is not to make major decisions; just make small, step-by-step decisions to enable the family members to feel safe and comfortable. It is best to involve the older children, if available, in such decision-making. This will help you to identify family strengths end resources and ideas for how to capitalize on those.

4. *Involve family members in every step of healing and recovery.* When you begin to see the family members as a resource, it becomes easier to work with them. Even young children can become an important source of valuable information for your ongoing assessment as the case moves along. Your goal in working with the family is to maintain its cohesiveness and integrity as a unit, if possible. When a crisis such as this happens, you want to be careful so that family members do not turn on each other with accusations and scapegoating, which could have a very destructive effect and result in the family's being "tattered and ripped apart," as one mother described the aftermath of a disclosure of sexual abuse. This is a very difficult time for everyone, including other children in the family. A worker can help by emphasizing how important it is for the family members to be patient with one another. Highlighting the evident strengths in the family and working to support appropriate cohesive bonds can be extremely useful to the family.

This kind of crisis can easily tear a family apart if a worker or a counselor focuses only on pathology and deficits. Some blaming and conflict may be inevitable in the beginning, but structuring a family group conference can keep family members from blaming and become destructive. It may be helpful to bring in other family members, identified by the victim and non-offending parent, for a group conference, where very clear guidelines are set forth to handle conflict and make decisions about future actions. When their conflict is habitual and longstanding, suggest family therapy, self-help, pastoral counseling, or individual and couple therapy.

WHILE YOU REMOVE THE CHILD

Removal of children from unsafe and abusive adults is only part of the journey toward long-lasting solutions and stability for the child. The unfortunate practice of separating the CPS and foster care programs administratively and often physically has reinforced CPS workers' belief that their task ends with the removal of the child. Unless CPS workers have experience and have seen the long-term consequences of removal, both positive and negative, they may believe that the child's problems are solved, at least for the time being. Now, they say, the child is safe. Removal, however, initiates a new set of issues for the child. How do we go beyond safety to protect the child's emotional attachments to the parent? This is especially important for infants and children under age 3. We believe the greatest challenge to CPS and foster care is how to insure both physical *and* emotional safety and health of young children. For many young children the removal from one caretaker to another can be damaging. A child may appear to go through emotional withdrawal, with devastating and long-lasting results. Therefore, it is crucial that the CPS worker involve the parent, if at all possible, while removing the child.

Birth parents need to know their rights to visitation and what they can do to begin the process of reunification while diminishing the risk that led to the removal. Often state laws dictate the minimum visitation to which a birth parent has a right; for example, in Michigan it is once every seven days. Informing parents repeatedly, in clear, simple language, how important they are to the child will motivate them to overcome obstacles. Also, CPS workers can immediately address the realistic logistics of frequent visits with the child.

It is commonly believed that the more frequent and longer the visits with the child, perhaps three or more times a week, the better the chances of maintaining the emotional bond with the parent. Consequently, we believe that the common one-hour supervised visit once every other week or even once a month in an office setting is woefully inadequate for all children, but particularly so for younger ones. This becomes especially troublesome when parents are unable or unwilling to make arrangements to remain in close contact with the child in care. When such close contact with the parent is missing, it is hoped that these children will become attached to foster care parents. The possible consequences of missing visitations should be set clearly to the parent, without threat or labeling.

For older children, who have memories of both positive and negative experiences with their parents, regular visits, phone calls, letters, and other means of staying in contact with the parent are important. The worker should also inform the children about the most recent court decision, what might be the next step, and how much progress and effort their parents are making toward getting them back home.

Being uprooted from one's surroundings is traumatic at all ages, but particularly so when the abusive and neglectful parent is the only adult the child has bonded with. In addition, even abusive and neglectful parents are not always so. There may have been many tender and loving moments between the parent and the child. When older children who are prone to running away from home are placed in foster homes or other alternative care, frequently they *run home to* their biological parent or siblings.

Such mundane but important tasks as learning new faces, names, rules, foods, bedtime routines, customs around dinner, where and when to do homework, whether to leave the light on in the hallway, and how to take turns in the bathroom in the morning—all these complicate their lives. They wonder how to make sure that their parents are doing okay. If a child is separated from her siblings, how will she contact them? When and how will they call or visit each other? Will the child be able to see her friends? Will she have to make new friends? What kind of friends will she have in the new school? What about the teacher? Will she be nice? Youngsters not only wonder about everything in their environment but also worry about their siblings and their parent's new life without them. Often children as young as 7 or 8, and especially adolescents, have been caretakers for their parents, so it is natural for them to wonder how everyone is holding up.

In order to reduce the uncertainty and the intense anxiety most children experience when they are abruptly moved from one place to another, we offer some suggestions:

- Allow the child to take as many favorite items as possible—a special shirt, shoes, toys, lunch box, etc. Parents can participate (when available and able) in the selection of special toys and other items that the child might like to have with her. Family pictures, picture of his or her school, and special documents such as a copy of a birth certificate stand as reminders to children that they have "roots" and a history.
- If the community has a group of emergency shelters or foster care facilities, there may be descriptive picture books available showing

the outside of the house where the child will live, foster parents and siblings, the child's bedroom, even a pet dog or a cat. Show these pictures as you transport him. Also, talk about the neighborhood the child will live in, even if it's for a short time. Any pertinent information will cushion the transition.

- Help the child make a list of things he wants the caretakers to know about him, including: favorite food for breakfast or dinner, favorite games or TV shows, favorite shirt or shoes, what he is best at in school, best friend's name, favorite activities, bedtime rituals, and so on. Knowing what makes the child unique will help the new adult in the child's life smooth the transition a little. The parent can also make a list of information about the child that he or she believes would be helpful for the new caretaker to know.

- Always inform the child about any new development that affects her life and solicit her ideas and reactions. For example, when you do not know how the court will respond, whether the placement will be a stable situation or for a very short duration, update the child on possible changes. While doing so, ask the child what her thoughts are, what her preferences are, and allow time to discuss these unknown factors and answer any questions in as simple and honest a manner as possible. Shielding the child or adults from potential bad news is not really protecting him or her; it compounds mistrust and increases anxiety. We find that children can handle unknown situations quite well when they are surrounded by calm, supportive adults who inform them every step of the way.

- If you are aware of any problems the child has, such as bedwetting, bad dreams, difficulty falling asleep at bedtime, speech difficulties, medical problems such as asthma or juvenile diabetes, or other needs requiring special care, find out from the child what has helped the most and how much the child is able to take of himself. This will be valuable information for the temporary caretaker so that disruption in care is minimized.

- Make sure that everyone involved in taking care of the child avoids talking about the child's parents in demeaning or derogatory terms. Children, even those badly abused by their parents, want their parents to be treated with respect and dignity.

Removal of children is traumatic not only to the children, but to the parent as well. Parents usually feel it is a crisis created by CPS against their wishes—as is true in most situations. Naturally it is appropriate that the worker's focus immediately turns to what the child needs, thus neglecting what the parents need. It is easy for CPS workers to believe that the crisis was brought on by parents themselves. There are very few services offered to a mother or caretaker whose children have been taken from her. Working from the assumption that crisis as a catalyst for change, a CPS worker who has training in crisis and trauma management could stay with the parent long enough to help her understand the implications of what has just happened and suggest ways that the parent can begin the process of changing behaviors immediately. This would give the parent a goal to work toward, a way to mobilize her energy and begin the change process immediately. (Keep in mind that her resolve may change several times during the coming weeks and months.) Not only is this kind of helping behavior a humane approach, but it is also efficient and effective in utilizing the opportunity to change as a step toward reunification with the children.

PLANTING THE SEED FOR REUNIFICATION

The majority of children (80%) who have been removed from their parent or caretaker return home within one year (Michigan Family Independence Agency, 1999b). Not surprisingly, many experienced professionals in foster care, residential treatment, and juvenile corrections facilities report that the longer a child has been placed out of home, the more difficult it is to reunite the family. Often children and families give up because they cannot meet the demands of the system or they themselves cannot make necessary changes to assure adequate safety. This is a particular problem when the children are teenagers, because many parents, even those with strong financial resources and supportive social and family networks, find teens difficult to raise. As much as parents love their teenagers, peer pressure and acting-out behavior often result in daily battles. The longer a child stays in an out-of-home placement, the more time parents have to adapt to a different way of life without the child. Then it is often difficult to reintegrate the child into the family. This is particularly the case if the child has been rather unmanageable to begin with. Life may be considerably simpler when there is one fewer body to feed, nurture, and keep track of. From the child's point of view, after the initial difficult period of adjusting to a new family or new surroundings, he or she may have found new social relationships. Disrupting this means that the child has to once more lose familiar relationships and start over. Usually, though, children want to be "home" and usually that means with their birth parents if that is at all possible.

Therefore, it is crucial to talk to both the parent and child immediately, or while they are just settling into the new environment, about reunification. Remember that, even if you are as clear as you can possibly be, there is no guarantee that the parent will absorb or understand everything you say. You must be patient and persistent as you explain what the court is likely to require, what CPS is looking for, what you mean by minimum level of safety. As soon as your common sense tells you that the parent can handle more than one issue at a time, assess his or her motivation for reunification and what it will take for it to happen. It is also important that the "system" give at least as much to the birth parents as it does to the foster families.

Most courts are very specific about the requirements for reunification, which may include treatment of drug or alcohol abuse, better housing, getting a job, and/or evicting the partner who may have been abusive toward the children. In reality, reunification often happens because of an unpredictable turn of events, such as the child's running away from the foster home, a new man or woman appearing in the parent's life, or the interim caretaker becoming ill and unable to care for the child any longer. Often, too, it is through steadfast dedication of birth parents who, despite their inappropriate behavior in the past, work hard to have their children returned. A child advocate recently told me (SK) about a mother whose parental rights to her three children had been terminated in New York City. The mother's five-year goal was to have the termination order overturned. Finally she succeeded. Now the mother's life work is to help other mothers break down barriers, especially by knowing their rights, and get their children back. The mother reported that neither the child welfare system nor the courts helped, but when she figured out that nobody was going to help her reach her goal, she kept at it until "they were a family again."

MAKE THE MOST OF YOUR TIME IN COURT

Often workers and clients show up for hearing at 8:30 A.M. only to find that all of that day's cases seem to have been scheduled for that 8:30 A.M. slot. The court hallways and waiting areas are crowded, with hardly a place to sit down. We have actually waited two to three hours for a 10–15 minute hearing! This could potentially be a waste of time for workers, who get further and further behind in their work and feel tremendous pressure on their time. We have observed that during these waiting periods, worker and client usually sit far apart from each other, usually not saying a word to each other, even when the court is not crowded. It seems this time might be used to talk with clients, helping them understand the court process or at least acknowledging how difficult this must be for them.

We once observed a very thoughtful, compassionate, highly respected worker sit far away from a crying mother and her male partner who was comforting her. The mother reportedly left her two children with a babysitter and did not come back to pick up the children for two days. The babysitter, who was also the alleged biological father of one of the two children, called CPS and reported that one child's medication ran out and he could not locate the mother; he wanted both children returned to the mother because he was running out of money for food and was no long able to care for them. We later learned that the mother and her partner were homeless and were living in her partner's truck during the last couple of weeks, and she did not want the children to live in the truck with them. They reported to the magistrate who presided over the hearing that they had been frantically trying to find a place for the four of them to live, and therefore did not have a way to contact the babysitter to let him know the situation. Before she showed up for the court hearing, she already made sure that the children's medication was handed over to the worker so that it was already at the foster home where the children were placed the day before. The mother cried for almost 45 minutes while waiting for the hearing to begin. Not once did the worker attempt to speak to or comfort her.

Suppose the worker had decided to use the waiting time to engage the mother, to review what alternative steps she could have taken and raise questions about her understanding of how searching for housing prevented her from staying in contact with the children or making sure the child had the medication he needed for his asthma. This would have opened a smooth path for them to discuss how she would maintain contact with the children if they were not returned home at the end of the court hearing and to review in detail what she might need to do if they were returned home. How did she see her new partner fitting into this picture? How and what kind of assistance could she count on from him? Where would they live? What did she plan to say to the court magistrate or the judge to indicate how she planned to maintain contact with the children? During the first chance to visit the children, what did she suppose the children needed to hear from her that would reassure them? What were her ideas about how to answer the children's questions about what happened during the past couple of weeks? What about future plans? What would happen to them? What did the mother want the foster mother to know about her children (if they were to remain there)? Since her partner was present at the hearing, the worker could have involved the partner in suggesting solutions and asked him how realistic these ideas seemed to be, given their circumstances.

REMOVAL OF CHILDREN AS A "WAKE-UP CALL"

Over the years we have met numerous parents, especially those recovering from drug abuse, who reported, "losing my children to CPS was the best thing that could have happened." They said that CPS intervention was a "wake-up call" and gave them reasons to turn their lives around by entering a drug-treatment program, getting out of an abusive relationship, finishing their GED (high-school graduation equivalency diploma), finding a job, and learning about themselves in many unexpected ways. Of course, until they lost the children, many of them did not quite realize how important their children were to them. The goal for them was to get their children back and to make their children proud of them again.

Some parents have even served time in prison because their neglectful behavior led to their child's death or some other disaster. So we know that at times the removal of children is necessary and we as a society will probably continue to remove children for their safety, however traumatic it might be for the young children involved. After a removal, the next step is, of course, to plan what will follow and decide with the parents how to make the most of this difficult situation for everyone.

But what about parents who do not see removal as a wake-up call? Occasionally you will come across parents who confess their love for the children, promise that they will enter the treatment program (or have entered or dropped out of multiple treatment programs), yet fail to live up to their contracts or agreements to change their behavior. These parents really mean it when they make promises. They probably do love their children, and you can even see that they have the potential to become good parents. Not only that, they really believe and want to do what they agree to at the time and are honest at the time they say it. But they keep returning to drugs or alcohol while their children lose valuable time developmentally because of neglect, ongoing chaos and deprivation, lack of proper stimulation, and lack of attachment. What, we are asked, do you do with them? What does your solution-building approach have to offer us when we are faced with such clients?

We had to stop a moment and think about this very appropriate question. We do not have a magic answer to make people do what they don't really want or are able to do. We are not sure if there is any approach that "works" to make people do something they do not really want to do. But then, we need to go one step further and ask, "Is it our job to make people do something they do not want to do?" We would like to challenge the notion that it is the task of CPS to make clients do something against their will or that they believe is not in their best interest (DeJong & Berg, in press). Substance abuse treatment does not "cure" people of their drug or alcohol use; it is the tool that they use to become sober. Twelve-step programs do not make people stop drinking; people use the model to get themselves started on a path of sobriety and then stay sober.

Be mindful that the solution-focused approach cannot perform a miracle (even though we do ask "miracle questions"); nor does it work to change everybody. At the same time, expecting parents to be responsible for their behavior is important and implies the possibility that they change. Holding parents accountable for finding solutions does not mean we give them unlimited chances or wait endlessly for them to get their life together. Their choices always affect the safety and well-being of their children. They need to be reminded of this. Respecting individual autonomy and dignity means that we hold clients responsible for the natural consequences of their choices, even if it means a mother will "lose her child" for the time being—or even permanently. Being a responsible adult means weighing a variety of options and choices and making decisions, then living with the consequences of those decisions. We cannot hold parents to less than this standard. We must ask, are these children safe and cared for in a way that we can be comfortable with and that is acceptable to our society? Our society will be judged on how we treat our children. We must set reasonable standards for caretaking for all parents to meet and exceed. To hold parents to a lower standard than what we would measure ourselves against is, we believe, demeaning to them.

The Future of CPS:
A Vision for Tomorrow

WHERE WE BEGAN

WHEN WE BEGAN THIS BOOK, WE WERE HOPING TO OFFER YOU SOME IDEAS about skills and strategies, as well as our observations about what we thought might improve the current practice of child protection—helping to fix it rather than setting forth a vision for shaping a radically reformed CPS system. We both believe it would be a miracle of sorts to have a reshaped, well-functioning CPS system all over the United States—a system in which skilled and competent workers and supervisors respectfully supported families in their solution-building processes. Our experience tells us that we have a long way to go to achieve such system overhaul.

Child welfare is not a high priority on the national agenda, nor does it garner much attention locally unless a high-profile media case catches the attention of the public. While there is good will, hard work, dedication, and enthusiasm present in many CPS teams, it seems that a minimally acceptable job is now the national standard. Over 21 states are under federal court decree to improve their child welfare systems (Cutler, 1996).

Even in our current robust economy there are many competing priorities on the national radar screen: Welfare reform, education, community and juvenile violence, prison building, and health care seem to keep child welfare issues in the background—except, of course, if a child dies.

Recognizing that we are a long way away from a state-of-the-art child welfare system, our hope is that what we offer may lead us closer to a more radically reformed system. As we have mentioned throughout this book, we have met many competent and skilled workers and some superb managers who facilitate the nuts and bolts well. There is quite a journey ahead for CPS to institutionalize solution-focused interviewing. Learning to engage families with respect for personal and cultural competence and understanding the special issues that add to the problems vulnerable families deal with everyday. Mental illness, domestic violence, substance use, and poverty, all complicate the task of CPS. CPS is difficult work, requiring many skills. We hope this book contributes to shaping a child protection system that can and should be known for its excellence, not its difficulties.

We challenge administrators and supervisors to support and model respectful, inclusive, solution-building behavior with their staff. Our suggestions are not a panacea and we know that in and of themselves they will not "fix" the system. The CPS system must continue to look within and find the values and beliefs that will help one family at a time.

WHERE TO GO? BEYOND SYSTEM
IMPROVEMENT TO SYSTEM REFORM

We have made many suggestions for an improved response by CPS. They include:

- reshaping training
- supervision that includes home visits, team-building, and case consultation
- learning to use risk and safety assessment tools as one part of determining a course of action
- implementing a "top-down, bottom-up" approach for administrators and managers
- using investigation as a preventive intervention during home visits
- including families every step of the way in determining their solutions
- recognizing that poverty brings many families to CPS because they need a helping hand, not necessarily because of abuse and neglect
- helping staff become aware of the richness of cultural and language difference

Beyond improving the CPS system from within by giving frontline staff the skills to help them respectfully and adequately protect children, there is a growing consensus that it is not just system improvement that is necessary, but also a radically new approach to child protection. Underlying the call for this new approach is the "belief that protecting children from harm is everybody's concern," not just the responsibility of CPS (Shirk, 1998). Those calling for this new approach do not dismiss the need for traditional tools of child protection, nor do they sidestep the need for a continuing effective government role. What they do suggest is that child protection needs to add other family-building tools to the toolbox such as "clear assessment of family strengths, case work built on achieving solutions, participation of parents, individualized plans for children's (and family's) safety, a system of integrated services, help from community groups, and even good old-fashioned neighborliness" (Shirk, 1998). In a multi-year executive session on "New Paradigms for Child Protection" at the Harvard University Kennedy School of Government (Farrow, 1996), a general direction for this community-based child protection movement was envisioned.

The current system of child protection is designed for the most extreme cases of abuse and neglect, yet in reality only a small percentage of CPS cases actually meet that criterion. Often these extreme cases, which should be in the CPS system, do not receive the attention they need because the system is so flooded with other, less risky cases. The result is that most families that go through the CPS system do not have their needs met thoroughly. The high referral rate to CPS and the relatively small percentage of actual removals by CPS are evidence of this reality.

Recognizing the human and fiscal cost of staying where we are, we ask, "What might a new approach look like?" The Harvard session suggested a vision including the following (Farrow, 1996):

- aggressively promoting safety at all points in the system
- emphasis on prevention *cost*
- a more flexible and comprehensive response once maltreatment is identified
- involvement of wider range of partner agencies, both in the public and private sectors
- reliably punishing criminal acts of child maltreatment *?*
- moving from a single agency accountability for child protection to a collective community-wide responsibility

How different it would be if CPS handled only the 20% of cases that needed CPS services and had readily available a full array of community resources to meet the needs of the other 80%!

Getting from the system we have to the system that we envision is no easy task. The current approaches to CPS are entrenched in custom, law, and policy. Thousands and thousands of CPS staff have a stake in the effects of a changing paradigm. It is not easy to move from a

deals in generalities
cost factors omitted

position of power that is based on child protection being almost solely the responsibility of the child welfare system to "a broadening of the overall responsibility for the mission of child protection (who is accountable)" (Farrow, 1996). That is to say nothing of the pervasive mentality and philosophy that question the competency of poor, under-skilled families, regardless of the safety risk, to care for their children.

There is no "right way" to begin to implement such a vision or reconfigure the system, although many jurisdictions are beginning to see the wisdom of such an approach. In Michigan, statutory change to the CPS law in 1998 created a "tiered CPS approach," ranging from mandated responses for those egregious and extreme cases requiring firm and swift action by CPS to those deemed appropriate for a community response and services. Additionally, the Michigan legislature authorized several million dollars for local communities to begin to strengthen the front end preventive services for families who do not need CPS intervention. Certainly law alone cannot radically change a system, but it can provide the context for developing new capacities. Time will tell whether state or local jurisdictions are willing to own a different and new approach. It certainly cannot be developed or implemented by the child welfare agency acting alone. The most powerful argument for implementing a more flexible and comprehensive system of partner is that the "one size fits all" approach has not worked. A more responsive system can only enhance our ability to increase child safety.

CPS needs to be "nested in a broader community system designed to support and strengthen families and improve overall outcome for children" (Farrow, 1996). If every change we suggest in this book were implemented but not surrounded with a supportive system of community supports, we would be right where we are, with CPS workers alone, and feeling a responsibility to protect children. What a different system we would have if neighbors, relatives, friends, community residents, police officers, school teachers and principals, doctors, nurses, domestic violence and homeless shelters, apartment managers, day care providers, school counselors, substance abuse treatment centers, therapists, representatives from the faith community, and sport coaches saw it as their responsibility *not just to refer at-risk families* to CPS but also to provide support and a helping hand.

What if families got the help they needed earlier?

What if parents believed that they could build the solutions that were best for their families?

What if CPS were reserved only for those most desperate cases?

What if communities came together to promote child safety because they believed "we are all in this together"?

What if CPS workers felt more supported in their work?

What if those who come to the attention of CPS were given what they needed instead of only what the system has?

What if?

A miracle? Maybe.

Possible? Yes, of course.

all hope, little realty!

References

Anderson, H., & Goolishian, H. (1992). The client is the expert: A not-knowing approach to therapy. In S. McNamee & K. J. Gergen (Eds.), *Therapy as social construction* (pp. 25–39). London: Sage.

Ban, P. (1993). Family decision-making—The model as practiced in New Zealand and its relevance in Australia. *Australian Social Work, 46*(3), 22–30.

Berg, I. K. (1994). *Family-based services: A solution-focused approach.* New York: Norton.

Berg, I. K., & DeJong, P. (1996). Solution-building conversations: Co-constructing a sense of competence with clients. *Families in Society: The Journal of Contemporary Human Services, 77*(6), 376–391.

Berg, I. K., & Miller, S. D. (1992). *Working with the problem drinker.* New York: Norton.

Berg, I. K., & Reuss, N. (1997). *Solutions step by step: A substance abuse treatment manual.* New York: Norton.

Brown, C. (1986). *Child abuse parents speaking: Parents' impression of social workers and the social work process.* School for Advanced Studies, University of Bristol.

Burt, M., & Pittman, K. (1985). The social policy context of child welfare. In J. Laird & A. Hartman (Eds.), *A handbook of child welfare* (pp. 77–99). New York: Free.

Cantwell, P., & Holmes, S. (1994). Social construction: A paradigm shift of systemic therapy and training. *The Australian and New Zealand Journal of Family Therapy, 15*, 17–26.

Chapin Hall Center for Children. (1989). *Study on foster care: The child's perspective.* Chicago: University of Chicago Press.

Corcoran, J. (1998). In defense of mothers of sexual abuse victims. *Families in Society: The Journal of Contemporary Human Services, 79*(4).

Costin, L. B. (1985). The historical context of child welfare. In J. Laird & A. Hartman (Eds.), *A handbook of child welfare.* New York: Free.

Cox, T. Jr. (1993). *Cultural diversity in organizations.* San Francisco: Berrett-Koehler.

Cutler, I. (1996). *The interests of the child.* www.CASAnet.org. Handsnet Resource Library.

DeJong, P., & Berg, I. K. (1998). *Interviewing for solutions.* Pacific Grove, CA: Brooks/Cole.

DeJong, P., & Berg, I. K. (in press). Co-constructing cooperation with mandated clients. *Social Work.*

De Panfilis, D., & Salus, M. K. (1992). *Child protective services: A guide for caseworkers.* Washington, DC: National Center on Child Abuse and Neglect.

de Shazer, S. (1991). *Putting difference to work.* New York: Norton.

de Shazer, S. (1994). *Words were originally magic.* New York: Norton.

de Shazer, S., & Berg, I. K. (1992). Doing therapy: A post-structural re-vision. *Journal of Marital and Family Therapy, 18*(1), 71–81.

Dobash, R. E., & Dobash, R. (1979). *Violence against wives.* New York: Free.

Dolan, Y. (1991). *Resolving sexual abuse.* New York: Norton.

Edelson, J. L. (1999). The overlap between child maltreatment and women battering. *Violence Against Women, 5*(1).

Fadiman, A. (1997). *The spirit catches you and you fall down.* New York: Noonday.

Fahlberg, V. I. (1991). *A child's journey through placement.* Perspectives.

Farrow, F. (1996). *Building community partnership.* John F. Kennedy School of Government, Harvard University.

Findlater, J., & Kelly, S. (1999). Reframing child safety in Michigan: Building collabration among domestic violence, family preservation, and child protection services. *Child Maltreatment, 4*(2).

Franklin, C., & Nurius, P. (Eds). (1996). Special issue: Constructivism in social work practice. *Families in Society: The Journal of Contemporary Human Services, 77*(6).

Furman, B., & Aloha, T. (1992). *Solution talk: Hosting therapeutic conversations.* New York: Norton.

Goffman, I. (1961). *Asylum.* New York: Doubleday.

Gonzales, G., Case, K., & Keggerreis, N. (1999). *CPS customer satisfaction survey,* Jackson County FIA, Jackson, MI.

Government Accounting Office. (1997). *Report to the Honorable Nydia Velazquez, House of Representatives. Child protective services: Complex challenges require new strategies.* GAO/HEHS-97-115.

Haley, J. (1973). *Uncommon therapy: The psychiatric techniques of Milton H. Erickson.* New York: Norton.

Hassal, I. (1996). Origin and development of family group conferences. In J. Hudson, A. Morris, G. Maxwell, & B. Galaway (Eds.), *Family group conferences.* Monsey: Willow Tree.

Hoffman, L. (1990). Constructing realities: An art of lenses. *Family Process, 29,* 1–12.

Hudson, J., Morris, A., Maxwell, G., & Galaway, B. (Eds.). (1986). *Family group conferences.* Monsey: Willow Tree.

Janis, I. L. (1969). Some implications of recent research on the dynamics of fear and stress tolerance. *Social Psychology, 47,* 86–100.

Jiordano, M. (in press). *Safe and responsible decision-making when working with alcohol and other drug issues in child welfare: Weaving help and hope into practice with the substance-affected family.* Washington, DC: Child Welfare League of America.

Kempe, G. H., Silverman, F. N., Steele, B. F., et al. (1962). The battered child syndrome. *Journal of the American Medical Association, 181*(1), 17.

Kotter, J. (1996). *Leading change.* Boston: Harvard Business School Press.

Kozol, J. (1995, December 11). Spare us the cheap grace. *Time,* 96.

MacKinnon, L. (1992). *Child abuse in context: The participants' view.* Doctoral dissertation, University of Sydney, Australia.

Mason, J. (1989). In whose interest? Some mothers' experience of child welfare interventions. *Australian Child & Family Welfare, 14*(4), 4–6.

Michigan Department of Education. (1998). *Free lunch data*. Lansing, MI: Author.

Michigan Family Independence Agency. (1995, 1996). *Children's fact sheet*. Lansing, MI: Author.

Michigan Family Independence Agency. (1999a). *ECO data*. Lansing, MI: Author.

Michigan Family Independence Agency. (1999b). *Kids count data book*. Lansing, MI: Author.

Michigan Governor's Task Force on Children's Justice, and Family Independence Agency. (1997). *Forensic interviewing protocol*. Lansing, MI: Author.

National Center on Addiction and Substance Abuse at Columbia University. (1998). *No safe haven: Children of substance abusing parents* (pp. 78–83). New York: Author.

National Center on Child Abuse and Neglect, U.S. Department of Health and Human Services. (1997). *Child Maltreatment 1995: Reports from the states to the National Child Abuse and Neglect Data System*. Washington, DC: Author.

The New York Times. (1998, August 22). Shake up at state agency after boy is found dead. 12.

Newberger, C. M., Gremy, L., Watermaux, J., & Newberger, E. H. (1993). Mothers of sexually abused children: Trauma and despair in longitudinal perspective. *American Journal of Orthopsychiatry, 63*, 92–103.

Ney, T. (Ed.). (1995). *True and false allegations of child sexual abuse: Assessment and case management*. New York: Brunner/Mazel.

The Packard (David and Lucille) Foundation. (1998). Executive summary. *The future of children, 8*(1).

Parad, H. J. (1965). *Crisis intervention: Selected readings*. New York: Family Service Association of America.

Poole, D. A., & Lamb, M. E. (1998). *Investigative interview of children: A guide for helping professionals*. Washington, DC: American Psychological Association.

Poole, D. A., & Lindsay, D. S. (1996, June). *Effects of parental suggestions, interviewing techniques and age on your children's event reports*. Paper presented at the NATO Advanced Study Institute, Recollections of Trauma: Scientific Research and Clinical Practice, Port de Bourgenay, France.

Ryburn, A., & Atherton, C. (1996). Family group conferences: Partnership in practice. *Adoption and Fostering, 20*(1), 16–23.

Saleeby, D. (Ed.). (1992). *The strength perspective in social work practice*. New York: Longman.

Schene, P. A. (1998). Past, present, and future roles of child protective services. *The Future of Children, 8*(1), 23–38.

Schorr, L. (1997). *Common purpose*. New York: Doubleday.

Sebold, J., & Uken, A. (1996). The Plumas Project: A solution-focused goal directed domestic violence program. *Journal of Collaborative Therapy, 4*(2).

Sebold, J., & Uken, A. (1999). *Treating domestic violence offenders* (audiotape). Milwaukee: BFTC Press.

Shirk, M. (1998). *We are in this together: Community child protection in America*. New York: Edna McConnell Clark Foundation.

Sternberg, K. J., Lamb, M. E., Hershkowitz I., Yudilevidch, L., Orbach, Y., Esplin, P. W., & Hovav, M. (1997). Effects of introductory style on children's abilities to describe experience of sexual abuse. *Child Abuse & Neglect, 21*, 1133–1146.

Swarms, R. L. (1999, January 30). Parents' suits says New York City needlessly put children in foster care. *The New York Times.*

Talmon, M. (1990). *Single session therapy: Maximizing the effect of the first (and often only) therapeutic encounter.* San Francisco: Jossey-Bass.

Thorpe, D. (1994). *Evaluating child protection.* Buckingham, England: Open University Press.

Turnell, A., & Edwards, S. (1997). Aspiring to partnership: The signs of safety approach to child protection. *Child Abuse Review, 6,* 179–190.

Turnell, A., & Edwards, S. (1999). *Signs of safety: A solution and safety oriented approach to child protection case work.* New York: Norton.

University Associates. (1995). *Final report: Evaluation of Families First of Michigan.* Lansing, MI: Author.

Van de Kamp, N. (1998, September). Great expectations. *Milwaukee Magazine.*

Wade, A. (1997). Small acts of living: Everyday resistance of violence and other forms of oppression. *Contemporary Family Therapy, 19*(1), 23–39.

Walter, J., & Peller, J. (1992). *Becoming solution-focused in brief therapy.* New York: Brunner/Mazel.

Watzlawick, P., Weakland, J., & Fisch, R. (1974). *Change: Principles of problem formation and problem resolution.* New York: Norton.

Wexler, R. (1996, May 20). *First do no harm: Child saving, family preservation and the role of the American media.* Presented at the Conference of the International Initiative: Protecting Children by Strengthening Families. Partnerships for Safety, Oslo, Norway.

White, M., & Epston, D. (1990). *Narrative means to therapeutic ends.* New York: Norton.

Whitney, P., & Davis, L. (1999). Child abuse and domestic violence in Massachusetts: Can practice be integrated in a public child welfare setting? *Child Maltreatment, 4*(1).

Whittaker, J., Kinney, J., Tracy, E. M., & Booth, C. (Eds.). (1990). *Rearching high-risk families: Intensive preservation in human services.* New York: Aldine de Gruyter.

Winefield, H. S., & Barlow, J. A. (1995). Client and worker satisfaction in a child protection agency. *Child Abuse & Neglect, 19*(8), 897–905.

Wulczyn, F. H., George, R. M., & Harden, A. W. (1995). *An update from the multi-state foster care data archive, foster care dynamics 1983–1994.* The Chapin Hall Center for Children at the University of Chicago: University of Chicago Press.

Yuille, J. C., Hunter, R., & Zaparnuik, J. (1993). Interviewing children in sexual abuse cases. In G. S. Goodman & B. L. Bottoms (Eds.), *Child victims, child witness: Understanding and improving testimony* (pp. 95–115). New York: Guilford.

Zellman, G. L., & Antler, S. (1990). Mandated reporters and CPS: A study in frustration. *Public Welfare, 48*(1), 30–37.

Appendices

Appendix A

Handouts

THE FOLLOWING PAGES MAY BE USED BY ADMINISTRATORS, MANAGERS, supervisors, workers, and advisory groups to assist in the implementation of a solution-focused approach to child protective services. They may be duplicated or adapted as necessary.

A VISION FOR CHILD PROTECTIVE SERVICES

To begin and end all interventions with respect for the family and their strengths.

To respond to and investigate reports of alleged child maltreatment, in respectful, client-driven, solution-focused ways.

To provide for child safety by enhancing family safety and autonomy.

To hold parents responsible for the safety of their children by providing them with collaborative, respectful, individualized services that promote and insure child and family safety and parental autonomy.

From *Building Solutions in Child Protective Services* © Insoo Kim Berg and Susan Kelly (W. W. Norton & Company, 1-800-233-4830).

GROUNDWORK AND GUIDING PRINCIPLES

Families know more about their situation than anyone.

Respect the dreams and aspirations clients have for themselves and their children.

Families are able to formulate their own goals and build their solutions.

Families tend to maintain solutions they create.

Families are doing the best they can in difficult situations.

Family strengths can be enhanced and change can happen.

Families are our partners and need our support.

Families can enhance and improve the well-being of their children, with assistance and support.

Safe solutions will be found in partnerships among parents, workers, supervisors, and other community partners.

Families have a right to be supported in their efforts to improve their children's well-being.

Most children can be protected by their parents.

Child protection must also focus on family protection.

SOLUTION-FOCUSED PARADIGM

The client takes center stage.

Assess solutions, not deficits.

Capitalize on what has worked so far.

Listen to the client's desired outcomes.

Join with the client to realize outcomes.

What are the client's existing strengths and resources? Use them to build solutions.

Using a client's own words and images will help the worker build on past successes (however small) and move toward solutions that last.

Collaboration is key.

Solutions will be generated by the client together with the worker.

Support goals of the client.

Respect and work with the unique individual, cultural, ethnic realities that each client brings to the situation.

Responsibility for the safety of the child becomes the parent's responsibility.

GOALS

A CPS system that does not pit child against parent, but aims for both child and family safety.

Whenever possible, CPS provides services to the family so parents can protect the child.

Services are customer-driven and outcomes are measurable.

All activities are performed to prevent first entry into the CPS system.

Respect is the hallmark of service delivery.

Family safety and parental autonomy are promoted.

HOPED-FOR OUTCOMES

Increased family satisfaction.

Reduced unnecessary out-of-home placements.

Reduced repeat investigations.

Reduced worker turnover.

Solution-focused paradigm.

Client-driven and collaborative.

Competency-based.

Focus on both family safety and child safety.

Enhanced morale within CPS teams.

GUIDELINES FOR WELL-FORMED GOALS

Goal(s) are always negotiated in collaboration with the client(s).

A goal is described in social, interactional terms.

A goal has contextual and/or situational features.

A goal is described as the presence of *some* behavior and/or the start of something.

A goal is small rather than large.

A goal is salient to the client(s) and, through negotiation, salient to the worker.

A goal is described in specific, concrete, and behavioral (therefore, measurable) terms.

A goal is both realistic and achievable.

A goal is perceived by the client(s) as involving "hard work" on his/her part to achieve.

From *Building Solutions in Child Protective Services* © Insoo Kim Berg and Susan Kelly (W. W. Norton & Company, 1-800-233-4830).

MOVING TOWARD SOLUTIONS:
A CHECKLIST FOR CPS TEAMS

1. Keep the child and their family first.

2. Be a great listener. Grow "big ears."

3. Show respect; it's key, it goes a long way.

4. Notice a job well done.

5. Thank people, appreciate them.

6. Celebrate your successes and those of your clients, families, staff. Talk about the job well done.

7. Exceed customer expectations and your own expectations.

8. Be a leader. Don't just talk the talk, walk it.

9. Value diversity, the fabric of our lives, race, culture, gender, religion. See diversity as the blessing it is.

10. Be solution-focused. Remove obstacles; don't create them.

TRY GETTING TO "YES" AND STAYING THERE

Try to put yourself in the client's place. This will help you to listen differently and better. Incorporate the following suggestions into a solution-building interviewing strategy.

Build a "yes set" at first and throughout.

Start by noticing something positive about clients.

Use the client's language, pick up his/her words and weave them into your next questions.

Assume the client is cooperative until proven otherwise.

Affirm what the client wants as valid and reasonable.

If conflicting stories confuse you, ask the client to help you understand.

Unrealistic expectations? "How do you know s/he/you can do this?"

Ask, "How would that be helpful to you?"

Ask, "What difference would it make for _____?"

Have the humility to say, "Gee, I don't know. What do you think?"

"What tells you that . . . ?"

"What have you thought about doing?"

OUTLINE AND QUESTIONS FOR WORKING WITH CPS CLIENTS

Goal negotiation (*setting well-formed goals*)

> Whose idea do you think it was that I needed to come to your home?
>
> How does _____ think my (coming here) will be helpful to you?
>
> What does _____ think is the reason you have this problem?
>
> How would _____ say this affects you (and her/him)?
>
> What would _____ say you need to do as a start?

Exceptions, past successes, hidden resources (*focusing on strengths and possibilities*)

> How does _____ know you can do this? How do you know you can do this?
>
> When was the last time you did this? How did you do this? What else?
>
> What would _____ say how you did this? What about you?
>
> How is that helpful for you? (between you and _____)?

Client's vision of a different life (circumstances, relationships, etc.) (*beginning to build solutions that last*)

> What is the first step you need to do to get this started again?
>
> How would _____ say it will be different when you do this again?
>
> What will be different between you and _____?
>
> What difference would it make in your life?

Client investment toward achieving desired outcome(s) (*experiencing progress toward the goal*)

> How confident are you that you can do this? (scaling questions)
>
> What would _____ say about how confident s/he is that you can do this? (scale)
>
> When was the last time you were able to do this? How did you do this?
>
> What would it take for you to do this again? (if there is exception)

continued

Moving toward termination (*supporting client's solutions and autonomy*)

How will you know you have done enough?

What will let you know that _____ notices that you have made progress?

What would it take for you to keep it up?

How confident are you that you can keep up the current level?

Suppose you were able to maintain this level (scale) the next three months. What will be going on in your life then?

CULTURAL SENSITIVITY AND CULTURAL COMPETENCE

Culture includes race, religion, ethnicity, family values, lifestyle, family composition, customs, values and beliefs. The family itself is the most important source of information about its unique characteristics, historical roots, and cultural values. Culturally competent workers:

Respect the client's perspective.

Listen well enough to learn about people who are different from themselves.

Avoid judgment from bias, stereotypes, or cultural myths.

Assess strengths and needs of families from various populations.

Ask the family to explain the significance culture has for them, especially regarding:
    family traditions
    child rearing and discipline practices
    spiritual beliefs and traditions

Every assessment interview will be affected by how effectively a caseworker understands and respects a family's history and culture. Some of the following questions may assist in eliciting helpful assessment information. They are by no means comprehensive, but may be helpful in thinking about how to approach a culturally different family.

Who usually makes decisions about the children in this family?

What types of discipline does the family consider to be appropriate?

Who usually is involved in child care responsibilities? Extended family? Informal kin?

What methods does this family use to solve its problems? How does it communicate?

How are cultural beliefs incorporated in the way this family functions? How does the family maintain its cultural beliefs?

continued

What role does religion play in this family? How do these beliefs affect child-rearing responsibilities?

What is the attitude or belief about health care?

What is the identification involvement with the tribe, race, larger group?

What family rituals, traditions, or behaviors exist?

This information and questions are adapted from: *Child protective services: A guide for caseworkers*. User Manual Series, U.S. Department of Health and Human Services, Administration for Children and Families, Administration on Children, Youth and Families, National Center on Child Abuse and Neglect, Washington, DC.

Appendix B

Visioning Process for Local Communities

THIS PROCESS WAS USED BY THE MICHIGAN PARTNERSHIPS FOR SAFETY Advisory Group to determine the goals for the reform of CPS services. The process helped identify the gaps between how CPS operates today and a more ideal system. This may be a helpful tool for child welfare systems to use when beginning solution-focused reform efforts.

VISIONING PROCESS:
THE PRESENT AND FUTURE OF CHILD PROTECTION
IN _____ COMMUNITY

SUGGESTED TIME: $1\frac{1}{2}$ hours

INVITED PARTICIPANTS should include but not be limited to:

social services administrators/
   managers
CPS supervisors/workers
hospital personnel
judges
prosecutors
educators (teachers, school
   counselors, nurse)
recipients of CPS services
faith community representatives
domestic violence advocates
business representatives
senior citizens

private child welfare staff
foster care/delinquency workers
police
media
politicians
foster care parents
court appointed special advocates
guardian ad litems
social workers
public health nurses
community mental health
volunteer organizations

Process

1. One-half of the group receives questions about the reality of the CPS SYSTEM in the present
2. One-half of the group receives questions about what the CPS WILL LOOK LIKE IN THE FUTURE.
3. Respondents quickly (10–15 minutes) write their responses to the following questions:

Present   1. What is the overriding philosophy of CPS?
Future   1. What will be the overriding philosophy of CPS?

Present   2. What do children and families need from CPS system now?
Future   2. What will children and families need from CPS system in the future?

Present   3. What external pressures are impacting on the CPS system now?
Future   3. What external pressures will impact on the CPS system in the future?

Present	4. What internal pressures are impacting on the CPS system now?
Future	4. What internal pressures will impact on the CPS system in the future?
Present	5. What do CPS clients say about us now?
Future	5. What will CPS clients say about us in the future?
Present	6. What is the community/public saying about us now?
Future	6. What will the community/public say about us in the future?
Present	7. How are decisions made about a referral?
Future	7. How will decisions be made about a referral in the future?
Present	8. What is the outcome of a CPS intervention now?
Future	8. What will be the outcome of a CPS intervention in the future?
Present	9. How do we measure success?
Future	9. How will we measure success in the future?
Present	10. What are we (CPS) proud of?
Future	10. What will we be proud of?
Present	11. What are we (CPS) sorry about?
Future	11. What will we no longer be sorry about?
Present	12. Who are the critical stakeholders in the protection of children?
Future	12. Who will be the critical stakeholders in the protection of children?

4. In groups of 4–8 (one-half who wrote about the present system, one-half who wrote about the future system), respondents share answers
5. Each small group is asked to analyze the collective responses and identify the gap between the *present* and the *future*.

A list of obvious themes will emerge. For example, in response to question 5 the following responses were generated from an actual focus group:

5. *What do CPS clients say about us now?*
    Help? "You've got to be kidding!"
    Not helpful to parents/family.
    We don't listen to them.

We take their children (threats).

We tell them what to do.

We're the enemy.

We don't help them.

Too intrusive.

Not doing our job; won't do anything.

Punitive.

Investigator/enforcement.

Inflexible.

We only do enough to make things worse.

5. *What will CPS clients say about us in the future?*
That we listen more but still try to dictate to them.

I was treated as a partner and respected.

They care about me.

We are more respectful of them.

We are positive about their dreams.

You really helped . . . thanks!

I am better off because you helped my family.

I know where to get help.

CPS is great!

Using true helping model.

My family is more involved.

There are more prevention services available.

Too busy to care.

You are supportive in what we want.

Analysis

Present	Future
You don't help	Respected
You don't listen	Helped my family
Punitive, inflexible	Support me to keep my children
Threats	Helped me reach my goals
Tell clients what to do	

Gap
Attitude adjustment: Moving from deficits to strengths focus
System needs to move from "parent" to "partner"
System needs to exist for better outcomes for families

Appendix C

Focus Group Process
For Local Communities

THIS FOCUS GROUP PROCESS CAN BE USED TO DIALOGUE WITH LOCAL communities to assess the perceptions of the comments about child protective services. It can also serve as a source of information for administrators, managers, and workers to help create a strategic action plan to enhance solution-focused strategies for families who come to the attention of the CPS system.

FOCUS GROUPS: WHAT DOES THE PUBLIC THINK OF CPS?
WHAT DOES THE CPS SYSTEM THINK OF ITSELF?

In 1997, as part of the Partnerships for Safety strategy, and to better ascertain a picture of the strengths, weaknesses, and future challenges of CPS, several focus groups were held in Michigan. This was part of a communication strategy to better inform the public about the role of CPS. Information gathered from the focus groups helped to develop content for a video, *Safe from Harm,* describing the roles of CPS and the community in protecting children. The video was distributed to all social services field offices to use with their board members for public meetings and to promote dialogue within their own CPS and agency staff.

Results of focus groups conducted by the Michigan Family Independence Agency during 1997 showed an inconsistent image about the role and effectiveness of CPS. Participants in focus groups were a wide rage of community residents, including:

- hospital personnel
- board members from services agencies
- neighborhood residents who make referrals to CPS
- grandparents raising grandchildren
- education personnel
- employment specialists
- CPS workers, supervisors, managers
- parents and family members

The questions asked during the focus groups were:

- Who are the key players in protecting children?
- What is the current public image of CPS?
- What is the *ideal* public image?
- What is a realistic public image?
- What should be the key messages of CPS?
- What external factors impact on CPS?
- What internal strengths does the CPS staff have?
- What accomplishments have been made for the protection of children?
- What challenges are ahead for CPS staff?
- What internal weaknesses exist within CPS system/staff?

Appendix D

Worker/Supervisor Surveys

PRE-POST BEHAVIOR SURVEY

Code Number _____
(last 3 digits of SS#)

Please circle the appropriate number
1. hardly ever, 2. seldom, 3. often, 4. most times, 5. almost always

Usually in my practice:

1. I use client's words and metaphors as well as my own. 1 2 3 4 5
2. I look for small successes that clients have made on their own. 1 2 3 4 5
3. I use neutral words in order to build rapport with clients. 1 2 3 4 5
4. I acknowledge client's frustration and anger at me as normal and understandable given the context or being investigated. 1 2 3 4 5
5. I go along with the client's tendency to put blame on external things as "joining" technique, and then encourage taking positive steps to find solutions. 1 2 3 4 5
6. I frequently normalize client resistance to investigation as natural and understandable. 1 2 3 4 5

7. I don't argue with the client, except in very
rare situations.   1 2 3 4 5

8. When setting goals, I help clients to state
what they want in concrete, behavioral,
measurable, and presence or something not
an absence problem.   1 2 3 4 5

9. I hold clients responsible for solutions, and
give them credit.   1 2 3 4 5

10. While I encourage some ventilation of feelings, I focus back on what the clients will
do about finding solutions.   1 2 3 4 5

11. I look for small exceptions to problems and
ask for the details of the solution generating
behaviors.   1 2 3 4 5

12. I look for ways to build on what clients have
done well already.   1 2 3 4 5

13. I ask miracle questions in order to find out
what the client's ideas of solutions are.   1 2 3 4 5

PRE-POST ATTITUDINAL SURVEY

Code Number_____
(last 3 digits of SS#)

Please circle the appropriate number
1. hardly ever, 2. seldom, 3. often, 4. most times, 5. almost always

Usually in my work as a protective services worker, I believe:

1. My primary function is to insure the safety
    of the children.   1   2   3   4   5
2. My primary function is to provide service
    to parents in such a way that they can insure
    the safety of their children.   1   2   3   4   5
3. Well-functioning families do a good job of
    insuring the safety of their children.   1   2   3   4   5
4. When parents feel good about themselves,
    they can help their children feel good about
    themselves; the opposite is true also.   1   2   3   4   5
5. All parents want to be good parents; some
    need more help than others.   1   2   3   4   5
6. All clients have strengths and resources if
    I look hard and carefully.   1   2   3   4   5
7. Even abusive and neglectful parents do a
    good job sometimes.   1   2   3   4   5
8. Building on successful parenting strategies
    is the beginning step to helping clients learn
    to be successful as parents.   1   2   3   4   5
9. There is no one "right" way to do good
    parenting; there are many.   1   2   3   4   5
10. The focus of child welfare is on what is
    changeable and possible rather than what
    is impossible and intractable.   1   2   3   4   5
11. Investigation for safety can lead to change
    for the client.   1   2   3   4   5
12. All problems have exceptions. When the
    problem does occur, repeating the excep-
    tion can lead to solutions.   1   2   3   4   5
13. It is not necessary to know a great deal
    about how a problem developed in order
    to solve it.   1   2   3   4   5
14. When clients are helped to recognize their
    own strengths and resources, it leads to em-
    powerment.   1   2   3   4   5

15. "Change is constant" means that clients' lives are in a constant state of change, both positively and negatively.   1   2   3   4   5

16. The helping relationship is a collaborative endeavor, and not just the worker dispensing opinions about what the client should do.   1   2   3   4   5

17. Sometimes it is not necessary to know the cause of the problem in order to solve it.   1   2   3   4   5

18. My primary task is to help clients to utilize their own resources.   1   2   3   4   5

19. Respect for clients' self-determination is best expressed through asking clients' opinions.   1   2   3   4   5

20. When clients have input in the outcome of the service, they are more invested in the solution, thus less resistant.   1   2   3   4   5

21. When clients define the problem, they are more invested in solutions.   1   2   3   4   5

22. When clients have input into the process of finding solutions, they can take credit for the successful outcome. This is empowering.   1   2   3   4   5

23. Whenever possible, a worker should stay close to the client's own definition of the problems and solutions to them.   1   2   3   4   5

24. My role is to help clients sort out what might be the best approach to take in coming up with solutions to their problems.   1   2   3   4   5

25. Treatment goals must be stated in positive language about what clients will do, rather than what they will not do.   1   2   3   4   5

26. Since the helping process involves the words we use it is important to use the client's words.   1   2   3   4   5

27. Clients will ultimately do what is in their best interest, from their point of view and not from the worker's.   1   2   3   4   5

28. I get better cooperation when I place myself on the client's side.   1   2   3   4   5

29. Some protective service investigation can be intrusive to clients.   1   2   3   4   5

30. Normalizing the client's reaction does not mean I condone it.   1   2   3   4   5
31. Understanding does not always lead to change. Doing something about it does.   1   2   3   4   5
32. Protective service investigation itself can be an intervention.   1   2   3   4   5
33. When I must take protective action, I do it in such a way that my clients see me as helpful to them, not interfering in their lives.   1   2   3   4   5
34. I make a positive difference in people's lives.   1   2   3   4   5
35. A client's problem is not an indication of a flaw in their character.   1   2   3   4   5
36. Motivation is related to how hopeful clients feel about themselves and their situation.   1   2   3   4   5
37. When the environment changes, the client is more likely to change.   1   2   3   4   5
38. People can change without admitting their guilt.   1   2   3   4   5

Tools for Supervisors

HALLMARKS OF THE CPS SUPERVISOR

Traditional Paradigm
Goal: To produce a competent worker

Hallmarks:
Supervisor is the source of knowledge
Worker is a neophyte who needs to be taught
Worker might make a mistake, thus needs overseeing
Supervisor is responsible for the welfare of clients
Supervision is situation and problem specific, thus, difficult to generalize learning
Emphasis on prevention of mistakes, not on developing skills
Authoritarian, hierarchical, linear, sole knowledge
Supervisor-driven, one-say evaluation, display of power
Climate of fear, criticism, thus avoidance

New Paradigm
Goals: To facilitate the development of a competent worker who will make good decisions and empower clients to make good decisions
To identify competencies and amplify them through supervision
To ultimately become peers and colleagues

Hallmarks:
Discovering worker competencies
Identifying and amplifying worker successes
Using the worker's cases to foster skill development

Using tentative and suppositional language
Holding worker responsible for his/her own learning
Create a climate of trust and safety in supervision
Developing a collaborative relationship with the worker
Using the worker's frame of reference to increase competency
Evaluation is ongoing, constant, and mutual

SOLUTION-BUILDING SUPERVISION AND EVALUATION
(for observation during home calls)

Evaluator: _____ Worker's Name: _____
Date: _____

1. What did the worker do that was effective? List 3 items.

2. How can you tell the worker was effective? Check all that are appropriate:
    _____ developed a "yes set," _____ used client's words throughout, was friendly, _____ said positive things about the children, _____ nodded a lot, _____ smiled, _____ talked in soft tone of voice, _____ noticed good things about client, _____ asked what client is proud of in his/her life, _____ asked client's view of safety issues, _____ gave full attention to client without correcting, _____ asked about natural support system, _____ worker agreed with client, _____ commented on existing safety measures, _____ assumed client good inten-tions, _____ asked about exceptions to problems, _____ looked for existing safety measures, _____ worker asked many relationship ques-tions, _____ accepted and acknowledged client anger without defend-ing. Others (Please describe):

    _____

    _____

3. How did the client respond to worker?
    _____ smiled often, _____ friendly, _____ relaxed quickly, _____ volunteered info, _____ attentive, _____ made eye contact with worker, _____ cooperative, _____ asked for help, _____ talked more than the worker, _____ expressed willingness to take steps, _____ acknowledged own shortcomings, _____ seemed genuinely relieved at the end of the visit, _____ has a plan of action, _____ confided in worker. Other: (Please describe):

    _____

    _____

CASE PRESENTATION AND CONSULTATION FORMAT

I.   Case presentation to team should last 15 to 20 minutes

II. For new cases:

1. Strength-based description of family
2. What is the family's understanding of why you are working with them?
3. Description of signs of safety in the home
4. What further indications of safety are needed to assure the family's well-being?
5. What goals has the family arrived at with the worker's help?

III. Consultation/supervision outline for new and ongoing cases:

1. What does the client want?
2. What are the signs of success(es)? List in detail.
3. What has been accomplished toward these goals so far?
4. How will clients/we know they can achieve these goals?
5. Who will do what, when, where, how to achieve the next step?

    List past successes—exceptions?

    Where does the client feel he/she is on the scale of 1 to 10 toward achievement of goals?

6. What is the confidence/investment level to achieve the goals?
7. How will we know it is good enough to terminate?
8. What did we learn from this case?

FAMILY ASSESSMENT FOCUS

Traditional Assessment	Solution-focused Assessment
Assess/evaluate the problem and the deficits	Assess/evaluate situation for strengths and possible solutions
Elicit history, symptoms, pathology	Elicit well-constructed goals
Category/classification	Client's desired outcome
Hypothesis, prognosis	Client's frame of reference
Emphasize solutions to match problems	Emphasis on exceptions, past successes
Emphasis on deficits	Coping strategies
Determine by worker what the client needs (to do, take, stop, change, etc.)	Listen for hidden resources with an emphasis on strengths
Worker as the expert	Client-driven solutions
Prescriptive relationship	Client investment in own ideas
Intervention (what to do and how to do it)	Collaborative relationship between worker and family members
Resistance will occur when client disgrees with prescription	Emphasis on what will work
	Individualized solutions
Client labeled uncooperative	Client owns progress
Good/bad, black/white dichotomy	Clients more self-revealing
Hopeless, discouraging, negative	Better and more useful solution when client is fully included in all decisions

BUILDING A SOLUTION-FOCUSED TEAM

The following questions might be used with supervisors to create a solution-focused framework, which identifies potential goals and action steps. These questions have been effective in supervisory meetings. They can also be adapted as a way to help workers assess their interactions with their clients.

1. What would your workers say they want from you?

2. What do you want from upper management?

3. What are your most pressing supervision issues currently?

4. How do you want things to be one year from now?

5. How will we get there?

TEAM-BUILDING EXERCISES

1. Divide staff into small groups (6 to 8 persons), which include workers, supervisors, managers, administrative and clerical staff.

2. Ask someone to act as reporter for each small group.

3. As an icebreaker, begin with "Life is Good" exercise. The question to which everyone responds is: "Since you got up this morning until this moment, what has happened to you that lets you know 'Life is Good'?" Each person is given a chance to respond. At the end of this exercise the small groups share with the whole group some of what was reported. (10 minutes)

4. Each person in the small group is asked to say aloud what she feels others would say that she has done to improve the working atmosphere in their unit within the last two weeks (all are encouraged to identify each and every talent). (20 minutes)

5. Allow everyone on the team to identify qualities, skills, talents, and special contributions anyone on the team did not mention. (10 minutes)

6. What needs to happen at the end of this meeting that will make this meeting worthwhile? How will the team work together to improve the working atmosphere and morale? Reporter makes sure that the conversation stays on track and focuses on concrete, behavioral, realistic, doable tasks. Make a list of these. Report to the larger group. (30 minutes)

7. When was the last time the unit, department, team has done this? How can we continue it? (10 minutes)

8. Detail a working plan: who, what, when, where, and how questions. Scale the confidence, ability, and resources among the team.

9. Scale the confidence of the team's ability to follow through with the group's suggestions.

10. What would the future be like if we were able to put our plan in action?

U.S. Child Protection Legislation at a Glance

Child Welfare Services Program, Title IV-B of the Social Security Act (1935) provides grants to states to support preventive and protective services to vulnerable children and their families. Initially, most funds went to foster care payments, since 1980, federal law has encouraged prevention of out-of-home care placements.

Foster care payments under the Aid to Dependent Children program, Title IV-A of the Social Security Act (1961) provides funds to help states make maintenance payments for children who are eligible for cash assistance and who live in foster care. Such payments go to foster parents to cover the costs of children's food, shelter, clothing, supervision, travel home for visits and the like. In 1980, this program was transferred to a new Title IV-E of the Social Security Act.

The Child Abuse Prevention and Treatment Act (CAPTA), Public Law 93-247 (1974) provides limited funding to states to prevent, identify and treat child abuse and neglect. It created the National Center on Child Abuse and Neglect, developed standards for receiving and responding to reports of child maltreatment, and established a clearinghouse on the prevention and treatment of abuse and neglect. Changes in 1996 reinforced the Act's emphasis on child safety.

The Social Services Block Grant, Title XX of the Social Security Act (1975) provides funds the states can use for social services to low-income

(Schene, Patricia A. "Past, Present, and Future Roles of Child Protective Services," from *The Future of Children* Spring 1998, Volume 8, No. 1). Reprinted with permission of the David and Lucille Packard Foundation.

individuals. A significant but unknown proportion of these funds pays for services related to child protection including prevention, treatment programs, and foster care and adoption services.

The Indian Child Welfare Act, Public Law 95-608 (1978) strengthens the role played by tribal governments in determining the custody of Indian children, and specifies that preference should be given to placements with extended family, then to Indian foster homes. Grants to allow tribes and Indian organizations to deliver preventive services were authorized, but have not been funded.

The Adoption Assistance and Child Welfare Act, Public Law 96-272 (1980) requires states that seek to maximize federal funding to establish programs and make procedural reforms to serve children in their own homes, prevent out-of-home placement, and facilitate family reunification following placements. This act also transferred federal foster care funding to the new Title IV-E of the Social Security Act, and it provides funds to help states pay adoption expenses for children whose special needs make adoption difficult.

The Family Preservation and Support Initiative, Public Law 103-66 (1993) gives funds to the states for family preservation and support planning and services. The aim of this legislation is to help communities build a system of family support and family preservation services to assist vulnerable children and families prior to maltreatment, and family preservation services to help families suffering crises that may lead to the placement of their children in foster care.

The Adoption and Safe Families Act, Public Law 105-89 (1997) reauthorizes and increases funding for the Family Preservation and Support program, while changing its name to "Promoting Safe and Stable Families." The changed name reflects the intention to make child safety the priority for all services. This law also requires states to move children in foster care more rapidly into permanent homes, by terminating parental rights more quickly and by encouraging and promoting adoptions. Financial incentives for states and penalties accompany the promulgation of this law.

Index

abstinence:
  practical approach to, 171–72
  single criterion of, 200
  see also substance abuse
abuse (childhood physical or sexual):
  assessing, 9, 29, 34, 58–59, 124–25 (*see also* risk assessment; safety)
  disclosure, aftermath of, 248–51
  domestic violence and, 34, 177–79, 245
  increases in reports of, 26–27
  medical model, role in identifying, 25–26
  by men, 179–80
  mothers with history of, 185–86
  non-offending parent and, 244–47
  reporting alleged, 4, 11 (*see also* caller)
  social context of, 231
administration (administrative):
  frontline staff, gap between, 52, 211
  as liaisons between staff and policy-makers, 52
  solution-based support of, 47–49, 51–52
  see also management; supervision
Adoption Assistance and Child Welfare Act, 27, 303
Adoption and Safe Families Act of 1998 (ASFA), 8–9, 303
Ahola, T., 16
Aid to Dependent Children (ADC), 25, 302
American Humane Society, 23, 24
Anderson, H., 81, 218, 236
anger:
  intervention, 77
  normalizing client's, 66, 72, 169
  questions sorting out, 126–27
Antabuse, 176
Antler, S., 86
anxiety (children's), reducing, 252–53
appreciation, management showing, 209–11

assessment:
  of abuse, 9, 29, 34, 58–59, 124–25
  of Child Protective Services (CPS) (Michigan), 37–38
  of home visit, 58–59
  of risks, *see* risk assessment
  of safety, 62–66, 108, 233 (*see also* separate entry)
  skills in, 39
  solution-focused vs. traditional, 299
  of strengths, 9, 63, 64–65, 194 (*see also* separate entry)
Atherton, C., 199

Ban, P., 199
Barlow, J.A., 86
"battered child syndrome," 25
Baveles, Janet Beavin, 97
Berg, Insoo Kim, xi, 5, 9–14, 16, 17, 42, 58, 59, 63, 69, 76, 81, 99, 109, 112, 119, 150, 176, 192, 216, 229, 236, 250, 258
Berns, David, ix
Booth, C., 228
Brace, Reverend Charles, 21
Brower, Shannon, ix
Brown, C., 86
burnout, 224
Burt, M., 26

caller, 4, 11
  maximizing call, 12
  as resource, 55, 56–57
Cantwell, P., 217
cars, agency's vs. own, 70
Carstens, C.C., 23, 24
case examples:
  of angry/hostile clients, 73–76, 226–27
  of coping questions, utilizing, 99–100
  of exception-seeking questions, utilizing, 105
  of human spirit, 163–64

case examples (*continued*)
    of managing noise/chaos, 76–77
    of not-knowing, 82
    of parent as expert, 129–30
    of removing children, 226–27
    of relationship questions, utilizing,
        102–3, 111
    of scaling questions, utilizing, 110–11
    of solutions that fit, 83–84
Case, K., 190
caseworkers:
    adversarial view of clients, 44–45
    blaming, 41, 204–5
    care and nurture of, 213–14
    concerns of, 94
    decision-making powers of, 6–7
    disparity between actions of different,
        228
    fearful of abusive clients, 68, 179–80
    intake/screening/gatekeeping, 10, 12,
        28, 39, 48, 55–56
    as part of family, 164, 165
    qualities of/needed by, 156–57, 162,
        171, 204, 206, 207
    relapse, responses to, 200–201
    as resource, 205–8
    self-evaluating, 223–24
    survey of behavior and attitudes, 290–94
    taking perspective of, 220–22
    training, *see separate entry*
change(s) (changing):
    behavioral, 93, 195–96, 244
    client/family responsible for, 61–62,
        151, 188
    client/family unable to make, 254–55
    compliance vs., 44–45, 80–81, 102,
        230–31
    concrete, vs. cause/etiology, 167, 195–
        96, 244
    language of, 77–87
    sustainable, 153
    within system, 7, 14
Chapin Hall, 32
checklist, worker observation, 43–44, 278
Child Abuse Prevention and Treatment
    Act (CAPTA), 26, 30, 302
Child Protective Services (CPS, Michi-
    gan), ix
    assessing, 37–38
    changes within system, 7, 14
    pilot study of, 11–14
    public's image of, 5, 38, 56, 79
    risks/strengths assessment, need for
        both, 9, 29, 34
        (*see also separate entries on* risk assess-
        ment *and* strengths)
    statistics of, 10–11

Child Protective Services (CPS, U.S.)
    advocacy frame as too narrow, 50
    criticism of, 204
    current issues facing, 29–36
    current status of, 3–7, 28–29, 37, 47,
        55
    domestic violence and, 34–35, 177
    "either/or" syndrome characterizing,
        45–46
    factors curtailing efforts, 4
    historical overview of
        18th and 19th centuries, 21–22
        1877–1920, 22–24
        1920–1959, 24–25
        1960–1980, 25–26
        1980s–1990s, 26–29
    mission/mandate of, 20, 142, 237
    political pressures affecting, 50–51
    proposed use of this book by, 7–9
    public's image of, 79, 141, 289
    reforming, xi, 5, 27–28, 36, 259, 260–63
    regulations of, 187
    "rescuing/saving" framework of, 6, 20,
        21–22, 23, 24–26
    resources within, 205–16
    training staff, *see* training
Child Welfare League of America
    (CWLA), 24
Child Welfare Services Program, 302
children:
    as caretakers of parents, 252
    contextual issues of, 131
    debriefing, 133–34, 135
    difficult, 183–84
    domestic violence, impact on, 177
    interviewing, 131–37
    miracle question and, 116
    recovery from relapse connected to,
        172, 173–74
    removal of, 251–54 (*see also* place-
        ments, out-of-home)
    story of abuse, pressure to believe,
        247–48
    teenagers, 254
    U.S. values the protection of, 20, 24–25
Children's Aid Society, 21–22
Children's Bureau, 24, 25
choices, offering, 72
Christofferson, S., 227
client(s):
    as adversary of caseworker, 44–45
    angry/hostile, 71–76, 239–40
    assessing own progress, *see* questions,
        scaling
    blaming, 79, 84
    commitment to children, 194
    complaints, of, 86–87

-driven services, xi, 17, 38, 48, 49
goals of, *see separate entry*
important others, working with, 198–99
interactional view of, 158
moral characterizations of, 189
preparing, for programs, 174–75, 197–98
responsibility of, 61–62, 90–91, 108, 151, 258
satisfied with services, 87, 190 (table), 211–12
traits, misconception of, 84–85
see also families; parent(s)
cognitive rehearsal, 166
collaboration (collaborative):
consultation as, 214–15
fosters change rather than compliance, 44–45
as key philosophy, 17–18, 48, 49, 169
in supervision, 217–18
treatment as, 85, 128
see also partnership
Common Purpose, 46
community (resources):
-based child protection movement, 261, 262
bridge-building with, 56, 57
focus-group process for, 288–89
reflect cultural/economic characteristics, 36
utilizing, 29, 48, 147
visioning process for, 284–87
confidence:
caseworker's loss of, 205
evaluating/scaling client's, 104–5, 109, 110, 145, 147, 155, 161, 165, 172, 280
confidentiality, 56, 132, 238
consultation (case):
domestic violence and, 179
format of, 155, 159, 164, 298
as resource, 205, 214–16
with supervisor, *see* supervision
cooperation, 85, 86, 89
Corcoran, J., 245
Costin, L.B, 23, 24
counseling, 105 (*see also* referrals)
court(s):
cases in, 13, 55–56
juvenile, 23, 24
-mandated changes, 109–10, 167
questions asked by, 8
reunification requirements of, 255
crises and emergencies:
abuse disclosed as, 250
dealing with, 180–81

goals underlying, 188, 191–92
precluding, 156–57
removal of children as, 228–31, 253–54
culture (cultural):
of CPS teams, 43
sensitivity, 35–36, 282
tragedy of overlooking, 233
curiosity, 81, 103, 119, 162, 166, 171, 218–19 (table), 223, 243, 244
customer satisfaction, 87, 190 (table), 211–12
Cutler, I., 259

Davis, L., 34
debriefing, children, 133–34, 135
de Francis, Vincent, 24
DeJong, Peter, 16, 17, 42, 59, 81, 236, 258
De Panfilis, D., 62
Department of Education (Michigan), 30
Department of Human Services (Milwaukee), 109
Department of Social Services (Massachusetts), 34
depression, in mothers, 184–85, 198–99
de Shazer, Steve, 16, 17
details:
eliciting from clients, 147, 160, 161, 166, 172, 200–201
management gathering, 208
dignity, 124, 233, 253, 258 (*see also* respect)
distraction, utilizing, 72
diversity:
respecting/training in, 29, 35–36, 260, 282
scaling questions and, 109
Dobash, R., 34
Dobash, R.E., 34
Dolan, Y., 17
dreams, miracle question eliciting, 112–16

Edelson, J.L., 34
Edwards, S., 17, 57, 108
emergency, *see* crises
empathy, for clients, 207
empowerment:
of clients/families, 128, 165, 186, 212, 230–31
culture of, 16–17
of staff, 50, 205, 212–13, 238
of supervisory experience, 218
English Poor Law of 1601, 20, 21
Epston, D., 16
Erickson, Milton H., 16

exceptions:
  clients offer, 151
  looking for, 152–53, 182, 196
  questions about, 102, 103–7, 280
  in substance-abuse cases, 170
expectations:
  of parents for children, 119–21
  of performance, high-quality, 209,
    211–12
  of workers for clients, 86–87
  of workers for selves, 146
expert(s):
  parents as, 45, 49, 81, 128–30, 178, 191,
    193, 243
  role of, 15, 45, 124

Fadiman, Anne, 233
Fahlberg, V.I., 6
failure:
  client's fear of, 200, 232
  of CPS system, 204–5
  incorrect focus on, 235–36
families (family):
  assumptions about, 273
  compliance vs. change in, see change(s)
  deficits of, vs. strengths, 63, 64–65,
    235–36
  fighting, dealing with, 77
  group conferences with, 231–32, 250
  home-based services for, 33
  preservation of, 5–6, 7, 23, 26, 27, 33
  as resource in abuse cases, 250–51
  violence in, see separate entry
  western European policy toward,
    27–28
  see also client(s); parent(s)
Families First (Michigan), ix
  domestic violence and, 34
  as model, 42
  philosophy/principles of, 5, 6, 16–17
Family Independence Agency (FIA, Mich-
    igan), 10, 30, 35, 37, 55, 189–90,
    206, 211, 254, 289, 303
Family Preservation and Support Act,
    The, 27
Farrow, F., 231, 261, 262
Findlater, Janet, ix, 177
Fisch, R., 116
focus groups (Michigan), 5, 211, 212,
    288–89
foster care (programs):
  alternatives to, 16–17
  CPS separated from, 251
  damage of, 29
  forerunners to, 21–22
  funding for, 25, 26, 31–32

growth of, 27
  see also placements, out-of-home
Franklin, C., 15
frustration:
  caseworker's feeling of, 148
  family's increasing, 157–59, 189
  normalizing family's feeling of, 106–7,
    148
Furman, B., 16
future, imagining different, 125–27, 140,
    145
Future of Children, The, 5n, 302

Galaway, B., 199
gatekeeping, 48 (see also intake)
George, R.M., 6
goals:
  of CPS system, 275
  defining/eliciting client's, 17, 149,
    180
  evaluation family progress, 188–93
    (table), 194, 199
  worker and client developing well-
    formed, 193–98, 277, 280
Goffman, I., 186
Goolishian, H., 81, 218, 236
Government Accounting Office, 10, 32
Governor's Task Force (Michigan), 131
Gonzales, G., 190
Gremy, L., 245
guilt, admission of, 90

Harden, A.W., 6
Hassal, I., 199
Hayley, Jay, 16
Hoffman, L., 81
Holmes, S., 217
home visit:
  assessing if needed, 58–59
  evaluation of, 297
  impact of, on client, 80
  positive, focusing on, 67–68, 195
  repeat, see reinvestigation(s)
  sensory assault of, on worker, 68–69,
    229–30
  setting the stage for, 66–77
  single, utilizing, 10, 116, 144–46
  see also interview(ing)
hope, 18–19
"hospital-hopping," 26
Hsi, Andrew, 192
Hudson, J., 199
Hunter, R., 131

"I-messages," 88
Indian Child Welfare Act, 303

information:
  on child-rearing, ways of offering,
    122–24
  educating while gathering, 234–35
  intervening while gathering, 58–
    59
  management sharing, 209
  from non-offending parent, 245
  in removing children, for new care-
    taker, 253
  in removing children, ways of offering,
    232–33, 237
  useful vs. complete, 55–56, 59–62
insight, 90
intake, 10, 12, 28, 39, 48, 55–56
intervention(s):
  anger, 77
  interview as, 64, 79–80
  strengths as central to, 17
interview(ing), solution-focused:
  balancing positives and negatives,
    135–40
  children, 131–37
  as cooperative endeavor, 79
  as core training module, 42
  in domestic violence cases, 178
  guidelines for, 87–93
  as intervention, 64, 79–80
  timing and, 105
investigation(s):
  language/implications of, 78–79
  as prevention, 143–47, 260
  special problem cases, 166–74
  see also reinvestigation(s)
Izquirdo, Elisa, 41

Janis, I.L., 228
Jick, Karen, 109, 110
Jiordano, M., 33, 237

Keggerreis, N., 190
Kelly, Susan, xi, 5, 14, 47, 177, 209, 210,
  255
Kempe, G.H., 25
Kinney, E.M., 228
Kotter, John, 49
Kozol, Jonathon, 41

Lamb, M.E., 131
language:
  of change, 77–87
  client's, using, 88, 149, 151, 279
  development of, in children, 131,
    134
  of supervision, 218
  tentative, 138, 220, 239, 240, 243

laws/legislature protecting children, 4, 5,
    22–23, 39
  as context for developing new capaci-
    ties, 262
  domestic violence and, 177
  government increases role in, 24–25
  state-mandated systems, 26–28
  summary of relevant, 302–3
Leading Change, 49
Leverington, John, 83
Lindsay, D.S., 135
listening:
  to client's side, 87–89, 180, 185, 190,
    207, 244, 282
  to reasons for harmful behaviors, 119
  solutions require, 77
loyalty, of children, 136

MacKinnon, L., 86
MacLean, Don, 65, 71, 191, 206, 226
maltreatment, see abuse
management:
  as resource, 208–12
  team-building exercise for, 210, 301
  see also administration; supervision
Mason, J., 86
Maxwell, G., 199
meaning:
  of experiences, 100, 139, 186
  of goals, 197
media, role of, 25, 94, 204
medical model, child abuse and, 25–26
medication, 182–83
mental:
  health practice, 16
  illness, and CPS, 181–83, 260
mentoring, 41, 42, 48, 69
methadone programs, 176
Miller, Jerome, 31
Miller, S.D., 17
miracle(s):
  promoting, 208–9
  questions, 112–16, 151, 186, 208, 258,
    262–63
Mondale, Walter, 30
Morrison, A., 199
motivation:
  of clients, 84–86, 152
  and gender differences in substance-
    abuse recovery, 172–74
  language/questions enhancing, 79, 86, 97
  for reunification, 255
  scaling, 110
  of staff, 211
  in termination phase, 202–3
Munro, Susan, ix

Nagy, JoAnne, ix
National Center on Addiction and Sub-
    stance Abuse (CASA), 32, 33
National Center on Child Abuse and
    Neglect, 26
National Coalition for Child Protection
    Reform, 31
neglect:
    addiction and, 33
    chronic, 142
    poverty and, 27, 29–32
    screening cases of, 39
Nelson, Barbara, 30
neutral(ity), 134, 136, 137, 159
New York Times, The, 40, 204
Newberger, C.M., 245, 249
Newberger, E.H., 245
Ney, T., 131
noise, dealing with, 76–77
noncompliance, see resistance
normalization (normalizing):
    of anger, 66, 72, 169
    of depression, 184
    of drug craving, 151
    of frustration, 106–7, 148
"not-knowing," posture, 81, 82, 103, 123–
    24, 125, 218, 235–36
Nurius, P., 15

openness (open mind), need for, 87
outcomes, hoped-for, 276 (see also goals)

Packard Foundation, 5n, 29, 142, 302
Parad, H.J., 228
paradigms:
    problem-solving
        limitations of, 14–16, 59
    solution-building
        basic concepts of, 61–62
        expecting, 211–12
        hallmarks of, xi–xii, 7, 8, 16–18, 48,
            167, 274
        institutionalizing, 260–63
parent(s):
    becoming better, 149
    believing nothing wrong with their
        parenting, 240–44
    coping strategies of, 184
    as "experts," 45, 49, 81, 128–29, 178,
        191, 193, 243
    mentally ill, 181–83
    non-offending, 244–48, 249–51
    as partners, 64, 65 (see also partnership)
    respite for, 234
    "terminating" rights to children, 227,
        228–31

visitation of children, see visitation
    see also client(s); families
partnership, with parents in removing
    children, 231–39
    see also collaboration
Partnership for Safety Advisory Group
    (Michigan), ix, 14, 37, 43, 289
peer networks, 207, 215
Peller, J., 17
permission, asking for, on home visits,
    71
physical abuse, see abuse
Pittman, K., 26
placements, out-of-home:
    and child, while removing, 251–54
    domestic violence and, 177–78
    foster care, see separate entry
    as last option, 29, 48
    overview of, 226–28
    percentage of, 141, 261
    policy statement on, 1909, 24
    preventing, 27
    problems with, 6, 10–11, 13, 189,
        190–91
    reasons given by workers, 38
    requested by parents, 198–99
    time limitations of, 143–44
Poole, D.A., 131, 135
poverty:
    abuse/neglect likelihood increased by,
        4, 25, 27, 29–32, 260
    rate of, in African-American families,
        35
power, 191, 233–34, 262
prejudice, 35
prevention (preventing):
    investigation/reinvestigation as, 143–
        47, 260
    placements, out-of-home, 27
problem:
    as client's attempted solution, 116–19
    definition of, connected to solution, 78
    focusing on successes vs., 83–84
    as resource, 150
"Promoting Strong and Stable Families,"
    27

questionnaire, for caseworkers, 224–25
questions (questioning):
    in abuse cases, aftermath of, 248–49
    in abuse cases, assessing, 124–25
    behaviorally specific, 166
    in case consultation format, 214–15
    caseworker asks self, 155–56, 187–88
    client relationship shaped by, 66
    commands vs., 89

coping, 97–100, 145, 151, 162, 178, 184, 247
courts, asked by, 8
courts, caseworker asks while waiting with client, 256
culture-related, 282–83
as curiosity in action, 218–19 (table)
exception-seeking, 103–7, 170–71
future-oriented, 125–27, 140
harmful behavior, 116–19, 169
information-imparting, 235
leading, 131, 135
miracle, 112–16, 151, 186, 208, 258, 262–63
open-ended, 95–97, 219
parents' expectations of children, 119–21
relationship, 100–103, 111, 114, 115, 137, 138, 145, 174, 201, 208–9, 219, 223
resource-seeking, 121–22, 127–28, 138
safety, 64 (*see also separate entry*)
scaling, 57, 107–12, 145, 152, 155, 156, 161, 162, 165–66, 180, 199, 201–2, 219, 223
solution-building, 60–61, 64, 137–40 (table summarizing), 145
supervisors ask workers, 219 (table)
tag, 96–97
termination-related, 281
"three wishes," 133
yes/no, 96, 279
"why?" 95–96, 215, 220, 244

rapport, building, with children, 132–35
Rea, Will, 132, 133, 134
recidivism rates
in CPS, 44, 51
in treatment programs for abusive men, 180
see also reinvestigation(s); relapse
recovery:
uneven process, 200
women and substance abuse, 172–74
referrals:
deciding to make, 146–47
inadequacy exacerbated by, 105, 121
jeopardizing (or not), 144
multiple, 40, 142
realistic, 175–76
reforms (reforming):
effective, xi, 36, 259, 260–63
parents, 23
reactive, 5, 27–28
reframing, 158
registry, of perpetrators and victims, 26

reinvestigation(s):
avoiding, 151, 152
family frustrated by, 157–59
family situation found to be worse, 156–57, 162–63
as new case, 148–53
as ongoing cases and later visits, 160–64
overview of issues, 11, 141–43, 147–48
as prevention, 143–47
as repeat visit for worker, 153–56
termination of, 146–47, 164–65
see also recidivism rates; relapse
relapse:
children as motivation to overcome, 172, 173–74
in families, in general, 199–202
in substance abuse abstinence, 171–72
see also recidivism rates; reinvestigation(s)
relationship questions, 100–103, 111, 114, 115, 137, 138, 145, 174, 201, 208–9, 219, 223
"removal," 227 (*see also* placements, out-of-home)
reporter, vs. partner, 55 (*see also* caller)
resistance, 18, 84–86, 158
resources:
caller/reporter as, 55, 56–57
community, *see separate entry*
in CPS unit, 205–16
exceptions as 103
within family, utilizing, 143–46, 199
friends as, 67
see also strengths
respect:
behavioral signs indicating, 118
for client, 71, 98, 100, 108, 123–24, 162, 169, 180, 190, 192, 197, 206, 282
for diversity, 35–36
institutionalizing, 260
narrow definition of, 120
for non-offending parent, 245
for parents whose children are being removed, 227–28, 236
among staff, 50, 216, 220
responsibility (responsible):
clients', 61–62, 90–91, 108, 151, 258 (*see also* solutions, clients)
non-offending parent held, 244–47
professionals', 79, 84, 86–87
reunification services:
enabling swift, 48
inadequate, 27
parents need to know how to begin, 251

reunification services (*continued*)
　planting seed for, 254–55
　scaling questions used in, 109–10
Reuss, N., 17
Reynolds, Deborah, 206–7
risk assessment:
　family-focused, 62–66
　mental illness and, 182
　overview of, 9, 15–16, 29
　in problem-solving paradigm, 16
Ryburn, A., 199
Rymarchyk, G., 231

Safe from Harm, 289
safety:
　assessing for, 62–66, 108, 233
　child's emotional, 251
　focusing on, 90
　on home visits, assuring, 68–69
　mental illness and children's, 181–82
　personal tips for, 69–71
　plan, detailed, 150–51, 154, 156, 178,
　　231, 232, 249
　questions determining level of, 60–
　　61
　signs of, 60–61, 153
Saleeby, D., 15
Salus, M.K., 62
scaling questions, *see* questions, scaling
scapegoating, 250
Schafer, Judith, 184
Schene, P.A., 24, 28, 29, 40, 62, 302
school setting, 131–32
Schorr, L., 46, 231
Sebold, J., 180
service:
　compliance vs., 80–81
　delivery methods, 49, 190, 208
sexual abuse, *see* abuse
"shadowing," 41, 42, 205
Sheeley, Neil, 70
Shirk, M., 261
Silverman, F.N., 25
Smith, Terry, 65
social action, 23
social constructivists, 15
social control, child-saving as tool of,
　21–22
Social Security Act:
　of 1935, 25, 27, 302
　of 1961, 302
　of 1975, 302
Social Service Agency (Michigan), 209
Social Services Block Grant, 302
social support, 33–34, 182, 199
social work field, empowerment culture
　affecting, 16–17

Society for the Prevention of Cruelty to
　Children (SPCC), 22–23, 25, 26
solutions:
　assessment of, 17
　clients creating/accountable for, 91–93,
　　95, 121, 154, 157
　fitting the family, 82–84, 197–98
　goals that include, 196–97
　supportive, 45–47, 51–52
　weaving miracle into, 114
　see also paradigm, solution-building
Spirit Catches You and You Fall Down, The,
　233
staff:
　administration and frontline, 52, 211
　development, vs. training, 224–25
　empowering, 50, 205, 212–13, 238
　meetings, importance/use of, 205,
　　212–13
　motivation in, 211
　policy-makers and, 52
　respect among, 50, 216, 220
　solution-focused, 300–301
　success, focusing on, 210, 218
　training, *see separate entry*
Steele, B.F., 25
Sternberg, K.J., 131
stereotypes, 36, 282
stigma, contact with CPS carries, 28
strengths:
　assessing, 9, 63, 64–65, 194
　questions acknowledging, 97–100
　utilizing, 14, 17
　see also resources
stress reactions to traumatic cases,
　213–14
substance abuse:
　exceptions in cases of, 170–71
　overview of, 32–34, 168–69
　preparing client for treatment, 174–75
　realistic referrals, need for, 175–76
　relapse, 171–72
　treatment programs and gender,
　　173–74
　wake-up call, when children removed,
　　257–58
　what parent wants/plans, 169–70
　women and, 168, 172–74
success(es):
　clients minimizing own, 104
　exceptions as, 103
　experienced via measuring, 164–65
　problems vs., focusing on, 83–84
　small, emphasizing/acknowledging,
　　105, 114, 123, 145, 146, 149, 153–
　　54, 167–68, 171–72, 185, 230–31
　staff focusing on, 210, 218

suicide (suicidal), 99, 171, 176
supervision (supervisors):
  blaming, 41
  consultation and support provided by,
    38–41, 45, 46, 47
  hallmarks of, 295–96
  new paradigm for, 216–25 (table)
  rules focusing attention, 46
  survey of behavior and attitudes,
    290–94
  techniques for effective, 222–24
  tools for, 295–301

Talmon, M., 202
TANF (Temporary Assistance for Needy
    Families), 42, 43, 173
termination:
  criteria of, clear, 187–88, 193–98
  goal-driven relationship with client,
    188–93 (table)
  of reinvestigated cases, 146–47, 164–65
  relapse, responding to, 199–202
  when and how, 202–3
  working with important others in cli-
    ent's life, 198–99
Third National Incidence Study of Child
    Abuse and Neglect, 31
Thorpe, D., 189
Time Magazine, 41
Tjhin, Martha, ix
top-down/bottom-up approach, 18, 43,
    48, 260
Tracy, E.M., 228
training:
  in assessment skills, 39
  in diversity issues, xi, 29, 35–36, 260,
    282
  divisions of, 42–43
  models of, 41
  as priority, highest, 40, 41–44, 45
  staff development vs., 224–25
treatment (programs):
  for abusive men, 180
  as collaboration, 85, 128
  for substance abuse, 173–75
Turnell, A., 17, 57, 108

Uken, A., 180
University Associates, 34
utilization principle, 57

validation (validating):
  caseworkers, of each other, 207–8
  of children, 137
  of clients, 100, 107, 120, 154, 239
  supervisors, of caseworkers, 221
Van de Kamp, N., 228
victims:
  not viewing client(s) as, 61–62
  registry of, 26
  women abuse survivors, 186
video conferencing, 41–42
violence (domestic):
  abuse and, 34, 177–79, 245
  on home visits, 68, 179–80
  mental illness and, 181, 182
  non-offending parent and, 244–47
Violence Again Women Act (VAWA), 34
vision:
  actualizing, 49–51, 261–63
  client's, 280
  principles of, 48, 272
  of training, 225
visit, see home visit
visitation:
  consequences of missing, 252
  parents' rights to, after removal, 251
Wade, Allan, 186
"wake-up call," 229, 257–58
Walter, J., 17
Watermaux, J., 245
Watzlawick, P., 116
Weakland, J., 116
Wexler, Richard, 30, 31
White House Conference on Children,
    24
White, Michael, 16
Whitney, P., 34
Whittaker, J., 228
Wilson, Mary Ellen, 22
Winefield, H.S., 86
women, substance-abuse and, 168,
    172–74
workers, see caseworkers
Wulczyn, F.H., 6

"yes set," 279
Yuille, J.C., 131

Zaparnuik, J., 131
Zellman, G.L., 86